# FOLLOWING *Balanchine*

ROBERT GARIS

Published with assistance from the Charles A. Coffin Fund.

Designed by Deborah Dutton.

Set in Adobe Caslon and Futura types by The Composing Room of Michigan, Inc.

Printed in the United States of America by Thomson-Shore, Dexter, Michigan.

**Library of Congress Cataloging-in-Publication Data**

Garis, Robert, 1925–

    Following Balanchine / Robert Garis.

      p.  cm.

    Includes bibliographical references and index.

    ISBN 0-300-06178-1 (cloth: alk. paper)

    ISBN 0-300-07059-4 (pbk.: alk. paper)

    1. Balanchine, George.   2. Choreographers—United States—

Biography.   I. Title.

GV1785.B32G37   1995

792.8'2'092—dc20                   94-34826

[B]                             CIP

A catalogue record for this book is available from the British Library.

F O L L O W I N G *Balanchine*

YALE UNIVERSITY PRESS / *New Haven & London*

# CONTENTS

# ACKNOWLEDGMENTS

I shared the experience of following Balanchine with many friends; the depth of that experience, as well as many ideas and observations about it, derive in part from conversation with them. I hope they will recognize themselves and their influence on many of these pages. Talking with Suki Schorer gave me valuable insights into Balanchine's thinking and working. Richard Poirier encouraged this project from the beginning and supported it in the most practical way by publishing parts of it. Other friends helped by giving my work critical reading as it was finding its shape: David Ferry, Constance and Richard Harrier, James Harvey, Timothy Peltason, Margery Sabin, William Youngren.

Wellesley College supported me with research grants on sabbatical leaves during the composition of this book, and has in many other ways given me aid and encouragement. The Guggenheim Foundation awarded me a grant at an early stage of the project.

The press officers of the New York City Ballet helped me attend all the performances I needed to see.

Portions of this book have appeared in *Raritan* and *Ballet Review*.

FOLLOWING *Balanchine*

O N E / *The* Apollo *Conversion*

I came to know George Balanchine's work by reputation in about 1944, and I saw my first Balanchine ballet, *Apollo,* in 1945. I wrote about his work first in 1946; by the middle 1960s it had become my chief subject. Now, eleven years after his death, as I watch the dissolution of his ballets at the New York City Ballet, I am still following his career and still watching myself do so. I believe Balanchine to be one of the greatest artists who ever lived. I am about to describe my encounter with his work in detail: how I got to know it, why I became attached to it, in what different moods and circumstances I watched its development, and with what difficulty or ease I revised my conceptions of it as it changed and as I changed. I don't offer myself as a representative follower of the arts or an average one—such categories are empty. But I do hope to make contact with readers, and in narrating the events and experiences that make up my following of Balanchine's career, I shall try to establish that contact by exploring the more general implications of some of my specific experiences. What I count on is that my reader will find what I say relevant to his or her own experience.

When I first became aware of Balanchine and of ballet in general, at the age of eighteen, I had already been seriously interested in the arts for about four years. I followed music and fiction and the movies closely and discussed my artistic experiences in great detail with my friends. These interests, in fact, formed my chief bond with these friends, and the whole enterprise formed the center of my life.

This is perhaps an unlikely adolescent identity to have developed in Allentown, Pennsylvania, in the late 1930s. My family was not highly educated (my father had a diploma from a correspondence school in civil engineering, and my mother had one from a business college) or particularly cultivated, though both my parents liked music and my mother read a lot of novels. There was pressure on me at home to do well in school but apart from that little encouragement toward any intellectual pursuit. But we had a piano, a big upright Hensel, a brand I've never encountered since, and when I was about eight I taught myself to play it by trying out hymns from our Baptist hymn book. This turned out to be an ideal way of learning how to follow different musical voices at the same time. Because a C-major hymn like "Jesus is tenderly calling me home" is so easy, with many repeated tonic and dominant chords, I learned to play it pretty quickly, and the immediate gratification this achievement gave me led me to attempt the easier pieces of Mozart, Haydn, Beethoven, Schubert, and Bach to which my repertory at the piano is still limited. Wanting to teach myself to play the piano shows a love for music and some musical gift, but it was also related to my lack of interest in sports. I was hunting for something of my own.

This part of my history seems relatively easy to understand. What may perhaps need more explanation is the degree of concentration, even semiprofessionalism, in the arts that I had reached at a fairly young age. I owe something of this to the curriculum of my junior high school, where in ninth grade I could get out of the "shop" courses I dreaded by choosing to take extra art or music classes. The surprisingly excellent training in sight-singing I received in elementary school and my own practicing of hymns had made me a good sight reader, and at the age of twelve I already knew some piano pieces pretty well—not just the hackneyed Beethoven Minuet in G, though I do remember playing that—and so I felt confident enough to study music; nothing was clearer than the fact that I *had* to escape auto shop and advanced mechanical drawing. My ninth-grade music major thus brought my interest in music into focus by allowing me to make it a conscious choice.

I owe even more to some of my public school teachers, who gave extra attention to students with special interests and abilities. I was one such student for two energetic, gifted, and generous English teachers. (Had the eighth- and ninth-grade music teachers showed equal interest in me, I doubt that I would ever have centered my professional work in literature.) But the most gratifying and influential attention came from my high-school French teacher. With a generous intuition for how education happens, she gathered together and invited to her apartment a group of students interested in music. This teaching succeeded, it now seems to me, because we all had about the same degree of interest and expertise that she herself had—if not, gratifyingly, a little more. She had an enviably grand floor model Philco radio-phonograph—the phonograph tilted toward you as you opened it, as I can still vividly see—which I seem to remember that she bought during my sophomore year of high school, in 1939. She did not have an immense record collection, for 78-RPM records still cost an expensive two dollars apiece, but enough for some real variety, and once a week, at 7:30 in the evening, she invited a group of between six and ten boys and girls to listen to her records and talk about music. These gatherings gave a kind of public extension to my interest in music and the arts. They established my sense that part of one's love for music and one's interest in it took the form of hearing it in the company of other people and of describing one's experience to them. Miss Swope must have chosen me and the other members of this group—some of whom were already my friends—because we had shown at school that we liked to talk about music. The formation of the group was not the first public ratification of my interest in talking about art, but being in the group brought what had been desultory and inchoate into steady practice and into consciousness.

Our group didn't cut much of a figure in the world of the high school, which was in fact rather big—Allentown was then as now a city of about 100,000, but it had only one high school, a large one with more than 3,000 students, among whom a group of six to ten music lovers made little impact. Yet I don't remember missing any larger kind of public acknowledgment. The fact that a teacher had formed the group helped us to believe that it represented an elite, and now it seems clear that it actually did so.

Music was only the center of our discussions; plenty of time went to talking about plays and novels. The level of the music we discussed was fairly high, since Miss Swope's records were those of the standard orchestral repertory of the day: too much Tchaikovsky (plus the Franck symphony) to be highbrow but enough Beethoven to be serious. Our discussions of drama and fiction, however, somehow centered not on the classics but on current popular works—the recent Broadway plays that might or might not come to Allentown on road tours and the novels which were reviewed weekly in the *New York Times Book Review* and appeared on the best-seller list, which, sad to say, was a respected guide. In a stern view of things, then, our group was an adolescent version of those middlebrow women's discussion groups endemic to exactly the kind of provincial city I grew up in. If, as I think, our group was better than those, it must have been because our discussions had the intensity of youth.

The group was not our only intellectual connection. We all had a few close friends who weren't members, with whom we had intellectual discussions. I had a not-quite-friend (we have since become close) whom I saw in the public library at night; and we would walk together after the library closed and talk about Dostoevski and, as I remember, German lyric poetry. And my closest friend was a tremendously difficult, brilliant, sad, furious, unclubbable, overweight, strong, and bullying young physicist with whom I discussed everything. We had an intricately structured symbiosis which gave us great power over each other's minds—what comes back to me now is the time he forced me to spend what felt like hundreds of hours soldering with infinite ineptitude the relatively few connections in the primitive hi-fi set that he had designed for me but made me build myself.

By the time I was eighteen, I had developed a special angle on all of this. I was still "interested in the arts," but in my case a more distinct motive linked all these concerns and ways of spending time: running through my interest in the arts, bringing it into focus, giving form to my discussions with my friends, and giving the whole enterprise its central motive and energy was a preoccupation with the very act of making aesthetic judgments. I thought of myself quite consciously as a person who did that, and I was aware that in this respect I differed at least in degree from most of my friends and from most of the members of my group. I didn't want to be a submissive appreciator but an active judge.

Another way of being active, of course, would have been to create works of art, and I had some hopes in that direction. But these were rather dim, and if Pound is right, and the way to go about being a poet is to write lots of poems, then I certainly wasn't one. On the other hand, the judging I did instead of making art did not seem negative or a substitute for something better. Many of my judgments were enthusiastically and excitedly favorable and—more to the point—I was eager to express and defend them. And the intensity of my negative judgments and the pleasure I took in expressing them made them too seem active, alive, essentially positive.

I was of course making something else in this procedure, though I wasn't making art—I was making myself, I was judging art in order to form and express an identity. And although this must have been a response to some uncertainty about some identity I feared I had or didn't have, there seemed to be a positive side to this enterprise as well. For while this self-making was certainly compensatory and imitative to a degree, it was not entirely so. It had the energetic, hopeful feel of a real project of the imagination.

What now seems problematic and a little awkward about all this is the relation between my preoccupation with judgment and my pleasure in the arts. With so much—my very identity—riding on it, each separate act of judgment became a test not only of my powers of discrimination but of myself, and so my experience of art was infiltrated by an anxious self-consciousness which, although it didn't destroy the pleasure I got from the works themselves, certainly complicated that pleasure—as for instance in my early dealings with Mozart.

I had become interested in opera very early—in seventh or eighth grade when I was eleven or twelve—through a boy whose own interest came from the unworthy circumstance of being a tremendous fan of the Jeanette MacDonald-Nelson Eddy movies. Although this friend later became one of the original members of Miss Swope's group, I didn't think him as smart as the other members, and I don't really link him to the way in which the group was important to me. I came to be rather ashamed of having him as a close friend, in fact, but ours had been a crucial relationship. Not only did he go to the movies, which I wasn't allowed to do, but he went all the time and, even more important, he went to the same ones over and over again, so that he knew the dialogue of many of them by heart. This was irresistible: he could give me exact, detailed information about a world to which I was denied access. Our talks, as I remember them, had mostly the movies as a subject—which was hardly a subject and they were hardly talks: what went on between us was his recital, with appropriate descriptive commentary, of the scenarios of the movies he had memorized, while I listened and imagined. His love for the movies of MacDonald and Eddy was a taste that was later held in contempt by my other friends, and I betrayed my movie friend shamefully by never acknowledging how well I too knew these unworthy films. I came to know them very well because my friend knew them completely, and he also knew something about opera, for Jeanette MacDonald sang bits from operas in these movies, and he bought records of the arias she had sung—the "Jewel song" from *Faust,* the first operatic record he bought, was the first aria I remember hearing. Soon after I got to know him he had singled out the Puccini operas as the ones he liked best. MacDonald had sung parts of *Tosca* in *Rose Marie* and he had found that immensely exciting; so be began buying *Tosca* record by record, and I too learned it, record by record—I still know it by heart. He followed this with *La Bohème* and *Madame Butterfly* and even made contact with the exotic world of the Gramophone Shop in New York to buy the imported Decca records of *Turandot.*

While I was learning and enjoying the Puccini operas through my friendship with this fan, I was at the same time beginning to learn from many other sources that ours was a low taste, not the right judgment at all, and when I began earning enough money from working in shoe stores on Saturdays to buy records, in 1940, it was Mozart's *Don Giovanni* I bought, followed by *Così Fan Tutte.* I find these operas completely beautiful and valuable today, and I believe I did so even at fifteen. But what stays in my memory about these choices has little to do with pleasure in the music and much to do with pleasure in making the right judgment. I have negative evidence for this. I did not buy *The Marriage of Figaro* at that time, and although I can't remember exactly why not, I'm pretty sure it had to do with my interest in making judgments. I somehow picked up the idea that the singing on the *Figaro* recordings was not as good as that on the other two sets, and I imagine I was thinking about the fact that the least gifted singer at the Glyndebourne Opera, Audrey Mildmay, sang the important role of Susanna—and I remember knowing that Mildmay was the wife of the director of the Opera, and I remember too the scorn I felt at this nepotism. Now I realize that all the singing in the ensembles, even Mildmay's, is perfectly integrated and that as an ensemble performance the Glyndebourne *Figaro* has remained unrivaled. My judgment against Mildmay's singing wasn't really a bad one, it was merely incomplete. But I was also making a judgment about the music itself, by default.

I didn't really know much of the music of *Figaro* at this time, although I had gathered from reading B. H. Haggin, an authority I was just beginning to discover, that it was a great work. But *Don Giovanni* figured more excitingly as "the world's greatest opera" in the writings of Shaw, Kierkegaard, and W. J. Turner, who were also important voices for me. *Così Fan Tutte* also had a special cachet because only people of the highest taste realized that it did not represent a lapse into artificiality and triviality after *Figaro* but rather a triumph of art through convention—or so ran Turner's powerful advertisement. My friend had bought *Tosca* because he loved the scenes that MacDonald sang in *Rose Marie,* but I bought *Don Giovanni* and *Così* because I had been told they were the best and I wanted to get to know and like them.

The upshot was that I knew only bits and pieces of *Figaro* by the time I had learned *Don Giovanni* and *Così* literally by heart. And then an extraordinary thing happened. For the first really intense pleasure in the music of Mozart that I remember took me by surprise by coming from *Figaro.* It was during a performance in 1944 under Bruno Walter's direction at the Metropolitan Opera, and what astonished and delighted me was Licia Albanese's "Deh vieni, non tardar" (not, as I might have expected, Eleanor Steber's "Dove sono"). Albanese was a universal favorite and very much one of mine, but she was not noted for her Mozart style and in fact rarely sang Mozart. I suppose that part of my surprise came from the fact that I didn't expect the great experience to come from her. But something else accounts for the force with which I still remember Albanese's ingenuous and touching byplay with a rose as she sang, and the way her utter conviction gave meaning to the summer-night atmosphere of the woodwinds and the plucked strings. I felt as if the motive of the whole event had become suddenly clear and coherent and as if I were in an immediate personal relation with everything that had brought the event into existence. I had felt in entire, admiring accord with the "great art" I had been listening to up to that moment, when suddenly I was seized with an intense and personal, an exhilarated and confident, pleasure. This transfiguration of acceptance into joy was something I recognized from my religious experience—I was feeling the difference between merely accepting my faith and being "born again" into it.

If my first intense pleasure in Mozart's art took both its force and its format from the Baptist religion in which I was raised, what is common to both experiences has nothing to do with particular religious beliefs and everything to do with my sense of the importance of "personal experience" and my keen awareness of the distinction between different states of mind. When in the years before my experience of salvation I accepted Baptist beliefs—that if I had faith in Christ's sacrifice I would be saved from damnation and given eternal life—I did so almost by rote, unlike my father, whose belief was literal and active. But when my father voiced his concern for the state of my soul he didn't stress guilt; rather, he urged me to think about what would save me from guilt: "the *experience* of salvation . . . the *personal* knowledge of Jesus as your Savior in your heart . . . *realizing* that Christ died for you." He emphasized not the beliefs themselves so much as the true experiencing of them, and this led to a constant search for the distinction between the real experience of salvation and the experience that wasn't real, for which there was no particular name but which my father associated with the kind of formal religion he thought of himself as being in rebellion from.

The upshot of all this was my development at an early age not of a set of beliefs but of a keen sense of the difference between experiences that were genuine and personally felt and experiences that were not. And this awareness wasn't the result of any particular experience of either doubt or anxiety; those famous signs of spiritual vocation never had as strong an appeal to me as the positive experience of assurance, the realization that I actually was in personal contact with the object of desire. I have some talent for anxiety, but my speciality is depression and its partner, exhilaration. I developed quite early a conscious sense of the beauty and value of exhilaration.

"Do I really, really feel Jesus here in my heart?" A question like this was a quite dramatic affair because I was also keenly aware of two almost contradictory truths: that one might want to have such a feeling, or *tell* oneself one had it, without actually experiencing it; yet the real thing, once it happened, was unmistakable. You *knew* you were saved. But you could lose your sense of personal relation with Christ, and then you were no longer saved, for the fact that you once had felt the reality didn't matter unless you continued to feel it. Other branches of fundamentalist Christianity believed in permanent salvation—"Once in Grace, always in Grace"—but my father was strongly opposed to it: this is in fact the only point of doctrine I remember from his continual wrangling in the various churches we entered and left throughout my childhood. I don't recall him looking askance at my having been baptized three times as a result of having twice lost my conviction of salvation; this pattern may even have seemed to him a sign of unusual spiritual sensitivity on my part—as I believe, in part, it was. All the emotions connected with my conversion, lapse, and reconversion were intensified by the fact that my father would always read the Bible and pray with me when I showed I was on the way to conversion or had just experienced it; since my relations with my father were otherwise distant, it will be easily understood that the possibility of personal contact with him impelled me pretty frequently to seek personal contact with Jesus.

But even when I was little I was offended—almost personally, as one says—by the particular nuance of personal feeling in the low-church hymn that was for many Baptists the central type of the religious experience:

> I walked in the garden alone,
> While the dew was still on the roses,
> And the voice I hear, chiming on my ear,
> The Son of God discloses.
> For He walks with me and He talks with me,
> And He tells me I am His own;
> And the joy we share as we tarry there,
> None other hath ever known.

I can still hear the sound of the awful music of this hymn played on the kind of home-electric organ people owned in those days, but it was to the words that I felt the strongest objection, one that is hard to define, although when I was older it was easy to spot the unfocused sexuality of the language, the wrong sort of intimacy hinted suggestively by "tarry" and "I am His own." I now believe that when I was young I thought there was something doctrinally wrong with the hymn, in the sense that Christians ought not to claim so exclusive a relation with the Savior. Yet some such claim was surely very close to the implication of any talk about personal contact with Jesus. There were many other hymns that struck similarly discordant notes; I despised "The Old Rugged Cross" at an early age, connecting its title with the calendar art of Norman Rockwell. And I soon began to find the bad taste, or whatever, of this kind of hymn to be a good reason to disconnect myself from a creed that could provide something so unworthy and cheap. In any case, my awareness of how taste and judgment enter into a matter like the expression of religious experience was an early instance of my perhaps innate sense of the connection between art and religion.

As I grew up I came also to value impersonality, some release from the limitations of "merely" personal experience or expression, in religion, art, or life. I much respected Catholic converts, who I believed valued impersonality too, although I couldn't ever take them quite seriously because I couldn't release myself from a village-atheist puzzlement about "what they really believed." My hyperawareness of the judgmental implications in the word *personal* made me vulnerable at first to T. S. Eliot's campaign against personality and his endeavor to get rid of his own—together with his self-congratulatory acknowledgment that only people with a strong personality could see the point of wanting to get rid of it. Yet however inviting I found Eliot's quest for impersonality in art and especially in religion, I ultimately, indeed repeatedly, in my development as a thinker and feeler on literary and other matters, found fear of the personal distasteful.

All this, of course, confirms my statement that I was much concerned with distinguishing between states of genuineness in both religion and art. When I begin to be interested in George Eliot in the late 1940s, I remained at first at a reserved remove from her Evangelical background and language, with its promptings and soul-searchings and other painfully familiar terms of discourse; my distaste passed quickly enough to make me see by the late fifties how crucial a part the drama of Evangelical salvation played in forming the kind of novelist of conscience and consciousness she was. Much later, reading and then teaching the works of John Donne sent me to Saint Ignatius and the spiritual exercises and showed me another brilliant instance, and clarification, of soul-searching.

What I don't mean to say at all is that art took the place of religion in my life—I never came to believe it was through art that I would be saved or find immortality, although I don't suppose I reject the idea that through art one can achieve transcendence. But one can do that in other pursuits too. So I'm saying something about a variety of *experience* rather than about a variety of *religious* experience when I connect my characteristic mode of experiencing art with the Baptist Christianity that filled my parents' lives and therefore my own life while I was growing up.

My parents came to their religious convictions during a series of painful experiences the whole family went through, which began at my younger brother's birth, when I was three and a half. He was anemic, requiring thirteen blood transfusions during the first year of his life (a much-cited family statistic), and my father was consumed with anxious love for him, as well as, I realized later, vague guilt about his sickness. During this same year my older brother also had to stay in bed all day with what they called a leaking heart, and this combination of circumstances put a lot of pressure on me, for it was perfectly apparent—I don't remember having to be told—that my job during all this anxiety was to be so well-behaved as to be invisible. The Depression hit a year later, and my father started taking salary cuts that continued until he was fired in the early thirties, which led to the loss of the mortgage on our house in the nice part of town.

All her deliveries had been difficult for my mother, but my younger brother's had led to serious complications. During these troubles, she sought help at a series of revival meetings during which she was saved, returning to the fundamentalist Christianity from which she had lapsed; she persuaded my father, who had grown up with hardly any connection with religion, to accompany her to one of these meetings. He too was saved, and the transformation governed his life almost entirely from then on. In due course, as hardly needs saying, pressure was put on all three of us boys to come "to the knowledge of Jesus as our Savior." I was a consciously born-again Christian by the time I was seven or eight, and in fact I first left the faith before I was ten, coming back at least twice, and it's the modality of these emotional states within our kind of Christianity that passed over into my experience of art during the rest of my life.

When I responded as I did to Albanese's singing of "Deh vieni, non tardar" at the Met, then, I was experiencing the difference between the high respect and admiration I had been feeling for the opera up to that moment, and my sudden personal conviction of the beauty and power of this aria. And I retained this sense of the distinction between the exhilarating personal experience of the power of art and the mere pleasure of acceptance or admiration of art. In the area of performance in the arts, this distinction developed into the sense that some performances had real musical instinct and others did not, some flowed from genuine musical conviction—which took the form of continuity and urgency of motive—and others, however worthy in terms of taste, knowledge, or technical proficiency in the use of the instrument, simply did not, and therefore were not, in a strict sense of the word that I enjoyed using at the age of twenty-one, *interesting*—that is, they did not interest me.

*Figaro,* as it happens, has come to seem to me greater than either *Don Giovanni* or *Così,* and my personal experience with "Deh vieni" led naturally enough to equally intimate experiences of such great, complex moments as the act 2 finale. Indeed, I have a dim memory from this first performance of rapidly rewriting everything that had come before "Deh vieni" to fit my new understanding and my new excitement—and in fact it makes good sense to say that I suddenly in retrospect got the point of it all: of "Dove sono," of the letter duet, and of the great act 2 finale. I have since felt equally exhilarated by most of Mozart's operas: I have come to love them, as well as to admire them and to give them high grades; and without this coming together of love and judgment I could feel no authority or authenticity as a critic.

My surprised reaction to Albanese's "Deh vieni" still seems to me the sine qua non, the experience without which I would never have become more than officially and generally involved in music instead of personally involved, and the same kind of thing was soon to happen with Balanchine. Before seeing any of his ballets I was ready to approve and like his work. I was even ready to fight for it, since I had conceived of him from my reading as a great artist whom it took unusually fine and bold and unconventional taste to admire. And yet my first experience with Balanchine was as powerful as my first experience of *Figaro* and as surprising. I had anticipated approving and loving *Apollo,* but I had not expected to be helplessly overcome by it to the point of shedding tears at the apotheosis.

I remember other excited surprises from these years. Some of them were far from the exalted nature of my discovery of *Figaro*. When I saw my first Preston Sturges film, *The Palm Beach Story,* for example, I could hardly believe I was watching something so witty and sophisticated in the Rialto Theatre in Allentown. Orson Welles's *The Magnificent Ambersons* was a tremendous event, too, and occurred at about the same time. Then there was my first Toscanini concert in Studio 8H at Rockefeller Center.

I am glad to remember such experiences because I am proud of them as judgments; no doubt there are less happy and wise enchantments that I have suppressed. But I believe I had relatively few great moments, and my surprise at them shows that my dealings with art and judgment were far less characterized by pleasure in art itself than I like now to realize. I spent a lot of time learning to like what I knew I ought to like. There was much anxiety and some hypocrisy in this, but my dealing with the arts mainly took place not at these extremes but in the middle ground between enchantment and that degree of anxiety or role-playing that would have inhibited pleasure altogether. I was always sort of at work on this judging business, but I felt that it was a fine business; I never doubted its worth to me and never tired of it; I regarded it as my special business, thought myself good at it, and knew I would succeed in it. Success—that bad word—was my goal, in a familiar American way, despite the supposedly disinterested nature of the aesthetic pursuit. I wanted to be, I hoped to be, and I pretty much knew I was going to be successful at making judgments about art, and this was the center of my pleasure in the arts at that time—this and the anticipated pleasure of seeing and hearing myself acknowledged as a good judge and of seeing my judgments carry authority and influence others' tastes.

My early experience with the work of Willa Cather shows how much I wanted acknowledgment and how curious a form that wish could take. When I was about fourteen I learned, first from one of my influential English teachers and then from a whole phalanx of middle-brow American literary journalists, that Willa Cather was a writer of special excellence. Looking back, I see many things working together to give such stature to an artist who is now identified as minor, although she remains interesting to me. The teacher and the critics I was obeying had themselves followed Cather's career with a strong sense of dedication because they thought of *her* as working with strong and pure dedication: hence the note of tribute in much of the writing about her. All my authorities accented Cather's style, never her insight or vision, her observation or her understanding, and this was the way I too described my judgment of Cather to myself. I admired *A Lost Lady,* for instance, because it was "beautifully written." Exactly what I meant by that is not easy to remember. *The Song of the Lark* actually appealed to me much more in my teens because of my interest in opera, and I still remember vividly my initial excitement at Thea Kronborg's glamorous operatic career in New York, her apartment on Riverside Drive, and other details. This didn't mean that I found the novel better than *A Lost Lady.* On the contrary, I whole-heartedly subscribed to the view that the later work was better. And yet I don't remember that the beautifully written element in *A Lost Lady,* its famous style, was in itself an object of my attention. I could have performed creditably if asked to specify what was distinguished about the style, but I don't remember savoring it or even thinking about it much. I would barely have had time; what I remember doing is something quite different: enjoying Cather's style indirectly through the medium of critical praise. I read about her more than I read her own work, I took more pleasure in seeing her art acknowledged than in experiencing the art itself, and when I saw her art acknowledged I felt acknowledged myself.

To put it concretely, I spent hundreds of hours during my teens in the periodicals section of the library, going through the bound volumes of the *Nation,* the *New Republic, Atlantic Monthly, Harper's,* the *Dial,* and a few others to find early reviews of Cather's novels. Of course, when those reviews were favorable, I was pleased, but I required more, since the novels always were praised. I required that special note of tribute to Cather's rare distinction as a stylist, and when I encountered it—quite often—I felt an unmistakably personal gratification. I had transferred the artist's power and worth to myself in a process as ordinary and as easy to understand in its psychological motivation and mechanism as it is now faintly shameful to contemplate.

I remember making a similar transaction at this age with two other artists, Mozart and Shakespeare, and their immense stature in the world of art helps expose the central dynamics of my need for such acknowledgment. Most critics praise the work of Mozart and Shakespeare in the highest terms, so it was a more intense kind of acknowledgment than mere praise that I hungered and hunted for and transferred to my own account. What I wanted to read was not only aggressive praise of the artists I admired but equally aggressive detraction of their rivals. I conceived of Mozart as being in rivalry with Bach and Beethoven, and when I saw his superiority to these rivals explicitly acknowledged I felt quite simply that I had won. Such anxious adolescent competitiveness (in my case transferred to a safer realm than the gym or the debating club) is callow enough but familiar too. And singling out favorites to cherish and to follow with personal investment and identification sounds pretty much like idolizing athletes or movie stars.

My parents' fundamentalist religion made them forbid me to go to movies or plays, although books and music were allowed. It is because of this that I valued my movie-fan friend so much and that I still feel different degrees of excitement about the arts. Literature has been my abiding, and has become my professional, interest, and I always thought of myself as destined to deal with it somehow—in fantasy by being a critic at least, a novelist at best, but in reality by being a teacher of literature. But because my parents prohibited movies and plays and approved of books, I have always considered literature to be the least glamorous of the arts. And there is a kind of logic, then, in how the excitement I might have felt about movie stars, had I been allowed to watch them, was transferred to other stars, the great people in the arts that I was allowed to experience.

Before about the age of thirteen my knowledge of movies and plays consisted entirely of hearing my friend running through *Rose Marie* and the rest of the MacDonald-Eddy movies and of reading reviews in newspapers and magazines—my introduction to the periodicals room in the library that made possible my later Cather research. I was an excited, in fact a deeply involved, participant, even without firsthand experience, and my guess is that a lot of my sense of participation came from the aggressiveness and competitiveness with which I practiced critical judgment of plays and movies I hadn't actually seen. At first the reviews I enjoyed most came from a theatrical magazine called *Stage,* and I can remember exactly why I loved them. The editors had devised a system of summarizing each review by appending little cartoons of a theatergoer who took one of four possible poses: standing up and applauding, sitting down and applauding, sitting down doing nothing, or leaving his seat in boredom or dejection—you saw only his back, so his mood wasn't completely clear. These cartoons seemed to me at thirteen an absolutely dazzling way of representing judgment, and the cause of this overestimation has to have been my vicarious pleasure in the assertiveness of the "statements" being made by this cheeky cartoon figure. And these characters were matched by an equal assertiveness, a verve of judgment, in the style of the writing throughout the magazine. I fear this would seem pretty crass were I to read it today, but I have been reluctant to check, out of a self-protective leniency toward my early self.

After discovering *Stage* I looked elsewhere for similar opportunities to participate in the experience of art through sharing aggressive judgment making. I wandered through the various magazines available in our library, and in due course (I no longer remember exactly when) I encountered the critic who was to prove decisive for me in so many ways, B. H. Haggin. The music critic of the *Nation* from the mid-thirties to the mid-fifties, Haggin brought the assertiveness, the aggressiveness, the competitiveness of the act of critical judgment to a strength and unremittingness that I hadn't encountered anywhere else. And in his seriousness, his power of intellect, he entirely—or so it seemed at the time—removed all taint of the merely aggressive or assertive from the process. With Haggin criticism was a matter of the utmost public urgency. And his anger (which at that time I didn't consciously hear in his writing, although I must have responded to it with alert intuition) was the anger of the righteous, if there ever has been such a thing in the world. This critic expressed his judgments with a force that made the little man in *Stage* seem just a joker; Haggin meant business, serious public business. He didn't simply leave his seat in disapproval, he fought back. He identified and attacked his critical enemies by name, and he identified their disqualifications by name—their inability to hear what was *palpably* to be heard, their vulgarity, their log-rolling, fantasy-spinning, system-mongering. And it was from Haggin that I heard about ballet and about Balanchine.

The terms of Haggin's recommendation gave it unusual power, even coming from a critic who always spoke with emphasis. He was a music not a dance critic, and he acknowledged his lack of special expertise in recommending artists connected with dance, the exciting point being that the sheer power of what he was calling to our attention had made him risk the charge of amateurism. The dancing of Alexandra Danilova and Alicia Markova and the ballets of Balanchine had given Haggin such pleasure that he could not restrain himself from writing about them for readers who had found his views persuasive on musical matters. These were marvelous conditions under which to encounter Balanchine. I was being invited, by someone whose taste I trusted by virtue of the power and accuracy of his critical assertiveness, to enter an entirely new language in order to experience works of art of great value.

Haggin's invitation to learn the language of ballet in order to appreciate a great artist wasn't as intimidating a challenge as it might have seemed, because reading his reviews had prepared me for such challenges. Haggin was not only a fighter, he was a teacher, the best I have ever known. In his music criticism I had already encountered, and been converted to, a mode of dealing with art as if one were following a mind thinking. In this mode, which has remained central with me ever since, one conceives of oneself as making contact with a mind that is carrying on a line of expressive thinking by making choices between the various directions in which its thinking might move. Art so conceived is a structure of movements that one becomes aware of because there might instead have been a different structure of different movements; as one gathers experience in the medium, one develops a sense of the range of its vocabulary, a sense of what is probable, and therefore one can measure the effect when the probable happens and the different effect when it does not. With this sense of how to go about following an artist's thinking, I went to see Balanchine, prepared to find an artist whose artistic thinking was interesting to follow. I was ready and able to learn the new language necessary in order to appreciate him because I had already been trained to conceive of an art medium as a language in which a mind could embody its movements—its choices—thereby causing the medium to come to life and become expressive.

Haggin's conception of the artist as a choice-making mind embodied in a medium had further implications about what made art interesting. For Haggin the most important kind of artist seemed to be the kind who made, to put it as plainly as possible, a lot of choices. The kind of art Haggin seems to have found most intensely enjoyable exists in a linear dimension and takes place in time and with a kind of narrative logic. And this narrative movement is enclosed in two frames: the known vocabulary and syntax of a language and, on a larger scale, the conventions of a certain art form. Inside these frames the movement of the expressive thinking is knowable because it can go only so far, and one can gauge pretty accurately the distance the mind has moved because of one's sense of the frame. And to gauge this distance, to feel the impact of that movement of mind, is thereby to sense a value—a force of imagination, a power generated by the distance the mind had moved, and a precise power controlled by the precision of the movement—using *distance* of course to stand also for such other factors as direction, angle, and momentum. Haggin's interest in the sheer quantity of choices and in the precise framing of the choice-making activity in order to enable precise measuring of the distance of the mind's movement showed itself in his pedagogical choice of the variation form—Bach's Passacaglia in C Minor, to be specific—as an introduction of the very concept of musical thought to his reader, whom he defines as the man who loves *Hamlet* but doesn't know how to connect with music. It is easy to get your bearings while listening to variations: keeping track of where you are by remembering where you've been, becoming conscious of the minor mode you are hearing by remembering the major mode you just heard, feeling the adagio of one variation by remembering the allegro of the one before. The exceptional legibility of these choices is due to the fact that alternative choices (the other variations) are immediately, or almost immediately, present in our mind.

In this way of experiencing art—and I am taking for granted that it applies to literature as well as to music—the artist is seen as making choices all the time; but some of these choices have a dramatic power of unexpectedness that makes them into events. Identifying events is of course the key process in understanding art, and it rests on the primary assumption underlying the whole concept: that you can derive (and that all people seriously and sensitively interested in an art will certainly derive) a secure sense of the normal choices available to an artist, a sense of the kinds of sentences the artist usually makes at this juncture or that—a sense of the good activity of a good mind. In the framework of a sense of good ordinary procedure, you derive pleasure from recognizing that a particular choice just made by the mind you are following is extraordinary. The upshot is that you not only *want* to measure and judge the brilliance of such choices but that the procedures of the art, and of the way you are following it, make you *able* to judge them and to take pleasure in so doing. In this way your participation in what Haggin would call the "operation" of the artist's mind combines judgment with pleasure.

Thus prepared, at the age of twenty I saw *Apollo,* my first Balanchine ballet and a particularly fortunate one to have lit on. My good fortune was half-accidental, for *Apollo* was available to be seen only because Ballet Theatre, despite its lack of enthusiasm for Balanchine's work, chanced to have revived it in 1943 for André Eglevsky—and the capriciousness of such chances in the world of ballet has not been exaggerated in the legends about the intrigues in this world. Another reason *Apollo* was my first Balanchine ballet, why I went out of my way, down to New York, especially to see it, was that it was one of Haggin's favorites. There was a good reason for this. Though I don't remember his explicitly saying so at that time, *Apollo* happens to be a particularly legible instance of the choice-making artist's mind at work. This piece might well have played in ballet the role Haggin had assigned the Bach Passacaglia in music: that of demonstrating the nature of the medium in itself, of showing what expressive thinking in that medium was like, and of laying out the range of vocabulary possible in that medium and the brilliant choices made by a great artist in a particular work—all at the same time. *Apollo,* more than any other ballet, is full of events.

The other critic whose work prepared me for *Apollo* was Edwin Denby, whom I learned about, significantly, through Haggin. For Haggin's aggressive and angry judgment making proceeded not only by attacking bad critics but also by praising good ones, those from whom he had himself learned, and in the field of ballet there was only one such figure to whom Haggin often paid tribute. When I saw *Apollo* I was equipped by Haggin to follow its thinking, and I was also equipped in a different way by having read Denby.

A key word in Denby's writing about *Apollo* and about many other Balanchine ballets in those days was *modesty.* In 1945 he called *Mozartiana* "another of [Balanchine's] unassuming pocket master-pieces." He was not coincidentally thinking about the kind of modesty one finds in Mozart. And when he wrote about *Apollo,* his accent on its modesty implied that Balanchine, like Mozart, could create art of great spiritual value not only with ungrandiose resources and in a nonheroic genre but also with qualities of grace, charm, and wit that are rarely thought to accompany or achieve profundity or spirituality.

The other important idea in Denby's writing about *Apollo* was that its deepest meanings come not through narrative or dramatic gesture or paraphrasable idea or motive but through the gradually increasing primacy, as the work goes along, of the formal devices and vocabulary of classical ballet. Denby completely accepted the fact that *Apollo* meant something about the birth and the triumph of the poetic impulse: a natural enough thing for a ballet called *Apollo* to be about. His special claim was that the ballet became a profound and powerful expression of this meaning by becoming more overt and explicit in its deployment of ballet vocabulary and structure. Instead of choosing rhetorical afflatus, emphatically noble gestures, and explicitly high purpose, Balanchine had chosen the road of conventional formal art, and Denby implied that this didn't just happen to be the mode Balanchine had chosen for this profound ballet but that it had been the necessary mode.

In this account of *Apollo* Denby was arguing (implicitly as always—for unlike Haggin's his rather Byzantine sense of courtesy forbade direct argumentation) against the view of *Apollo* offered by John Martin, who therefore also had something of an effect on my first experience of Balanchine. Martin, who wrote for the *New York Times,* was the best-known dance critic in America during the thirties and forties, and his views on dance had considerably wider circulation than those of Denby or Haggin. Denby had written for the small audience of *Modern Music* in the thirties and came to greater prominence only when he substituted for Walter Terry as dance critic on the *New York Herald Tribune* for a couple of years during World War II; Haggin had a faithful audience at the *Nation* but it was never large, and in any case he rarely wrote about dance. Martin's judgment was that *Apollo* was decadent: chic, trivial, and artificial—a contraption of empty formalism. This view now seems absurd, and it wasn't easy to account for back then. Of course, one saw easily enough that a generally negative response to *Apollo* was part of Martin's campaign for the kind of expressionistic modern dance and ballet, like the work of Martha Graham and Antony Tudor, in which he was interested. Dance expressionism seems peculiarly boring and faded today, but there is no reason to doubt that Martin loved it; it therefore is not surprising that he should have been antagonistic to *Apollo.* Not that his was a sensible judgment, but this is the way people's tastes do work: only exceptional critics can really see something they are fighting against, much less give it justice. Martin's tone was another matter—a note of waspish, weary, Clifton Webbish outrage emerged from the way he deplored Balanchine's ballets. When he saw *Symphony in C* in 1948 this was his response: "Balanchine has once again given us that ballet of his, this time for some inscrutable reason to the Bizet symphony." Martin was so committed to Graham and Tudor and Doris Humphrey that he just couldn't like Balanchine, one could see that. But something impure in his commitment to these artists showed up in the nastiness with which he did not so much judge Balanchine as revile him.

Whatever his motives, Martin's hostility to *Apollo* in the 1940s usefully fed into my sense that making critical judgments was an excitingly aggressive and competitive business. Martin on *Apollo* proved that everybody was involved in a battle about its value, not just the habitually quarrelsome Haggin. And so in this respect too I was lucky in having encountered *Apollo* as my first Balanchine ballet. Its disputed status made it the subject of the important controversy in its field—just my meat, and I knew which side I was on.

John Martin's hatred of Balanchine owed something to Americanism: first and simplest, Balanchine just wasn't American—what do we need these imports for anyway? Balanchine stood for RUSSIAN BALLET, which Martin thought American ballet companies had to get out from under; furthermore, he represented the late rather than the heroic early period of the Diaghilev Ballets Russes and therefore was a more dangerous influence to have around than the earlier choreographers, Michel Fokine or Léonide Massine—more Parisian, less powerfully Russian, and therefore, in the logic of this sort of thinking, less American. I remember deciding that this objection to Balanchine was foolish, but my judgment now seems to have had little substance to it. My lack of interest in Americanism as such can't count for much, since I had had virtually no experience with the American dance scene before my encounter with Balanchine. It seems unlikely that I would have been more interested then than I am now in Doris Humphrey or Martha Graham, and I also turned out to be uninterested in ballets with American subjects, such as Agnes de Mille's *Rodeo* and Eugene Loring's *Billy the Kid,* when I finally saw them.

On the other hand, I was something of a chauvinist in my proud pleasure that the great Willa Cather was an American, as were my favorite film directors, Preston Sturges and Orson Welles. One of the first facts I learned about Balanchine was that he had worked successfully on Broadway and in Hollywood, and for me today this aspect of his talent—the way he has been able to incorporate American dance impulse into his classical vocabulary— seems immensely important, even crucial and central, which is, of course, a way of saying that I find Balanchine to be a particularly American kind of artist. But I didn't understand any of this in 1945, and I think I considered Martin's campaign for American ballet simply provincial—and I still do.

There was an anti-Wagnerian angle to the *Apollo* battle too that fitted in with many of my other tastes. In loving Mozart and hating *The Ring*, I was flashing my credentials as a person of advanced taste as I had come to conceive of it from my various authorities: I was against rhetoric, against high lyric or heroic afflatus, against the overt intentionality of the expressionistic aesthetic. Through Denby's suggestions I thought of Balanchine as sharing this taste and therefore as being on my side of this battle. I was on the periphery of what I am calling anti-Wagnerism, so much so that Wagner himself—fifty years after his death!—was still at the center of the battle as far as I was concerned. I had not yet read T. S. Eliot and I didn't have that central interest in painting which would have led me to question the importance of subject matter; I was utterly unaware of the "no more masterpieces" cult in Paris and other such aspects of modernism. What I really had a feeling for on this issue was music. I thought *Parsifal* at the Met at Easter was boring and hollow and intolerably tyrannical over its audience. I regretted having missed what sounded like the best opera of the twentieth century, *Four Saints in Three Acts,* with a libretto by Gertrude Stein, music by Virgil Thomson, and choreography by Frederick Ashton, that had been staged only a few times in 1934, with cellophane decor by an all-black cast, to a select and knowing audience.

The bravado and uncertainty of my advanced taste shows also in the way my anti-Wagnerism extended to a denigration of middle-period Beethoven. I was running all of Mozart against Beethoven but I was also committed to the accepted idea, with which I still agree, that late Beethoven was supreme, and perhaps it was as a way out of this dilemma that I chose to single out middle-period Beethoven for detraction. I claimed to find this music overextended, uneconomical, rhetorical, overtly expressive, too earnest, provincially "heroic," naively individualistic. So foolish a mishearing and misjudging of art that seems to me now incontestably major and beautiful is hard to credit, and in fact I hardly know what I meant by it. I suppose I was thinking about the *Eroica* and the Fifth Symphonies, yet I remember no specific dissatisfaction with these works. Practically the only thing I do remember about the Fifth Symphony in those days is being amused by Oscar Levant's calling the way the last movement winds up a "Roxy finale"—and the reason I was amused was that the quip made me hear for the first time the joyous extravagance in this "over-extended" passage. I do hear something a bit thick about the texture of the *Appassionata* Sonata that still keeps me from really liking it, but that's all I can think of on the negative side, and my memories of the expansiveness of, say, the first movement of the string quartet Op. 59, no. 1, are entirely positive. My anti-middle-Beethoven campaign had no real substance to it, but as a negative gesture I think it had a stimulating and clarifying effect. More to the immediate point, it played its role in making me welcome Denby's preview of

Jacques d'Amboise, Allegra Kent (left), Patricia Wilde (right), and Melissa Hayden (obscured) in *Apollo*, ca. 1960 (photo ©1994 Martha Swope; choreography by George Balanchine ©The George Balanchine Trust)

the modestly, sweetly, wittily sublime *Apollo* and in recognizing those remarkable qualities when I experienced the ballet myself.

When I saw *Apollo* for the first time, after having been prepared for it by my critics, I saw with the greatest satisfaction most of what I had expected. I saw a multitude of extraordinary, surprising dance images which represented striking movements of Balanchine's mind, brilliant choices on his part, which is to say that I saw what Haggin had prepared me for; and I also recognized the combination of modesty and profundity that Denby had prepared me for. But there was something else that seemed to take place in another realm: I was enchanted, ravished with pleasure by what I saw; and in the apotheosis, when Apollo and the muses ascended to Parnassus, my eyes filled with tears. I was weeping for the beauty of the moment and for its tragic meaning, Stravinsky's special tragic note of eternal loss that Balanchine had corroborated so simply and affectingly in his choreography. Apollo and the muses represent our art, our capacity for expression, and

Jacques d'Amboise and (from left) Suzanne Farrell, Patricia Neary, and Gloria Govrin in *Apollo,* ca. 1965 (photo ©1994 Martha Swope; choreography by George Balanchine ©The George Balanchine Trust)

therefore they are ours, us, and their immortality is ours too; yet in the lamenting phrases of the music at the end and in the accompanying movements of the dancers these presences are leaving us behind, alone in our mortal human situation, as they ascend into an ideal realm. So this was not only one of my first experiences of the enchantment of art, it was my first intense experience of tragedy.

What I don't remember recognizing at this first encounter is the increasingly explicit formal organization as the piece proceeds that Denby had also prepared me for. I was of course a novice in the language of ballet and had little sense as yet of what explicit formal organization in ballet might look like. But my lack of experience might have made it equally hard for me to judge Balanchine's dance imagery, the boldness of his choices, the distance of the movements his mind was making throughout the ballet. Why could I see the one but not the other? The answer, I think, is that the events, the brilliant choices I was aware of, were not quite, not exactly, embodied in the vocabulary of ballet classicism. They were

Allegra Kent and Jacques d'Amboise in *Apollo,* ca. 1960 (photo ©1994 Martha Swope; choreography by George Balanchine ©The George Balanchine Trust)

strokes of wit and fancy which were embodied in the movements of ballet dancers, and they took place in a classical ballet and in a mode not antithetical to ballet classicism—but they were not exactly classical ballet.

These strokes are everywhere in *Apollo* and they form its mode: the nymphs unwind Apollo's swaddling clothes in a maypole dance; Apollo frees himself completely by a bold balletic pirouette; the nymphs turn themselves into one nymph and a wheelbarrow when they bring the lute to Apollo; in the *pas d'action* Apollo pushes the three muses off on a little bourréeing ride; in the variations for the muses, Calliope has a stomachache of poetic inspiration, Polyhymnia hushes herself into mime with her finger to her lips, and Terpsichore paws the ground like a horse before she begins to dance; in Apollo's variation, Apollo clenches and unclenches his hands in time with the music's pulse (a gesture Balanchine says he picked up from the flashing signs in Piccadilly Circus); the pas de deux begins with a Michelangelo imitation—God touching Adam's finger is metamorphosed into woman inspiring man; later on in the pas de deux Terpsichore sits on Apollo's knees, they play a game with hands and elbows, and at the end they share a kind of swimming lesson; the coda makes Apollo into a charioteer with three horses; at the end of the coda the muses clap their hands suddenly and Apollo falls asleep for a second on the pillow formed by their palms; before the final procession he performs a ritual blessing of the muses' pointe shoes; and in the apotheosis a sunburst figure passes before your eyes like a cloud formation (rather than what it has become in the current version, a brilliant Apollo-logo to ring down the curtain).

These events may have been what John Martin particularly hated in the ballet when he saw it first. In 1957 he came around to liking *Apollo;* the reason he gave for the change was that the recostuming of the ballet in practice clothes had at last revealed its beauties. At the time my invidious reading of his change of mind was that he took the occasion provided by the recostuming as a pretext under which to change to the side the money was on. Later I learned from the beautifully perceptive writing about Balanchine's work Martin was doing in the fifties but which my prejudice was keeping me from reading, that his taste had actually changed. If in 1957 he still thought that "some of the invention remains self-consciously over-inventive," this is a wrong judgment but not a foolish one, for these inventions are indeed directly and proudly offered for pleasure and admiration—and admiration is what they got from me in 1945. The fact that Haggin has chosen to record so many of the inventions in *Apollo* in his *Discovering Balanchine* and that Denby referred to several of them suggests that they were important for both writers. They were important for Stravinsky too. In the official, diplomatic language of the *Autobiography* (essentially a ghosted work, to be sure), he wrote that "Balanchine had arranged the dances exactly as I had wished—that is to say, in accordance with the classical groups, movements, and lines of great dignity and plastic elegance." But one of Robert Craft's books of conversations with Stravinsky, *Dialogues and a Diary,* shows that what Stravinsky remembered from Balanchine's dances is not the classical movements or lines but two of these images, the wheelbarrow and the charioteer, which he naturally calls a troika.

These strokes of fancy were noticed and described because they are particularly noticeable and describable, to be sure, but I think it is also true that they form the special mode of *Apollo.* Terminology is a problem here, and I don't want to seem to be saying that *Apollo* is not a classical ballet. But classical structuring is not the leading feature of its identity, nor is it what seized my interest in 1945. *Apollo* was a lucky first Balanchine ballet for me, then, because it captured my attention by these not-exactly-balletic strokes of dance imagery and then, beneath the level of my consciousness, it began to teach me how to read ballet by inspiring me to follow, and therefore gradually to understand, the logic of its formal dances. I don't remember anything in Terpsichore's variation from 1945 but Alicia Alonso pawing the ground like an elegant horse. Now the wide fourth position, tremendously *contrapposto*, from which she begins the dance proper seems to me in its promise of further movement one of the most eloquent moments in the whole ballet. I have come to understand the way ballet language works.

My education in ballet proceeded rapidly enough so that within just a few months, as I remember, I was able to follow the expressive thinking in *Concerto Barocco* (1941), composed thirteen years after *Apollo*, in which there is almost no vestige of the witty and fantastic dance imagery that had so seized my mind in the earlier ballet. In fact, since *Serenade* in 1934, Balanchine had gradually been abandoning the wit and fancy of *Apollo*, which had also been the mode of *The Prodigal Son* (1929) and apparently of *Cotillon* (1933), a lost Balanchine masterpiece which I have never seen. There is some evidence that this change in style amounted to a deliberate self-criticism. After the 1972 Stravinsky festival Balanchine lost interest in *Apollo*, and when he revived it for Mikhail Baryshnikov in 1978 he seemed to have turned violently against it—mostly because of its narrative elements, I am sure, but conceivably also because of these strokes of wit and fancy which his taste had long before discarded. The distinctive imagery of the great neo-classic masterpieces he made in America is quite different.

In a 1945 review of *Concerto Barocco* Denby describes one of its most powerful images: "the final adagio figure before the coda, the ballerina being slid upstage in two or three swoops that dip down and rise a moment into an extension in second—like a receding cry . . . another image that corresponds vividly to the weight of the musical passage. But these 'emotional' figures are strictly formal as dance inventions." This kind of image, figure, movement, choice, event was to become the essential vocabulary of Balanchine's language, and it will be perfectly clear how different it is from the muses' handclap in *Apollo*. The image in *Concerto Barocco* is arguably greater, and Balanchine's choice to work almost entirely in the mode of the later imagery is probably what made possible the extraordinary breadth and depth of his development as a classical artist. But the imagery of *Apollo* is wonderfully beautiful and the invitation it extended to me was irresistible. When I first saw *Concerto Barocco*, I felt what Denby had promised I would at this eloquent moment, but it had taken a lot of learning of ballet vocabulary before I could do so, and my learning was hastened and made exciting by my first experience of *Apollo*. That is why this marvelous work has kept a special place in my love—for what it is and for what it made possible.

# T W O / *The Monte Carlo Immersion*

*Apollo* made me eager to see more of Balanchine's marvelous art, and his work happened to be abundantly visible in the mid-forties. His great early success had taken place in a world doubly disordered, first by the Russian Revolution and then by the chronic unsettledness of ballet in the West in the first half of the century. Balanchine defected from Russia in 1924 on an almost casual impulse with a small troupe of dancers that included his wife, Tamara Geva, and Alexandra Danilova, who later became his common-law wife. The three met the impresario Serge Diaghilev in Misia Sert's famous drawing room in Paris only a few weeks later, and after another brief trial in London, Diaghilev installed him at the age of twenty as balletmaster of the world's most famous ballet company (the title balletmaster also meant resident choreographer). In this capacity and among many other assignments in both ballet and opera, Balanchine produced his first masterpieces, *Apollo,* at the age of twenty-four, and *The Prodigal Son,* at twenty-five. But Diaghilev's death in 1929 scattered an enterprise that had depended entirely on his personal presence for financial viability, and Balanchine's career was derailed. In the next three years he served briefly as balletmaster of the Royal Danish Ballet before forming companies in Paris and Monte Carlo, which did not last, although two important works were composed—*Cotillon,* now lost (despite the recent attempt to revive it), and the original *Mozartiana,* which was superseded by the 1981 Tchaikovsky festival setting of the same score.

Even after 1933, when Balanchine accepted Lincoln Kirstein's inspired invitation to come to America to found a ballet school and eventually a company, the progress of his career remained uncertain. In the thirties Kirstein and Balanchine formed several different enterprises—the American Ballet, the American Ballet Ensemble, Ballet Caravan, American Ballet Caravan—but none of them lasted. Masterpieces disappeared almost immediately after the making: *Serenade* in 1934 and *Le Baiser de la Fée* and *Card Game* in 1937 for the American Ballet, *Concerto Barocco* and *Ballet Imperial* in 1941 for Ballet Caravan, and, also in 1941, for the Original Ballet Russe, *Balustrade*, which I am calling a masterpiece on trust, since I never saw it. One or two earlier Balanchine ballets remained uncertainly in the repertory of the companies into which the Diaghilev organization had splintered,* but when they were performed they were attacked almost poisonously by John Martin of the *New York Times*. As a result, when in 1939 a new company, Ballet Theatre (after 1957 called American Ballet Theatre), was formed, with much publicity from Martin, Balanchine was one of the few established choreographers who was not invited to make new ballets. (A couple of years later Ballet Theatre did mount *Apollo* for their new star, André Eglevsky, which is the production I saw in 1945.) At the end of the thirties, then, although Balanchine was doing good work and making good money on Broadway and in Hollywood, his career in serious ballet was something that few people followed or even thought about. It was only through special insight and persistence that Edwin Denby, B. H. Haggin, and a few others kept his reputation alive.

Even these knowledgeable people were surprised, however, when Balanchine was invited in 1944 to become balletmaster of the Ballet Russe de Monte Carlo (replacing Bronislava Nijinska, the same choreographer he had replaced twenty years earlier in the Diaghilev company), but by the time I began seeing ballet in earnest, this happy accident had produced an effect that fitted my new interest exactly. Balanchine had immediately, as is the practice in such circumstances, installed some of his older ballets in the Monte Carlo repertory, while creating new ones. Unluckily, I missed the biggest new ballet, *Danses Concertantes* in 1944 to a Stravinsky score, but I saw the older ballets. Then, in August 1946, just after Balanchine had left the company, I was in New York when the Monte Carlo

---

*After Diaghilev's death, two Paris-based impresarios, René Blum and Colonel de Basil, gathered many of the Diaghilev artists (including Balanchine) together in 1932 in a new company, the Ballets Russes de Monte Carlo, which became the "Russian Ballet" that toured in the thirties. Balanchine left the company in 1933 to form his own company, Les Ballets, and later that year he came to America. In 1938 the name of the Ballets Russes was changed to the Ballet Russe de Monte Carlo. In that year a splinter organization, called the Original Ballet Russe, was formed under the direction of de Basil, and it was he who retained the rights to the ballets Balanchine had made in the early thirties—*Cotillon, Concurrence,* and *Le Bourgeois Gentilhomme.*

company decided at the last minute to give a late summer season at the City Center ("air cooled," as advertised—big fans somewhere in the theater blew air across blocks of ice, making the theater marvelously cold when you came in but awfully warm by the third number). I went every night, and the Balanchine repertory was still intact: *Mozartiana, Serenade, Le Baiser de la Fée, Ballet Imperial, Concerto Barocco, Danses Concertantes, Le Bourgeois Gentilhomme,* and *Raymonda,* together with *Night Shadow,* later retitled *La Sonnambula,* another major work of the Monte Carlo period.

I had been in New York all summer, following a first year in graduate school at Harvard that had gone well. My friend Bill Hardy had just been discharged from the navy, where he had served at the Bell Telephone Laboratories in New York (in the building that has since been turned into the artists' complex Westbeth) in a research group that worked on radar and other war technologies. His first act on being demobilized, before starting graduate work in physics at Columbia, was to buy a sailboat and invite me to New York to help him recondition it. I was the least likely candidate in the world for such an enterprise, but my relationship with Hardy had involved a similar project before, when he had forced me to put together that hi-fi set. This time what got me to agree to help him was the idea of spending months in New York—heat didn't seem to bother us at all in those days. Every day in late May and June we took the subway to Flushing and scraped paint off the boat. When it was ready to be put into the water, I helped with the launch, and then, perhaps an hour after embarking from Flushing harbor, I became seasick—probably a delayed objection to the slavery I'd endured for so many weeks. Hardy put me ashore at Port Jefferson, I took the Long Island Railroad back to Manhattan, and I never saw the boat again.

But in the evenings after our work in Flushing we enjoyed a marvelous New York life, centered around our connection with Haggin and Denby. I had written Haggin a fan letter in 1943, and we became good friends; through him I had come to know Denby, and I had introduced Hardy to both of them. They were in their mid-forties, we were twenty-one, and the amount and kind of attention we received from these remarkable intellects ought to have been more surprising than in fact it was at the time. But their response is not really hard to understand. Haggin's interest in contact with his readers often led to his quoting their letters in his column, so my genuine fan letter was exactly the right approach to him, as I had meant it to be. He was uniquely dogmatic, but his mind was extraordinarily acute. The almost entirely unironic strength of his convictions made disagreeing with him a task of considerable anxiety, although he never seemed to have understood this. His fierce, often enraged honesty (he never, of course, agreed with this reading of his tone) made a wonderful contrast with Denby's blend of sweetness, subtlety, malice, wit, and gentleness, combined with a bafflingly hidden social and sexual agenda. As I list these attributes, it seems that Denby ought to have proven dangerous to deal with, and I should say more openly that both men were quite obviously difficult people, but Denby's elusive style yielded in practice an amazing capacity to listen to young people with interest and respect. His central role in New York culture a few years later, as guide to the New York school of poets as well as painters, did not surprise me. The friendship of these two major critics was undeniable but puzzling, and Hardy and I speculated often about what they really thought of each other. As for our part in the relationship, both of us had the insight and common sense back then to understand that our intense and overt interest in being disciples went a long way to explain why we were accepted as disciples.

Through Denby, Hardy had met other New Yorkers, most excitingly Willem de Kooning and his wife, Elaine. This was just before de Kooning's fame. De Kooning had abandoned figurative painting and was beginning to paint abstractions with oval shapes in pale lavender and yellow; I can't remember how or whether Elaine was painting, but I read her criticism. I didn't get much out of either the paintings or the criticism, but the de Koonings were terrifically interesting people to talk to and to watch as they led their New York lives. Denby shared a loft on West 21st Street with the photographer and filmmaker Rudy Burckhardt, exactly the right place for him to live, it seemed to me; the de Koonings lived in a four-story walk-up on Carmine Street in the Village, which seemed exactly the right place for *them*, emphasizing the complete lack of conventional aestheticism in their art, their conversation, and their marriage. During the summer I came to know Denby better. On our walks through the New York streets he would tell me how to look at what we were seeing. It was he who first showed me the special visual excitement of the New York cityscape, which he contrasted with the official handsomeness of the European capitals—and so I began my discovery of American culture, after having aspired more to a European model earlier. Burckhardt's film *How Wide Is Sixth Avenue?* fell into place with Denby's tips, as did the visual excitement in the photographs of Birmingham steel mills by Haggin's friend Walker Evans.

This intellectual excitement was a daily curtain raiser to the feature performance of the summer, which took place at the City Center on 55th Street: the Ballet Russe de Monte Carlo in its Balanchine repertory. During these weeks I watched the ballets in the evening and thought and talked about them with my friends the rest of the time. And however important my first experience with *Apollo* had been in 1945, I believe it was this total immersion in 1946 that was responsible for my commitment to the medium and to Balanchine—I enjoy using the words *total immersion* about the experience because they connect with my Baptist upbringing.

The Ballet Russe de Monte Carlo is said to have been in bad shape when Balanchine took it over in 1944—there is a story of his saying in his patient voice while rehearsing *Scheherazade* or some other war-horse, "Lift your legs, it's the finale." By the time I saw the company, it was generally agreed to be vastly improved, but I lacked the experience to have an opinion on this matter; all I can report is that it gave me entirely satisfactory experiences of Balanchine's ballets. The soloists made a distinct impression but not one I feel much confidence in. I saw *Ballet Imperial* danced by both the capable, rather soft-edged Nathalie Krassovska, who had been with the company since the late 1930s, and the brilliant, sharp Mary Ellen Moylan, one of Balanchine's new discoveries, but what must have been the immense difference between them didn't really register. Maria Tallchief's dance power did register, very memorably; her distinctive Native American face and bearing made her easily identifiable to an unpracticed eye. But the heroine of the whole experience was exactly who it should have been, Alexandra Danilova, the prima ballerina of the company. I was not, as an inexperienced ballet watcher, able to ignore the signs of age visible in her trembling arms when she was supported in arabesque, but these weaknesses made even more moving the taste and tact with which she presented (rather, it seemed to me, than *impersonated*) a character or a style—poignantly in her enchanting image of youthfulness as Swanilda in *Coppélia* or the bride in *Le Baiser de la Fée*, heroically in *The Nutcracker*, gloriously in *Mozartiana*. In the role Balanchine made for her in *Night Shadow* she was a great dramatic actress: her intensity as the Sleepwalker was electrifying; nobody since, neither Allegra Kent nor Suzanne Farrell, has made anything close to that effect on me.

*Mozartiana* inevitably became a particularly important ballet for me: the music, Tchaikovsky's Fourth Suite, is an orchestration of some of Mozart's piano music and of his motet "Ave Verum Corpus," and the combination of these four artists—Balanchine, Mozart, Tchaikovsky, and Danilova—couldn't have missed. *Mozartiana* lingers in my memory as a uniquely fragrant ballet. I had read Denby's praise of its modesty in the *New York Herald Tribune*, and that attribute came to seem enchanting to me too. I loved the overt fancifulness in Balanchine's macabre setting of "Ave Verum Corpus," which combined wonderfully with the sublime music—this was related to the Mozartian wit I had experienced in *Apollo*. Best of all was the spontaneity and charm with which Danilova presented the character and the style of its grand ballerina. When the ballet disappeared, as it soon did, my special memory of it led to a special sense of loss. And here I come to one of the hazards of following Balanchine's career so intently.

When I first saw Balanchine's new version of *Mozartiana* on the opening program of the Tchaikovsky festival in 1981, I didn't take to it at all, although I was by that time an experienced judge of Balanchine's new ballets and although the new *Mozartiana* later

Alexandra Danilova in *Mozartiana,* ca. 1945 (photo courtesy the Dance Collection, New York Public Library for the Performing Arts, Astor, Lenox, and Tilden Foundations)

Suzanne Farrell with members of the School of American Ballet in *Mozartiana,* 1981 (photo ©Paul Kolnik; choreography by George Balanchine ©The George Balanchine Trust)

became in Suzanne Farrell's performances one of the greatest of all ballets for me. Denby had described the original *Mozartiana* as sunny, but the new ballet was about as far from being sunny as possible, with its ballerina dressed in somber black-tinged tulle, her cavalier in a dark purple vest, and the nine other dancers in black. "Ave Verum Corpus" was now the first movement (Balanchine had rearranged the order of the Tchaikovsky suite for his new version), composed in the form of a prayer that was not only completely serious in tone but danced with naturalistic gestures. I was deeply disappointed, almost personally offended. Even worse, Farrell injured herself seriously during the premiere and had to take a long leave; it was thus more than a year before I was released from the tyranny of my own formulation of what *Mozartiana* ought to look like.

Back in 1946, however, *Serenade* with the Monte Carlo company immediately became and has remained a ballet for which I feel a familial affection—it is often called the signature ballet of the New York City Ballet. Its unique capacity to define the identity of dancers comes from its origin. Balanchine made it in 1934 to give his students in the School of American Ballet encouragement in practicing their steps and a comfortable way to appear in public, and the spontaneity with which it was created has never been lost. One of the most famous pieces of ballet lore is that *Serenade* opens with a formation of seventeen girls simply because that is how many students were in the studio the day Balanchine started making it: everyone who knows this experiences the pleasure of secret knowledge in watching the extra girl slip away into the wings when the corps separates into four groups of four. The original structure consisted of group dancing, with several short solos by different members of the group—this too fitted the academic setting and purpose. For more professional performances later Balanchine created a version that concentrated on a single soloist throughout the ballet, something hard to conceive of after one has seen the ballet danced by three major dancers in three separate roles. But at a 1989 Balanchine conference in Florida, the ballerina Marie-Jeanne reported that she had never had any problem with stamina in this immense role; my conversation with her later that day showed her to be so marvelously direct and honest a person that I took her absolutely at her word.

The present version, which Balanchine had first mounted on the Monte Carlo dancers in 1940, uses three soloists to exhibit what seems the whole range of ballerina style: the heroine, who loves and suffers, who "is to bear the burden of fate," in Yeats's phrase, is a lyrical dancer; the angel of death, who steals the heroine's lover, is taller and more sophisticated sexually; and the third lead, whom I call the jumper, comes to the fore in the "Russian dance" that Balanchine added in 1940. She leads a tender, sisterly conversation with four demi-soloists; elsewhere she is brilliant and sharp, full of body power. When a new ballerina appears in one of these roles she identifies herself unmistakably as a certain kind of dancer, and the New York City Ballet uses *Serenade* as a graduation or promotion exercise for this purpose. No dancer in my experience has succeeded in more than one of these roles, although various angels and jumpers throughout the years have aspired to heroine status— Merrill Ashley, a terrific jumper, persuaded Peter Martins to let her try the heroine role after Balanchine's death, but Balanchine had been right, it wasn't her style.

*Serenade* was a general favorite and was scheduled frequently; that I saw it so often and so early helped me develop my own eye for dance identity, a faculty that has given me as much pleasure as anything in my experience of ballet. There have been many wonderful casts over the years. Right now you can occasionally catch spectacular performances by the three major dancers of the City Ballet, Darci Kistler, Maria Calegari, and Kyra Nichols. For me the greatest cast ever came together in the mid-sixties, consisting of Suzanne Farrell, Mimi Paul, and Violette Verdy, in the order described above—this happened during the period of Balanchine's infatuation with Farrell, and as I think about it, I see that it may well

Karin von Aroldingen (center) and four corps members of the New York City Ballet in *Serenade,* ca. 1970 (photo courtesy David Lindner; choreography by George Balanchine ©The George Balanchine Trust)

have represented a rare moment of respite for the dancers from the competitive tensions of the ongoing crisis. I once saw Danilova dance the heroine, and I wish I could really remember it—her grandeur must have been utterly without "heroine" airs.

The Monte Carlo phase of Balanchine's career, so important to me, has been expunged from the official version of the Balanchine story given in the writings of Kirstein and his followers. Here, for instance, from her splendid and essential *Repertory in Review: 40 Years of the New York City Ballet* (1977), is Nancy Reynolds's account of the period during which Balanchine was with the Monte Carlo:

> During the war years, there was no employment, although sporadic attempts were made to give concerts. The New Opera company presented a month of *Ballet Imperial* in November 1942. The American Concert Ballet, made up of Balanchine

alumni, gave one performance in 1943. In 1945, Balanchine took a group to Mexico to appear in operas, and he staged *Apollo* at the Belles Artes. But there were hiatuses everywhere. Then, late in 1945, Kirstein got out of the Army. On 5 November 1945, he and Balanchine presented some students at Carnegie Hall—

and the story continues as if what took place at the Monte Carlo had nothing to do with Balanchine's career.

Reynolds's book claims to be an account of "all the works performed by the New York City Ballet and its predecessor companies from the first *Serenade* in 1935," and the logic for omitting the fact that many of Balanchine's ballets appeared in the Monte Carlo repertory, and remained there until the end of the 1940s, must be that only the work Balanchine did in partnership with Kirstein contributed to the founding of the New York City Ballet. But this cannot be true, for the Monte Carlo experience must have been an important part of the background for the City Ballet in many ways. Getting his hands on a large ballet company again, however briefly, must have taught Balanchine a lot about the management of people, time, and money. Mounting *Ballet Imperial* on the Monte Carlo would have shown him more about how to teach his own dance style than producing it with his own dancers for the New Opera company could have, just as mounting *Apollo* for Ballet Theatre in New York taught him more than showing it with his own dancers at the Belles Artes in Mexico. Several key dancers from the Monte Carlo company—Maria Tallchief, Patricia Wilde, Todd Bolender, and Nicholas Magallanes, to name the most prominent—were brought over to Ballet Society and then to the New York City Ballet when that was founded, giving a continuity of dance style between the Monte Carlo experience and what followed in Balanchine's career.

More deeply resonant was Danilova's presence as prima ballerina of the Monte Carlo company. The renewal of her matchless powers under Balanchine's inspiration and guidance during these years, together with the great roles he made for her in *Danses Concertantes* and *Night Shadow*, tied his whole career together, linking his early relationships with Danilova at the Maryinsky Theater and at the Diaghilev company with their later relationship when she taught at the School of American Ballet (where she continued to teach after his death). Balanchine's vital connection to his Russian heritage passed through those months at the Monte Carlo. The fact that Kirstein played no role in the Monte Carlo episode is sad for him but cannot negate the importance of what happened there to what finally happened at the New York City Ballet.

After my immersion in the Monte Carlo repertory, I became as regular a member of the

Balanchine audience as I could afford to be. I saw all the Balanchine ballets the Monte Carlo and Ballet Theatre brought to Boston, and I went to New York fairly often to see them there, as well as to see the beginnings in 1946 of Kirstein and Balanchine's new enterprise, Ballet Society, which in 1948 became the New York City Ballet. I always checked my reactions to Balanchine against those of Haggin and Denby, my teachers, and I continued to do that until the end of the sixties. But I was having strong personal reactions to Balanchine myself, for his powerful work reached me easily. Who has ever failed to grasp the beauty of the rich outpouring of designs and images in *Serenade* or the grand calligraphy of the lifts at the opening of the pas de deux from *Concerto Barocco?* I was experiencing moments such as these, dozens of them, with such force that I seemed to myself to be having a brilliant career as a ballet watcher. Balanchine had become one of the most important concerns of my life.

Talking about Balanchine at the Sixth Avenue Delicatessen, or the 57th Street Automat, or back in Cambridge was a crucial element in my experience of his ballets, but I never tried to ground my approach to ballet in a systematic study of its vocabulary or grammar. This choice helped save me from two vices of the ballet world—obsession with academic correctness and excitement over athletic feats and world records. But it has of course deprived me of the technical language in which to describe what I see, both to myself and to others. On the other hand, my lack of terms of easy reference in writing about particular movements in ballet has forced me to describe dancing in the everyday language I actually prefer to use. I am more troubled by the possibility that I might see the movements of ballet more clearly if I could fix them in my mind by naming them. Yet although I am skilled at such fixing and naming in the medium of language, I have never considered my expertise to be of great advantage. I learned to read music and play the piano at an early age, but I do not believe that these skills much enriched my response to music or my ability to describe what I hear. True, my ability to read a score helps me *remember* the sequence of events in a piece of music, so since it is through my musical memory that my memory for ballet chiefly functions, I know I would remember ballets better if I could follow their syntax more consciously.

Nevertheless, if I continue to believe that my amateur standing hasn't much cramped my response to Balanchine's work, I have partly his own relation to academic correctness and to tradition to thank. He is like Mozart in having had such a happy childhood in the tradition in which he grew up that he followed its rules without oppression and disobeyed them without rebellion, and in consequence his extension of ballet technique and style became a natural outgrowth of the ballet language he had inherited rather than a break with it. My approach to his ballets took advantage of this in the sense that instead of learning ballet grammar from books or from class, I learned it from watching Balanchine's ballets. His ease with the medium taught me to read its syntax if not to name the elements I was beginning to recognize. For some time after I first saw *Apollo*, for example, I continued to be particularly struck by the witty, often mimetic, images that are so important to that early ballet. Balanchine had timed and placed them to make it easy to measure the distance and the angle of departure between these strokes of invention and the normal syntax of ballet language in which they occur. As I saw *Apollo* again and again, I developed an eye for that syntax, which carried over into later ballets that contained fewer of these images. I was learning from the artist, from Balanchine himself, how to look at the art he was in the process of making.

Both Denby and Haggin had some personal acquaintance with Balanchine, but I didn't really want one. Watching Balanchine make one of his ballets was said to be one of the great experiences in the world I was now on the edge of, however, and in 1947 Denby took me along to a Ballet Society rehearsal; we saw Balanchine making a section of *Renard*, a new setting of Stravinsky's "Ballet Burlesque for Singers and Dancers" (1915–16), a clever Parisian animal skit. Todd Bolender was at the rehearsal (he danced the Fox), and Lew Christensen must have been as well, because I remember a tall dancer (the Rooster)—but I have to confess that I don't remember studying Christensen to try to bring his historic performance of *Apollo* from the thirties to life in my imagination, although I knew the photographs well. I was so frozen by anxiety that I couldn't have had much of an experience even if there had been one to be had. But in fact I cannot imagine anything less central to my interests than seeing *Renard* in rehearsal: it did not have a score I cared about, nor was it "dance" in the sense I had come to know and love, and it did not survive—it was given only five times. My great opportunity misfired completely.

I remember more clearly talking with Balanchine and Denby some years later, as we stood on the right side of the lobby near the stage door of City Center. Denby and I had just seen a performance of *Concerto Barocco* with Melissa Hayden, and my memory is that we had agreed that it had not been good, although this now seems doubtful when I consider how elusive, even evasive, Denby was in expressing judgments in conversation. In any case, it hadn't been a good performance for me, but when Denby spotted Balanchine and took me over to talk with him, Balanchine immediately began praising Hayden's performance in detail, whereupon Denby very inventively and—as it seemed to me—very disingenuously proceeded not just to agree but to add falsely enthusiastic details of his own. That wasn't an experience likely to encourage me to think I would ever be good at talking with Balanchine.

Haggin reported conversations during breaks in rehearsals which had given him great pleasure, but I had a slightly different response to these talks. They sounded as if they would have been rather painful for me and as if they would have left me feeling teased or let down. I am sure Balanchine was marvelous to talk with if you had the right sort of fluency and confidence, but he seemed difficult and even painful to converse with if you didn't.

The personal relationship I wished to have with Balanchine was similar to what Haggin had taught me to experience with Mozart:

> The special circumstances which produced Mozart's concertos made them some of the greatest and the most fascinating of his works. They were produced for the occasions at which he presented himself to the public as the greatest musician of his time—the greatest performer displaying his capacities in music written for the purpose by the greatest composer. Mozart wrote a concerto as an actor might write a play for himself to act in, or a dancer might compose a ballet for himself to dance in; and his concerto is in fact highly dramatic in character. Listening to the first movement of the Piano Concerto K. 482 in E Flat we hear, in musical terms, the curtain raised on a stage on which the orchestra performs with increasing suspense in anticipation of the moment when it bows itself from the center of the stage and the piano makes an impressive first entrance, holds attention for a while, makes a brilliant exit, and thereafter reappears and disappears until the last brilliant flourish of the last exit. And the special fascination of the form is that while the piano is on the stage we are in an especially immediate and personal contact with Mozart—that in the piano's every phrase of melody, every brilliant passage of rapid figuration, every trill, every ornament, we are aware of Mozart himself, showing us everything he is capable of as a musician, attempting to impress us, to dazzle us, and actually succeeding, not with flashy, empty exhibitionism, but with the inexhaustible flow of an invention that is infinite in its variety—now miraculously lovely and poignantly expressive, now deliciously witty, now tremendously powerful, but expressive or powerful with grace, distinction, nobility—in short, with the qualities of a great person and quite the greatest musical artist who ever lived. (*Music on Records*)

Haggin is for me a great critic because in a passage like this he completely and exactly serves the function of criticism as I understand it. This passage taught me how to achieve the experience it described, and that experience proved as valuable to me as the power of his writing showed it to have been for Haggin himself. His account of feeling in contact with Mozart's mind in the concertos helped form my central conception of the way one encoun-

B. H. Haggin (©Walker Evans Ar-
chive, Metropolitan Museum of Art)

ters what E. M. Forster, at a symposium on music criticism at Harvard in the spring of 1946, called "the life of a work of art." Contact with the mind, the spirit, the life of the artist in his art is one of the things I most value. It is not the only thing that matters, but one must be ready for it: susceptibility to this contact is an interest and an ability no one is required to have but important for thinking and writing about art. My 1965 book about Dickens's art, *The Dickens Theatre,* represents a development and adaptation of Haggin's metaphor of the theater, as its title indicates.

With Balanchine, who is, of course, literally a theatrical artist, I happen never to have experienced quite the sort of contact Haggin is describing. Indeed, the contact I have experienced with Balanchine through his art has come to me in a long and complex process that is only now, in this book, yielding its result.

There was another difference between my experience with Mozart and my experience with Balanchine, a difference which I also shared with Haggin and perhaps learned from him. In writing about Mozart, Haggin followed his usual practice, in his books about phonograph records, of discussing the piano concertos and other pieces in a hierarchy, from

"The Greatest Works" (Mendelssohn was awarded only "Best Works") to his legendary artistic dump, "Uninteresting and Unimportant Works." But Haggin did not rank Balanchine's works this way, nor did I. Perhaps the excitement of following a career in progress, of watching invention actually happening, distracted him from his customary preoccupation—some would say obsession—with establishing a hierarchy of value. This was certainly the case with me. I was as interested as Haggin in making value judgments of Mozart's work (although I differed from him in concentrating on distinctions among great works rather than between greater and lesser works). I was proud of my judgment that Mozart's last string quintet, K. 614, while less painfully moving than K. 516, generates an equivalent musical energy; Haggin seemed simply to think K. 614 less great.

With Balanchine I made no such comparisons. I imagine I took it for granted that *Le Bourgeois Gentilhomme* was a lesser work than *Concerto Barocco,* but the judgment simply didn't seem important to think about or even to notice. At this juncture in following Balanchine's career, I was less a judge than a missionary. And so it was that my first extended piece of criticism, written in the fall of 1946, was about Balanchine.

# THREE / *Bearing Witness*

I originally came up with the idea of writing about Balanchine because I had fallen in with a group of graduate students at Harvard who had founded a magazine called *Foreground,* for which I wanted to write because they were impressive people whom I wanted to impress in turn. I had first met them through Haggin, who during the war had become friends with a Vassar student named Jackie Steiner, a wonderful mimic of European art historians in exile. She moved on to graduate studies in philosophy at Harvard but had switched to sociology by the time I arrived, and she was on her way out of graduate school altogether and into pick-up jobs while she devoted herself to Progressive Party politics. We became friends immediately through our interest in music. I was impressed to learn that she was on the editorial board of a magazine and became eager to get involved myself. When I suggested an article about Balanchine, whose work the board did not know, I felt lucky to have so brilliant a subject to offer.

Jackie had just begun living with the most powerful figure in the group: a young French poet, André du Bouchet, who had spent the war years in college at Amherst and was listlessly gathering together an M.A. in English literature at Harvard while waiting to return to France. He was a nephew of Georges Auric, a friend of André Masson, a disciple of Pierre Reverdy and René Char, and an enthusiastic lover of high French romanticism: Berlioz, Théodore Gericault, and Delacroix. His imperious certainty of taste excited and intimidated me; it made me nervous about my own tastes and judgments and leery of expressing them in front of him—all the more so since I was in the process of developing them. André disdained the difficult English poetry and fiction I was learning to understand and like and the close analytic criticism I was learning to practice, and in consequence I led a double life. In his presence I joined in scorning what he called the "incessant sterile ironies" of John Donne, T. S. Eliot, and the New Criticism, but in other settings I felt and expressed a love for this irony; fortunately, my sense of reality as an American graduate student made me keep on trying to understand Eliot's art and criticism better. Carrying on this double life helped me develop a rather unworthy intellectual agility. Although arguing with André could have strengthened and clarified my understanding of Eliot, I. A. Richards, and William Empson—and in fact of André himself, his taste and his judgment—I just couldn't take the chance. Whatever I hoped to learn from André would have been inaccessible had I argued with him; his temperament would not have found disagreement interesting, whereas he obviously liked being looked up to and listened to respectfully.

If, despite my immense respect, he taught me surprisingly little in the end, it was perhaps because I never became fluent in French and therefore never got a really inward experience of his great enthusiasms. I had no trouble with Berlioz—it was through shared enthusiasm for Berlioz that the friendship began. But although I tried hard to appreciate Delacroix (where my inadequate French didn't matter either) and certainly took some pleasure in his work, I never accepted this artist as the model of free creative genius he was for André, and when I see his paintings now they have an almost purely nostalgic interest; Gericault matters more to me. André's most urgent enthusiasm was for the poetry of Char and Reverdy, which my lack of French entirely kept me from joining. I half-realized back then that his excitement about French romanticism expressed his poignant eagerness to return from exile, and this realization may have played a part in keeping me from being converted to his tastes. The fact of the matter, though, is that I am, by temperament I believe, somewhat alien to French culture, as my experience with literary theory in the sixties and seventies showed.

But Balanchine wasn't connected with any of these ambiguous issues. Neither André nor Jackie, nor any of the other people involved in *Foreground,* had any experience of ballet, and they readily accepted my Balanchine piece, partly, I believe, because his name was unsullied by the wrong kind of approval, and partly because it was connected with the glamorous name of Diaghilev, who had had so much to do with forming the taste of Parisians in the early part of the century. But their most important reason for accepting my article was pleasurably visible at the time: they recognized my excitement about Balanchine as being the real thing. My piece was couched in a tone and vocabulary of open enthusiasm that amounted to a form of self-definition. That tone expressed a conviction that the right

way to be interested in art was to be interested in experiencing it as it happens and that the
right terminology to use to describe that experience was the large and unguarded language
of immediate response.

My *Foreground* piece now strikes me as genuine and not unperceptive. I claimed more
knowledge than I actually had about ballet and other matters—something I have fruitfully
done all my life as a way of acquiring the understanding I am pretending to have. And I
slightly misrepresented myself in another way—I wrote as someone who had been following Balanchine's career with great pleasure for some time and had found in this activity a
major component of my experience. The truth, of course, was that I had been interested in
his work for only a short time, and in the literal sense of the word I had not been following it
at all—through a lucky fluke in the politics of the ballet world, I had been catching up on a
career of which the artist chanced to be conducting a retrospective. But if I wasn't telling the
truth about my experience, I was telling the truth about the experience I planned to have.

The main interest of this article in relation to my following of Balanchine's career lies in
the odd way it reflects the critics who influenced me and the effect it subsequently had on
my understanding of the ballets I discussed. I followed both Haggin and Denby in comparing Balanchine with Mozart; in fact, I quoted Haggin. I cited a different passage from the
one quoted earlier, however, and then almost entirely misapplied it. Haggin wrote that
*Concerto Barocco, Ballet Imperial, Danses Concertantes, Mozartiana,* and *The Four Temperaments* were similar to Mozart's piano concertos in the sense that "the creative mind and
personality, the language and style in which these express themselves, the formula which
they fill out with the language and style—these are always the same; but the completed
forms are constantly new and fascinating" (*Music Observed*). But the ballets I chose to
describe at length were *Concerto Barocco* and *Le Baiser de la Fée,* a pairing—of a plotless
ballet and a narrative ballet—that does not show an artist following the same procedures. I
don't think I missed Haggin's point, nor do I think I was simply using the name Mozart as a
blurb. I paired these ballets because doing so made my task easier. I couldn't say much about
*Concerto Barocco,* but I could describe *Le Baiser de la Fée* at length, and fairly accurately,
because at that juncture I found narrative ballets much easier to think and write about than
plotless ones.

The following twenty-one-year-old's description still seems a decent account of an
episode in *Baiser,* a little heavy on the pedal, perhaps, but that may be due to the riveting
dancing of the young Maria Tallchief:

The gypsy moves in the quiet of evil, circles throbbingly about the bridegroom,
hushes the whole stage with the curious lift of her arms and the sway of her body.

One feels with terrific force that the happy village band is no longer playing, any-where, in this world. The young man has come, under some evil compulsion, into another world, a tight breathless world, which closes a circle about him, in the gypsy's movements, until she pounces on his hand. They struggle briefly. The strange, airless passion erupts in a fierce dance of seduction and of the triumph of seduction.

My account of the relation between dance and music in *Concerto Barocco* is less exact, but I was attempting something much harder to describe: "The two girl soloists in the first movement correspond obviously to the solo violins. But the second movement is a *pas de deux* of a boy and one of the girl dancers, with an occasional entrance of the other, which does not correspond in any obvious way to the musical structure—yet we feel a relation-ship." The last phrase isn't an entirely empty gesture. I was reporting that although I *might* have felt a sense of discrepancy between music and choreography in the second movement, in fact, I didn't; that report was and remains a true account of *Concerto Barocco*. But I did make a serious mistake in saying that the second soloist makes "an occasional entrance," since she returns only once. I was writing from memory, of course, as one had to do in the days before videotapes (and as one still often needs to do with ballet), but this alone does not explain my mistake; for when I finally paid attention to the second soloist's return, I saw that it came at the moment of musical recapitulation—something I would not have failed to notice had I really taken it in back in 1946.

When I wrote those vague sentences about *Concerto Barocco* I had just begun to think about Balanchine's musicality and about his conception of the pas de deux. Now, in order to present that thinking about the pas de deux, which is a major element in Balanchine's work, I must temporarily change my narrative mode: what I shall trace now is not my year-by-year experience of his new ballets but how my conception of his identity and his procedures as an artist changed, for these changes took place according to their own logic and timing and not in correspondence with the new ballets I was seeing.

This way of following an artist's career does not fit into a linear chronological presenta-tion. Some distinctly "new" understandings happened at particular moments, but the process often took the form of a recircling back to earlier realizations, which could now be experienced more deeply, more sharply, more subtly. Nor can I remember all the junctures at which I made this or that discovery. I can remember some of them, to be sure, but the discoveries always brought with them a new understanding of other aspects of Balanchine's art, aspects that I must at some level of awareness have been thinking about all along. Approximately thirty-five years after I wrote the piece for *Foreground,* for instance, there came a performance at which I actually *saw* the return of the second soloist in the slow movement of *Concerto Barocco;* that moment instantly refocused my thinking about the movement and then brought other general issues to clarity and fruition. Another important clarification came only recently, when I was in the Wellesley swimming pool, taking a break from trying to formulate the discussion you are now reading: I had the experience of seeming suddenly to realize that the pas de deux in *Concerto Barocco* was the first of its kind in Balanchine's career. Yet I had known this all the time. Such is the case with many of my "realizations" about Balanchine that took place while I was following his career, as it is the case with all "discoveries" about works of art that we keep thinking about: we circle back again and again to some version of our initial response and understanding, but with new awareness, new sharpness of formulation. With no hope of tracing my steps exactly, then, I must offer my conception of how Balanchine's musicality relates to his understanding of the pas de deux as it appears to me now, rather than as it gradually developed.

When Balanchine choreographed *Concerto Barocco,* the slow movement of the Bach Concerto in D Minor for two violins and strings was one of the world's most sublime utterances: I present this not as an aesthetic judgment but as a fact in the history of taste. For me, the movement remains sublime, but in 1940 we all thought so. Classical disk jockeys then would have introduced it as *the* Concerto for Two Violins. The eminence of the music presented a big risk to Balanchine. It had been one thing back in 1934 to make a ballet to Tchaikovsky's Serenade for Strings, Op. 44—this adorable concert piece was by the composer of the world's greatest ballet music and thus seemed comfortably inside the domain of ballet. But the exalted Bach concerto was another matter entirely. It required special handling, which is what I want to show that it got.

I think Balanchine may have chosen in 1941 to set the Bach concerto precisely because he thought he was at last ready for such a risk. And he set the slow movement as a pas de deux because he knew that he was finally able to compose the kind of pas de deux the music required. He had set the first and third movements as duets for two ballerinas because nothing in the duet format was inconsistent with the emotional weight of the music of these movements. But he knew this format would not suit the emotional weight of the slow movement; whereas the kind of pas de deux he was confident he could now compose—and actually did compose—would match the music completely. And so it did, to a degree that erased any sense of discrepancy between the pas de deux form and the structure of the double concerto.

Pas de deux is the central form of ballet in a way that needs no arguing—everyone knows that adagio is the heart of classical dancing. With Balanchine, this centrality emerges from the fact that so many of his pas de deux are unmistakable love duets that contain openly dramatic and expressive gestures of human relationship on the part of both the man and the woman (although in Balanchine, the woman's role is always infinitely more interesting than the man's). We see this in the duet from *Baiser* (1937) that I described above and, in a quite different tonality, in the playfully tender pas de deux for Apollo and Terpsichore in *Apollo* (1928), where Terpsichore sits on Apollo's knees and practices swimming balances on his back. Balanchine made love duets throughout his career; they ranged from the tense self-conscious experimentalism of *Agon* (1957) to the exotic but frank and full-bodied eroticism of *Bugaku* (1963). The last great Balanchinian pas de deux are the one to Gluck's solo-flute Underworld music in *Chaconne* (1976), the duet the ballerina dances with her fantasy lover in *Vienna Waltzes* (1977), and the duets between Clara and Robert Schumann in *Robert Schumann's "Davidsbündlertänze"* (1980).

Some pas de deux in Balanchine seem more like rites than dramatic relationships: the way the couple enter the stage in "Diamonds" (1967), for instance, and the kind of attention the man pays to the woman suggest a ritual of heroic, aristocratic courtship. The duets in *Who Cares?* (1970) are real love duets, but they are public dancing too, show dancing, exquisitely calibrated not to overread the emotional weight of the Gershwin songs. Balanchine's most disturbing ballet of love is the pas de deux called *Pithoprakta* (1968), in which the black dancer Arthur Mitchell was not allowed to touch the white Suzanne Farrell—this powerful and successfully focused work was the most upsetting ballet generated by the crisis of Balanchine's infatuation with Farrell; his more alarming plans for a Salome ballet set to Berg's *Lulu* never came to anything.

But the pas de deux in *Concerto Barocco* is of another kind, deeper inside the idiom of classical ballet, in which the male dancer makes no expressive gestures toward the ballerina but is virtually invisible. He appears to be—and Balanchine has said as much—only the instrument by means of which the woman can dance on a larger scale than she could by herself. Yet these abstract pas de deux generate great emotional power in Balanchine's hands, and they are the locus of his highest art. Examples abound: the several pas de deux in *The Four Temperaments* (1946), the slow movement of *Symphony in C* (1948), the chain of five pas de deux that makes up the slow movement of *Divertimento No. 15* (1956), the six pas de deux in the second half of *Liebeslieder Walzer* (1960), the pas de deux in the act 2 divertissement of *A Midsummer Night's Dream* (1962; the deepest moment in the ballet), the huge minuet and variations in *Chaconne*, and the apotheosis of this kind of pas de deux—which is also Balanchine's farewell to the form and his last gift to Suzanne Farrell—the pas de deux in the 1981 *Mozartiana*. But the pas de deux in the slow movement of *Concerto*

Suzanne Farrell and Peter Martins with Judith Fugate (left) and unidentified dancer in the pas de deux from *Concerto Barocco*, ca. 1969 (photo ©1994 Martha Swope; choreography by George Balanchine)

*Barocco,* as I fully realized only in writing this book, was the *first* such purely abstract pas de deux in Balanchine's work.

The pas de deux of *Concerto Barocco* consists of a continuous series of lifts and arabesques and turns in attitude and in arabesque—familiar, elementary steps and positions and sequences, in which the man's support enables the woman to extend one leg or the other, backward or forward, to different heights and at different angles, to one side or the other. The chain of these figurations covers the entire stage and intertwines intricately with the corps of eight women—sometimes the couple thread themselves through a line of dancers, sometimes they form an arch under which the dancers pass, sometimes they become a pivot to which the dancers attach themselves. The figurations gather power and command hushed attention because one couple dances the entire chain. The single trajectory of the couple's movement enacts one long relationship of engagement and commitment, unfolding in time, in which a man watches, holds, steadies, lifts, supports, displays a

Suzanne Farrell and Conrad Ludlow with members of the New York City Ballet in the pas de deux from *Concerto Barocco,* ca. 1967 (photo ©1994 Martha Swope; choreography by George Balanchine)

woman. Lacking gestures of declaration and avowal, the pas de deux in *Concerto Barocco* does not carry the implication of courtship; and the lack of variation in tonality, the fact that man and woman maintain the same emotional distance from each other throughout, means that the pas de deux makes no overt reference to lovemaking, although it generates an equivalent intensity. The emotional power which the pas de deux in *Concerto Barocco* generates is similar to what the music produces, in the sense that it comes from structure, from the creation of a long, deep, sustained, and developing continuity. This, of course, is why it so entirely suits the emotional weight of Bach's movement.

The pas de deux in *Swan Lake, Giselle, The Sleeping Beauty,* and *La Bayadère* are models for the pas de deux in *Concerto Barocco.* Yet these earlier pas de deux, although deeply similar to the slow movement of *Concerto Barocco* in structure, are quite dissimilar in another respect: they derive a large part of their power from the fact that we encounter them in narrative ballets, where they become love duets. This is not to say that they lack the highest eloquence in themselves and in their structure, but that we can never experience them "in themselves": even if we were to see them in practice clothes on a bare stage, they would still for all of us represent the love relationships of the characters they were originally designed to represent.

Balanchine himself had not really diverged from the pas de deux as love duet until 1940. The pas de deux in *Apollo, The Prodigal Son, Cotillon, Serenade* and *Le Baiser de la Fée* were all at least semi-dramatic, filled with gestures of love, and, in addition, given special point by those strokes of witty invention I found so attractive in *Apollo*. But in *Concerto Barocco* Balanchine pared the pas de deux down to a pure state; he removed the context of narrative which would have let the audience evade the eloquence of the form in itself, and at last he arrived at the deep center of his art. Later he pared the pas de deux down still further: *Concerto Barocco* had originally been danced in rich costumes by Eugene Berman; when Balanchine took those costumes away in the early 1950s, the classic Balanchine ballet took its final form.

He was ready to try this great form in 1941, I think, because he was confident of his own capacity for it and also confident of the capacity of his dancers, those products of the School of American Ballet who had been trained in his technique and style until they were capable of the sustained tension without which the depth of *Concerto Barocco* could never have been achieved. It may have been specifically Marie-Jeanne in whom Balanchine was confident— his mistreatment of her when she decided to marry and have children shortly afterward is a clear though horrifying sign of his special esteem for her.

If Balanchine knew that he had made the right choice in setting the slow movement of *Concerto Barocco* as a pas de deux, he nonetheless had to do some arranging to persuade his audience to accept it. He had first of all to make an easily visible transition from the first-movement format to the second. At the end of the first movement the two soloists and the eight members of the corps freeze into a pattern which they hold until the second movement begins. Then all ten dancers move about the stage in beautifully legible reformation: the soloists circle each other, acknowledge each other, walk together through the corps to the back of the stage, and then separate, in order, it would appear, to leave the stage; but only one leaves, to the left; the other walks to the right, where she is met by a male dancer who carries her to the center of the stage in a great lift, one of the most glorious movements in ballet, to dance the adagio pas de deux by which the movement is essentially structured. About seven-eighths of the way through the movement, there is a passage of especially poignant music, followed by a recapitulation of the opening statement. Balanchine sets to the poignant music the most daring movement of the dance, in which the man thrusts his partner ahead of him, sliding her on her toe, while she ends the phrase with an extension in second; and it is just here that the second soloist returns, at upstage right, as the male dancer leaves and the initial formation of two female soloists and eight corps members is reassembled, then disassembled, exactly as at the opening. The second soloist walks off to the left, the first soloist to the right, the male dancer reappears, and the heroic opening lifts are repeated, but in a compressed sequence which matches the compression of the musical structure.

When Balanchine brings the second soloist back because he needs her in order to match the music, he is also calling attention to his choice of setting the movement as a pas de deux. He had rightly, and with his usual effortless tact and assurance, dropped the correspondence between violins and ballerinas in the first movement to achieve the intensity of feeling demanded by the music of the slow movement that is possible only in the form of a pas de deux; now with the same finesse he brings the second soloist back and restores the initial correspondence to match the recapitulation in the music. The return of the other dancer reminds us that we are listening to a *double* concerto. The reminder comes about in the limpidly unemphatic way normal both to Balanchine's art and to all classical art, but noticing that entrance for the first time gave me a thrilling sense of contact with Balanchine's mind.

What I was most moved by that first time was that I felt in contact with how his mind operated when he was *at work*. And it was exciting to catch another meaning created with the same ease by this return: the reentry by the second soloist upstage right rather than left, where she had exited, creates an almost subliminal suggestion that she has been leading an independent life while we have been following her counterpart—as if we were suddenly experiencing another dimension in the illusion, glimpsing another space, although the feeling disappears as soon as it is recognized. This last is the kind of meaning that may seem farfetched and obtrusive to some, even people who love the ballet and this moment in it as much as I do, but *Concerto Barocco* will survive all of these speculations, which are only a tribute to its power and beauty.

I have taken it for granted that Balanchine could not have achieved the powerful continuity of the slow movement in a duet for two women, or even as a pas de trois for a man and two women, although those forms more obviously correspond to how the line of the melody is first passed back and forth between the two violins and then deepened by an intricate intertwining of the two voices. But my next step in thinking about Balanchine's handling of pas de deux and of the general relation between choreography and music in his ballets was to wonder how I had the right to take this for granted, how I had come to know the capacities of the pas de deux form and the limitations of the pas de trois form. The answer to this question brought to a conclusion my thinking about this element of Balanchine's work and career. It was he himself who had demonstrated the limitations of pas de trois, in the slow movement of a ballet made in 1945, *Symphonie Concertante*. And now I understood why this charming piece is not one of his great works, although it resembles *Concerto Barocco* in so many respects that it ought to have been its equal.

Balanchine alerted me first to the form of pas de trois—to its meaning, its location in the ballet lexicon, and its weight—at a marvelous juncture in *Ballet Imperial*, his masterly 1941 setting of what is not quite a musical masterpiece, Tchaikovsky's Piano Concerto No. 2. This concerto is seldom played, which ought to be surprising in view of the popularity of the first concerto and the constant search for new repertory to fill compact disks—in fact, two decent recordings of the piece came out in 1991. But its lack of popularity is no mystery when you experience it without the dancing. After Tchaikovsky's death, the pianist Alexander Siloti published a revised version of the concerto, almost entirely excising a weirdly long concertante passage for violin, cello, and piano in the second movement, which turns out to be a lovely and original inspiration. Balanchine used Siloti's version, probably the only one he knew, but even in edited form the first movement is too long and diffuse, with painfully bombastic writing for the piano. Balanchine's success in solving its problems makes this movement one of his greatest large structures, and his solution of a particularly difficult problem was also the occasion for one of my proudest insights during the Monte Carlo performances.

About three-quarters of the way through the movement, Tchaikovsky alarmingly begins a completely new episode, after he has already made us listen to twenty minutes of first-movement material, tempo, and style. Balanchine covers for Tchaikovsky's awful decision by an inspired change in format. The original, and basic, format of the ballet was pas de deux and ensemble, the ballerina and her cavalier in balance with a large corps de ballet; now, to acknowledge the new section formally and to divert impatience about it, Balanchine offers a pas de trois, one woman between two men. (At the Monte Carlo performances this was a marvelous Tallchief role, a great memory indeed.) The opulent rhetoric of ballerina and cavalier as they enact their relationship before us—a princess and her consort displaying themselves to their subjects—modulates at a stroke into an elegant *social* lyricism perfectly in accord with the new musical material, which turns out to be exceptionally attractive, worth the attention Tchaikovsky and Balanchine gave it. And Balanchine's first lesson in the difference in emotional weight between pas de trois and pas de deux succeeded with this particular pupil: I loved getting the point of it. Later ballets continued my instruction in pas de trois and showed the variety the form was capable of in his hands. He made it one of the most idiomatic and various entries in the ballet lexicon—I think particularly of the skating pas de trois in the last movement of the *Divertimento No. 15,* the witty twin pas de trois in *Agon,* the three interlocking pas de trois in *Liebeslieder Walzer,* and the lovingly full paradigms of the form in *The Figure in the Carpet* and "Emeralds."

The pas de trois in the slow movement of *Symphonie Concertante,* on the other hand, does not belong with this company for me, because there Balanchine disobeys his own instincts about the form. The slow movement of Mozart's Sinfonia Concertante for Violin and Viola, K. 364, is almost as central to the work of Mozart as the slow movement of the double violin concerto is to that of Bach—an unending, plangent outpouring of deep, instinctive eloquence. But Balanchine's choreography had never carried the same weight as the music for me, and my thinking about the decision to use a pas de deux in *Concerto Barocco* now shows me that when Balanchine set the Mozart movement as a pas de trois he simply denied himself access to what the music demanded.

Wondering how this lapse could have come about—for I feel such comradeship with Balanchine in musical taste that I find it hard to accept his having a different conception of that movement from mine—I come to the conclusion that I am once again in contact with Balanchine's mind at work, but this time in another role, that of a pragmatic man of the theater. When he created *Concerto Barocco,* for American Ballet Caravan, he had on hand a dancer of the very highest caliber, Marie-Jeanne, of whose power he could take advantage to set the slow movement as a new kind of pas de deux; and since she was the prima ballerina of the company, he could use a less important dancer as the second soloist without giving offense or creating an imbalance. But *Symphonie Concertante* was created for students of the School of American Ballet, whom he was using, as the program booklet promised, "to show the relationship between a classical symphony and classical dance" at a program of the National Orchestral Society entitled *Adventure in Ballet.* It was probably simply out of the question to attempt a major pas de deux without a major dancer; it may also have been inappropriate to single out one student as the "ballerina," which is to say that he may have chosen the pas de trois form in full awareness that he was undersetting the music. There was another issue as well: the sense of two quite different voices in antiphony is far stronger in the Mozart concerto than it is in the Bach, because of the difference in timbre between violin and viola in the Mozart. So it may have seemed not only practical but logical, even musical, to employ the pas de trois, in which the antiphony could be made visible. And if Balanchine noted the limited emotional weight of the pas de trois compared with the power and density of Mozart's music as a problem, he may have argued to himself that the graceful intertwinings of the movement he planned nevertheless suited the limited emotional resources of the student dancers; and he may have concluded that this solution was all he could hope to achieve on that particular occasion.

When he revived the piece for Ballet Society in 1947, however, there were two supreme dancers at the top of the roster, Maria Tallchief and the young Tanaquil Le Clercq, who differed both physically and temperamentally in a way that wonderfully matched the difference between viola and violin. It was practical and musical to use them both. (Let me add, by the way, that my discussion of this ballet is entirely based on the superb Tallchief–Le Clercq performances of the fifties; the lifeless revival by American Ballet Theatre in 1984 raises questions about the permanence of the Balanchine repertory that cannot be addressed here.) But Balanchine's decision to stay with the lightweight loveliness of the choreography he had composed for the students instead of attempting something deeper was a choice to stay with choreography that is neither the masterpiece the music demands nor even correct for that music. I make this judgment at the level of Balanchine's own standards, of course, but I feel licensed to do so, since a later development showed that Balanchine had not convinced himself that all was well with *Symphonie Concertante*. For he dropped the piece from the repertory in the late fifties—perhaps for the reasons that my sense of its limitations suggest.

After the moment in which I really saw the reentry of the second soloist in *Concerto Barocco*, I wondered why it had taken me so long to see it. It is likely that my *Foreground* article had something to do with the delay. Just as my memory of *Mozartiana* from the Monte Carlo experience blinded me temporarily to the 1981 version, so the very process of formulating my understanding of the relation between music and choreography in *Concerto Barocco*, vague as it was, may have put the question out of my mind for a while, and may have had the more serious effect of putting that moment of reentry, and all its implications, *out of sight*. I say this because I know for a fact that my formulation of *Le Baiser de la Fée* in *Foreground* helped close my books on that ballet for a long time, so much so that it blinded me for a couple of seasons to the beautiful ballet Balanchine made when he composed the *Divertimento from "Le Baiser de la Fée"* for the 1972 Stravinsky festival.

Balanchine's revival of *Baiser* for the New York City Ballet in 1950 showed that he continued to be interested in the piece, as did I. He may have had another motive as well. This ballet had never quite worked; despite Stravinsky's and Balanchine's genius and experience in theatrical matters, the basic structure of the ballet never came across in the theater. In genre it is a full-evening narrative ballet but in epitome: four scenes are separated by entr'acte music that is played while the curtain stays upraised on a darkened stage. In the opening scene, a mother loses her child in a storm; the child, a boy, is discovered by a strange, cold fairy, who seals her possession of him with a kiss. Some peasants find him and bring him up. In the second scene, the boy, now grown to manhood, celebrates his coming marriage outside a mill; when he is left alone, the fairy enters, disguised as a gypsy, and seduces him, then sends him into the mill to dance with his bride. In the third scene the bridal couple are dancing when another bride appears, the fairy in a black bridal gown, come to take possession. In the final scene the fairy holds the young man forever in her eternal realm.

In practice, these scenes were slightly too short to capture the audience's attention fully enough to keep them from talking during the beautiful entr'actes; bringing the curtain down made things worse, and there was no other solution, since the ballet required sets and set changes. There was another problem, too, in Balanchine's eyes if not in mine—he never found choreography for the last scene that satisfied him. I remember two versions, and I liked both: in the first the fairy made majestic gestures of domination on a high platform toward which the young man endlessly tried to climb up a rope netting. The second was a trompe l'oeil pas de deux behind a scrim: the youth knelt inert and submissive in front of the fairy as she bourréed around him, lifting first his one arm, then the other, in an infinite and eternal act of possession. But Balanchine liked neither of these endings, and he dropped *Baiser* after a few years.

Granted his problems with *Baiser,* Balanchine had a hard choice to make for the Stravinsky festival in 1972. It was out of the question to omit so important and beautiful a score, but it may have seemed tactless to assign a score he himself had attempted to one of the other choreographers who were also composing for the festival. His solution, in the *Divertimento from "Le Baiser de la Fée,"* was to use the 1934 concert suite, fleshed out with additional music from the original ballet—chiefly from the mill scene—and to set that music with a suite of dances that presents the theme, the mood, even an approximation of the situation of the original scenario but in a structure that satisfied his current taste in ballet form. In the original ballet the scene began with a dance of the bride and her bridesmaids, followed by a classical pas de deux for the bride and groom: entrance, adagio, variation for the bride (but none for the groom), and coda. And here came the new creation: an additional variation, for the groom, which balances the structure (I've never heard an explanation for the imbalance in the original ballet)—a shifting, restless, uneasy dance that amazingly succeeds almost by itself in recapturing the anxiety of the original ballet.

But because this variation was danced to the music for the gypsy pas de deux I described above in the quotation from my *Foreground* piece, I simply couldn't accept it. I had formulated a conception of *Le Baiser de la Fée* to get clear in my mind and on the page the ballet I loved; and now my own formulation made me think Balanchine's new use of the gypsy music "wrong." I associated the jabbing musical pulse of this section so closely with the struggle between the gypsy's pull and the bridegroom's fearful fascination that I felt a sense of incorrectness about the new solo, as if the musical rhythm demanded a duet. I remember going so far as to argue that this music subtly suited the form of a pas de deux but not the form of a male variation (I may have argued with perverse exactitude that it was *precisely* a male variation that the music did not suit). I had a more rational objection to the new setting for the soft flute scales at the end of this passage. In the complete ballet, Balanchine had set those scales with one of his great inventions—the gypsy coming up behind the bridegroom and pushing him toward his bride by extending her pointing finger again and again over his shoulder—an invention I admired even before I saw the ballet, since it was Haggin's favorite example of what he called "fantaisie Balanchine." I still hear the music as a gesture, and I still think it weakly represented by the lack of gesture in the new exit.

I continued loyal to my own formulation when a couple of years later Balanchine added a further pas de deux and a finale, which were set to the hypnotic cold rapture of Stravinsky's rhapsody on "None but the Lonely Heart" followed by the frozen eloquence of the *Berceuse des Demeures Eternelles*. They also seemed to me wrong, and this time I believed I had on my side the discordance between the hauntingly somber music and grave choreography and the bright colors of the peasant costumes. But it was I who was wrong, pushing at a door that opened inward; eventually Balanchine's art proved strong enough to convince me. Once I felt the tragic irony in the image of those ballerinas in their short, bright peasant dresses moving in stiff-backed bourrée as they implacably separate the lovers, I saw that the *Divertimento* was one of Balanchine's most adventurous and successful mixtures of modes.

As I try to see this image in my memory, I realize that I will never have the experience of *Divertimento from "Le Baiser de la Fée"* again. What I have been describing existed only in ephemeral performances in the theater and it is perhaps that fact that accounts for the urgency, perhaps the willfulness, with which I tried to formulate an image of *Le Baiser de la Fée* in my mind—certainly it is the main explanation for the loyalty to my own formulation that made me resist the later ballet. I didn't want to give up something I had rescued from the passage of time. And the harder truth is not only that these ballets exist only in performance but that they had full reality only in performances Balanchine himself rehearsed. Patricia McBride and Helgi Tomasson were the first performers of *Divertimento from "Le Baiser de la Fée"* in 1972; they were marvelous dancers, and their performances were sensitive, imaginative, deep, intelligent, skillful in the last degree—everything one could want. But "their" performances were also what they achieved together with Balanchine in rehearsal. Like most dancers, they had subtle and exact bodily memories—McBride's greatest gift, perhaps, was an uncanny ability to keep her initial performance of a role as she was taught it absolutely intact in later performances—and both of them continued to dance this particular ballet marvelously until they retired, so that their part of *Divertimento from "Le Baiser de la Fée"* continued to come into existence on many afternoons and evenings after 1972. It is conceivable that other dancers some day will dance these roles as well as they, although the inspired exactitude with which Balanchine matched choreography to dancers makes it rather unlikely. But the dancers' infinite skills of style, of nuance and timing and shading, and their capacity to impart them, by means of which Balanchine brought *all* the elements of this ballet, all its discordant tones, into unity—which produced the eerie doll-like inhumanity of those implacably bourréeing peasant girls—will not come again. The ballet I've been trying to describe, which my own description of its antecedent for a time kept me from seeing, will never be seen again. You'll have to take my word about it.

# F O U R / *Ballet Society*

While I was experiencing my August 1946 immersion in Balanchine's work and writing my *Foreground* article, his career took a turn that might well have increased the excitement of my enterprise but didn't quite do that. Lincoln Kirstein returned from war service in 1945, after which Balanchine joined him in forming Ballet Society, a subscription organization dedicated to the production of "lyric theater." Ballet Society gave six programs in two years; it mounted three major Balanchine works—*The Four Temperaments* in 1946 and *Symphony in C* and *Orpheus* in 1948—and it came to figure as a major entity in the history of ballet when it was renamed the New York City Ballet in 1948 and took its place as the ballet branch of a group of publicly supported institutions for the performing arts called the New York City Center of the Arts. Ballet Society may now seem to have initiated a major change of mode and status in Balanchine's art, in which he made the transition from showing his works under haphazard or ad hoc circumstances to special interest groups, to working as the full-time director of a public institution for a large general box-office audience. But although I was excited by the two Ballet Society programs I saw, I did not believe that I was watching a major metamorphosis. In fact, despite, or perhaps even because of, my excitement, I didn't really get much out of either experience beyond that excitement. I wasn't yet good at formulating first impressions in ballet; but I have come to believe that neither the spirit of Ballet Society nor the actual programs it presented were central to Balanchine's art, either as I conceived of it then or as I conceive of it now.

Ballet Society gave its debut performance on November 20, 1946, in the auditorium of

Mikhail Baryshnikov and members of the New York City Ballet in *The Four Temperaments,* 1979 (photo ©1994 Martha Swope)

the Central High School of Needle Trades, an odd setting, which gave a special accent to the excitement I felt at participating in so important a New York event. The program consisted of a restaging of the Ravel opera *L'Enfant et les Sortilèges*—which Balanchine had staged first at its premiere in Monte Carlo in 1925—along with the premiere of *The Four Temperaments,* set to a Hindemith score that Balanchine had commissioned in 1940 with money he had made in Hollywood and on Broadway. (Apparently, he had not originally intended the score for dancing but had commissioned it simply to become, in a modest way, a patron of the music he admired. By 1941, however, according to Bernard Taper, he was beginning to consider how he might set the piece.) The atmosphere of this event, which emphatically represented the "lyric theater" to which the new institution had dedicated itself, differed strikingly from what I had come to love in Balanchine's work and was not, in fact, representative of his future, nor of his essential and abiding interests.

Although my excitement at attending a glamorous New York premiere may have hindered my concentration on the works performed, there were other inhibiting factors as well. Ravel isn't one of my enthusiasms, and I have never found his little opera a work of even mild interest, much less consequence. Years after this performance I found in Nancy Reynolds's *Repertory in Review* an enchanting picture of Tanaquil Le Clercq as the Princess, from which I concluded that the 1946 version of the opera may have had sharper focus and greater distinction than the version I saw in 1975, when Balanchine produced it for the Ravel festival of the New York City Ballet with Christine Redpath as an emptily pretty Princess and not much excitement anywhere else. But I'm not even sure of this—perhaps it's just a wonderful photograph. That Balanchine mounted the opera three times in expensive and theatrically complex productions may, but does not necessarily, mean that he thought it an interesting and important score. The 1925 production certainly must have mattered to him: it was one of his first assignments after emigrating to the West and one of his first connections with an important twentieth-century composer. The later revivals may have been, so to speak, tributes to that early part of his career, just as his final setting of Stravinsky's half-spoken, half-danced version of *Perséphone* for the Stravinsky festival of 1982 was a tribute not only to Stravinsky and to one of Balanchine's wives, Vera Zorina, who spoke the title role, but also to his entire theatrical past. In any event, whatever his motives may have been for mounting *L'Enfant* three times, neither of the versions I saw showed me how or why it mattered to him.

But from its first revival in 1950 *The Four Temperaments* became an important work for me, and I feel disappointed in myself for having gotten so little out of it at the premiere. I failed to spot the pas de deux set to the third theme of Hindemith's theme and variations structure, which became a dance Balanchine repeatedly used—both as rite de passage and as pedagogy—to signal interest in a new dancer; even something as appealing and accessible as Phlegmatic's languidly jazzy dance with his four girlfriends passed me by. What I remember most vividly from the premiere, in fact, is the ending, which Balanchine changed when he revived the piece for the New York City Ballet. On opening night he formed the entire cast into a seething volcano out of which William Dollar erupted three times, in time with those final strokes of music that are now marked by traveling lifts of the four principal couples, who are borne across the stage like projectiles through the lines of the rest of the company. It is foolish to feel ashamed of having liked this bona fide Balanchine invention so much, and I don't remember other people considering it vulgar or coarse at the time. But after Balanchine discarded it, the volcano came to seem rather a cheap trick; the fact that I remember it virtually alone from the entire work does imply that despite my baptism in Balanchine's language a few months earlier, I was still more responsive to special effects than to dance values.

Also soon to be discarded from *The Four Temperaments* were the atrocious costumes by a neoexpressionist painter named Kurt Seligmann. I won't claim that it was these wretched bunches and strips of wadding that kept me from seeing Balanchine's choreography, but they are notorious for the way they hid the steps. What now strikes me as more important is that the very existence of these obtrusive costumes shows how little connection the opening program of Ballet Society had with the direction Balanchine's interests were to take. It is true that in 1946 he was not yet known for his indifference to ballet decor; perhaps he had not as yet developed it. Apart from *Serenade,* all his early American works had been presented with fairly elaborate sets and costumes: *Ballet Imperial* had a Mstislav Doboujinsky backdrop representing St. Petersburg; *Concerto Barocco* featured decor and costumes by Eugene Berman in his own "neo" style. The existence of these sets seemed acceptable and even natural at the time. The *Ballet Imperial* drop fitted the homage to Petipa in Balanchine's choreography, and it was spacious and quiet enough to allow an unobstructed view of the dancing; when Balanchine revived the ballet in 1964 at the New York State Theater, he seems as a matter of course to have commissioned a new backdrop by Rouben Ter-Arutunian. (Conceivably, only the company's puzzling failure to dance the piece well led to the eventual abandonment of decor and the simplification of costume.)

The Berman costumes for *Concerto Barocco,* on the other hand, in particular the bobbing headdresses, had been distracting from the beginning, but that does not seem to have been why the Monte Carlo company danced the revival in unusually ugly black leotards; apparently there was some hitch in negotiating the transfer of the Berman costumes from Ballet Caravan to the Monte Carlo. When Balanchine revived the piece for the opening program of the New York City Ballet in 1948, the Berman sets and costumes returned. In 1951, however, they were again replaced by black leotards, which were used steadily until the sixties, when the elegant white costumes and brilliant lighting that make the ballet so beautiful now made their appearance. All this suggests a conventional acceptance of decor on Balanchine's part before Ballet Society. But there are anecdotes about his furtive attempts at dress rehearsals of *The Four Temperaments* to thin the Seligmann costumes down without Seligmann's being aware of what he was doing. That this action was necessary so late into the production suggests that Balanchine had paid no attention to the decor, even though the company had commissioned it. All this also suggests that the importance of decor in Ballet Society, and its purpose to produce lyric theater, was less Balanchine's than it was Kirstein's.

It is Balanchine's lack of commitment to "total" lyric theater to which I venture to ascribe what seems to me the failure of *Orpheus.* My view is a minority one, since *Orpheus* continues to be a favorite with audiences and was the most widely publicized work mounted by Ballet Society—in fact, the triumph of *Orpheus* motivated Morton Baum to invite Kirstein to form the New York City Ballet. But in 1948 my eye for dance had developed to the extent that I immediately and confidently knew that the new work was not going to be one of my favorites. I was impressed by the unity of the whole production of *Orpheus,* but it seemed to me to have been achieved at too great a cost to what mattered most to me in Balanchine's art.

The actual event of the premiere was thrilling, though. I already knew and loved the Stravinsky music, which I had heard at a concert of the Boston Symphony Orchestra and which Stravinsky had already recorded, and the fact that he himself was conducting the ballet that night increased the excitement. The decor was by Isamu Noguchi, whose paper lamps I later came to love and to buy but whose stage work I had already encountered with the strongest distaste in the abominable *Cave of the Heart* that Martha Graham premiered at a symposium on music criticism in Cambridge in 1946. His powerfully sculpted shapes in *Orpheus*—dinosaur eggs, as they soon came disrespectfully to be called—had the authority to command attention, yet I couldn't take them as seriously as they were meant and still don't, though I share the general admiration for the panache of his lighting, the scrim, and another curtain effect that looked to me like a giant teardrop. Actually, for this Balanchine lover it was the choreography that disappointed most, and my response has remained unchanged. There are good taste and eloquence in the grave *plastique* Balanchine chose as his essential mode; it is fully appropriate to the music and was clearly prescribed by it. But these "correct" choices meant that *Orpheus* lacked the kind of dancing for which I had come to love Balanchine—dancing of highly stylized artifice, with a wide range of speed and nuance and brilliant detail.

Indeed, the mode of *Orpheus* has become more rather than less mysterious to me since its premiere. The evidence suggests that the Orpheus myth had great power over Balanchine's imagination, at least since his days as opera choreographer in Monte Carlo; as ballet director at the Metropolitan Opera in 1936, Balanchine mounted Gluck's opera *Orpheus and Eurydice* with Pavel Tchelitchev sets; during his association with the Hamburg opera, he mounted it again in 1963, then brought the production to Paris in 1973; it is from this production that he derived the 1976 *Chaconne* for Suzanne Farrell. As I think about all these ventures and look at photographs of key moments, eager to discover the exact terms of Balanchine's interest in this material, only with *Chaconne* can I see why the story mattered so much. As a scenario about the nature and source of art, the Orpheus myth has many possibilities, but they have never seemed Balanchine's kind of possibilities. The tremendous power of the human relationship rendered in the opening "swimming" pas de deux from *Chaconne* make it one of the great Balanchine creations and also suggest that the dramatic relationship between the characters interested Balanchine most in the story.

But here is exactly where *Orpheus* is most puzzling. I can't find a moment in the whole work when some accent or note or tone in the dance suggests special attention, concentration, focus, even any significant degree of interest on Balanchine's part—rather the opposite: there is a depressingly moderate competence throughout that suggests duty rather than inspiration. For years I heard myself exempting the central pas de deux, in which Eurydice tries to persuade Orpheus to look at her, from this general indictment; I remember making up an explanation of why and how this dance acquires a particular eloquence from being performed in the narrow space at the front of the thrillingly dropped scrim that hides the scene change. But eventually I allowed myself to blow sophistry away in the frank confession that even the pas de deux seemed to me from the beginning thoroughly conventional in its realization of the famous dramatic situation—what almost any choreographer would have done—and I now see that Balanchine was in the most obvious way strapped and handicapped by not having the full three-dimensionality of the stage to work with.

From the beginning I had been struck by the painful discrepancy in style and value between the music and the choreography for the Furies and the Bacchantes: while Stravinsky was reworking his ostinato rhythms into the silkily menacing refinement of a new *danse sacrale*, Balanchine was marking time with feeble jumpings and dartings. Perhaps Stravinsky's rhythm on this scale did not attract him—one remembers that he never wanted to make his own *Sacre du Printemps*. As for the extraordinarily original timbre of the serene music with which Stravinsky begins and ends the ballet, the best that can be said for Balanchine's choreography for Orpheus grieving with his friends, or for the ascent of the lyre into the stars at the end, is that these quiet movements allow one to hear the marvelous music without competition—but these are pitiful terms of praise for a Balanchine ballet.

The meat of my experience at the *Orpheus* premiere came after the performance, when the young composers with whom I had driven down and I went to the Sixth Avenue Delicatessen (on the East side, since demolished to make way for Eero Saarinen's CBS building), which I knew to be a haunt of Balanchine's. We were not disappointed, for there soon appeared in a booth near ours not only Balanchine and Maria Tallchief but a bald man whom one of us—perhaps myself—was knowledgeable enough to identify as Eugene Berman. We didn't consider Stravinsky's absence remarkable, nor do I remember his taking a bow after the premiere, although he must have. Perhaps we realized that he simply wasn't the man to go to the Sixth Avenue Delicatessen after a premiere, whereas it was terrific that Balanchine and the glamorous Tallchief were the sort of people who did.

The transcendent experience at the delicatessen seemed at the time ample justification for the special pains I had taken to get to New York, but now the fact that I remember this part of the experience with greater pleasure than I do the performance indicates the degree of my disappointment in *Orpheus*. Another indication is the realization that I have no memory of my first experience of another Balanchine masterpiece, *Symphony in C*, which I first saw on the same program. Balanchine had originally mounted Bizet's recently discovered youthful Symphony in C on Tamara Toumanova, Tallchief, and others at the Paris Opera Ballet in 1947, under the name *Le Palais de Cristal* and with brilliantly colored costumes; the American premiere under the new name, with white costumes against a blue drop, had come in March 1948. When I saw it in April I had probably exhausted myself handling the experience of *Orpheus*—exhausted not merely physically: I must have been depressed by disappointment. There is negative evidence for this. Tallchief danced the first movement of *Symphony in C* that night and Le Clercq the second; the excitement of the event must have produced great performances, but I remember nothing of them. Even stranger, I don't remember Tallchief or Le Clercq in these roles at all, although I saw the two of them dance them many times with the New York City Ballet.

My having missed the impact of *The Four Temperaments* and *Symphony in C*, then, two of Balanchine's greatest works, was due to factors quite irrelevant to those works in themselves and does not suggest that I was not following his career with interest and excitement in the late 1940s. I did not fail to appreciate *Theme and Variations*, which Balanchine had made for Ballet Theater in 1947, and I retain distinct memories of Alicia Alonso and Igor Youskevitch in this ballet. As for the work itself, I eventually decided its opening sections were unsatisfactory (although everything after the adagio *danse d'école* for the ballerina and four demi-soloists is marvelous). But my more important experience of Balanchine in the late forties was not with Ballet Society or the New York City Ballet, partly because it was impossible for me to go to New York regularly enough to have settled and calm experiences there, but at performances of Balanchine ballets by the Ballet Russe de Monte Carlo and Ballet Theatre when they came on tour to Boston. There, I really followed Balanchine's work, and if this means that I was actually concentrating on catching up on past work rather than focusing on work in progress, it was nothing new for me; that was a pattern I followed in dealing with other artists I was interested in at that time.

My response to the formation of what became the great artistic institution of my life, the New York City Ballet, was not very prescient. Institutions did not interest me at the time, not even the Hollywood studio system, the one artistic institution from which I might have learned something in the 1940s. In the case of the New York City Ballet, however, perhaps only Lincoln Kirstein saw what was possible. It was he to whom Morton Baum, after the premiere of *Orpheus,* offered the connection with the City Center, and it was he who spoke the famous words, "I will give you in three years the finest ballet company in America." But even had I known of it, this claim would not have impressed me; I was (and still to some extent am) under the influence of B. H. Haggin's scorn for and distrust of Kirstein, which was as unbounded as was his reverence for Balanchine. As Haggin's editor at *The Hound and Horn* Kirstein had mangled Haggin's copy, an unforgivable offense, but he had also imprinted himself indelibly on Haggin's mind as a classically irresponsible "idea-spinner." Haggin had devastating anecdotes to prove his case. Throughout the thirties and forties Kirstein had followed many bursts of optimism about the future of ballet in America with ensuing drops into pessimism, and what he told Baum, although a completely accurate prediction, sounded at the time no different from earlier claims. Then again, my view of *Orpheus* was such that I wouldn't have much respected Baum's judgment in having been so excited about it as to want an institution formed to make more ballets of its kind. In any case, the founding of the New York City Ballet amounted at the beginning merely to the renaming of Ballet Society, so my experience at the theater remained much the same: what I was interested in still were the Balanchine ballets from Ballet Society, which were still performed by the same dancers and musicians, for the same brief weeks, and in the same inadequate setting—the City Center. It was thus hard for me to feel the difference that was to revolutionize ballet history.

Haggin's influence had something else to do with the fact that I wasn't yet interested in the concept of artistic institutions: how they work and why they matter. He had cast himself with such conscious pride as the gadfly of institutional misbehavior in the arts (*gadfly* is hardly adequate to describe the furious vehemence with which he attacked the way the powers-that-be ran the arts) that it would hardly have been possible for a disciple like myself even to conceive of the idea of a benevolent institution, much less one run freely and inventively by a genius.

I had never had the experience of living with a great ballet company and didn't know what I had been missing or what I could look forward to. I was mildly interested in ballet history and had read in a scattered way about the Diaghilev company and its various derivatives which had toured America in the thirties, but theirs was a dying tradition, and when the Colonel de Basil company came to Boston in the late forties, showing Léonide Massine and David Lichine ballets of the thirties, it was all too clear that the tradition had already died. (This company owned Balanchine's *Cotillon* and *Concurrence,* but they did not bring them to Boston; there were rumors about burnt sets and costumes. For whatever reason, these versions of his ballets never reappeared.) Although I had had great experiences with Balanchine ballets and certain of the dancers at the Ballet Russe de Monte Carlo, I didn't think of this company as a valuable institution in itself but rather as a haphazard enterprise that happened to be exhibiting some work that I valued. Nor was I wrong in this conception; when Balanchine left the company in 1946 it never recovered its artistic momentum, and when Alexandra Danilova retired in the early fifties it lost its distinction.

Ballet Theatre, the rival company, did have a clear, strong institutional direction, but not one that suited my taste—in fact, I think I associated the idea of an artistic "institution" with the kind of boring and pompous ideological tendentiousness characteristic of Ballet Theatre. Granted that its performances of Antony Tudor's psychological ballets and ballets with American themes were important theatrical events, nonetheless I didn't much like these ballets and felt no loyalty toward or much interest in the institution that had sponsored them. The reason I went to Ballet Theatre was to see Alicia Markova and Alicia Alonso, but mainly it was to see *Apollo* and the two ballets Balanchine had created for the company in the late 1940s, *Waltz Academy* and *Theme and Variations.* When the Sadler's Wells Company came to America in 1949 I loved what I saw of it and respected Ninette de Valois's valiant creation of the institution of British ballet, but hers was not an institution I could be committed to in any practical way. Also around this time, travelers were bringing back what seemed like tall tales about fabulous dancers at the Bolshoi and the Kirov, particularly the men, but this experience was beyond my reach and really beyond my interest—I doubted I would like these Russians all that much, and, apart from my great pleasure in the dancing of Galina Ulanova and Alla Sizova, this turned out to be more or less my response when I finally saw these companies some time later.

I was interested not in ballet in general but in one choreographer in particular, although I made an exception of the great classics as performed by the dancers I had learned to admire, like Markova and Danilova. I scorned and perhaps feared the idea of being a balletomane. Edwin Denby liked to call himself a "fan" in his writing, but I thought the word campy. I never did become a balletomane. In most of my dealings with the arts I have preferred to hang on the edges of the crowd rather than commit myself easily or early to enthusiasm. There is a mixture of bad and good in this, of independence and fear; my preference for individual response, or for response shared with just a few others, clearly owes something to anxiety about my status in larger groups. Yet I am still uneasy about people who derive their sense of identity from being insiders in the world of the arts.

I see a big distinction between my way of following the movies, for example, and the way of the *Cahiers du cinéma* people. I have mixed feelings about them, and as usual these feelings are connected with competition. When I first heard in the sixties the term *film noir* used to refer to the crime movies I had liked in the forties, I refused to be thrilled by the discovery that I had been speaking prose all my life, à la Molière's M. Jourdain, and I still often avoid the term. I appreciate the degree to which that term and other habits and procedures connected with French movie criticism represent value judgments I share. On the other hand, there is something unappealingly systematic about the critics' way of going about value judgment; I do in some sense of the word acknowledge and like a category I call "Hollywood crime movies of the forties and fifties," but what I *think* I mean by that is that I certainly don't discard such movies as beneath critical notice, that I like some of them but not others, and that I don't consider it any more interesting to think about the ones I don't like than it is to think about any other works of art I don't like. Likewise, *auteur* criticism, especially as coarsened by American imitators, seems to me, despite its claim to be interested in individual works of art, to be in fact interested exactly not in individual works of art but rather in the systematic advancement of an idea. I have respect for the intensity of its type of interest in movies or in any kind of art, but its overriding tendency to theorize always seems in danger of threatening the spontaneity and the flexibility of the kind of interest in the arts that I like. Perhaps, despite my professional status as a teacher of the arts, I don't really approve of or like to practice the *study* of art.

A sounder but more everyday reason for my lack of excitement at the formation of the New York City Ballet lies in the fact that there was no strong reason to believe that this institution would last, much less grow into the major enterprise it later became. The survival of so complex an institution as a ballet company, not to mention its achievement of major work, depends on many factors besides hope and enthusiasm, and at that time I had no idea of what those factors might be. For what Balanchine achieved with the City Ballet took qualities, circumstances, and sheer experiences that could not have been predicted at the beginning of the enterprise. Kirstein's role, on the other hand, has remained something of an enigma to me. He has always figured on the masthead and in the public eye as codirector of the New York City Ballet, and ballet lovers are immensely in his debt for handling the relationships with the patrons and the trend- and taste-setters without whom the company might not have survived. But exactly what he contributed to its day-to-day artistic workings has never been clear either to me or to the world in general.

Only Balanchine's choreography mattered to me in the forties, fifties, and sixties. Not until the 1970s did I gradually develop an interest in Merce Cunningham and a selective interest in Frederick Ashton, Jerome Robbins, Paul Taylor, Twyla Tharp, Mark Morris, and a few other figures; along with many other Balanchine admirers in the seventies and eighties, I have learned to love August Bournonville.

# F I V E / *Balanchine and Stravinsky*

Before *Orpheus* I had assumed that the relationship between Balanchine and Stravinsky was a wholly positive and admirable phenomenon. But *Orpheus* was only the second Balanchine-Stravinsky ballet I had seen, and I knew neither Balanchine's choreography nor Stravinsky's music well at that time. I had loved both *The Firebird* and *Petrouchka* in my teens but had only admired *Le Sacre du Printemps*—I can't quite figure out what kept me from loving that masterpiece too, beyond the possibility that I thought it so famous a musical watershed that it must be inaccessible: when I did finally connect with it, its power and beauty seemed so absolute and incontestable that I felt I had always known it. But Balanchine's choreography for *Apollo* was what provided the entry for me into post-*Sacre* Stravinsky, a region in which I advanced as quickly as new recordings and concerts brought the music to me. By the time of *Orpheus* I had become acquainted with a group of undergraduate musicians at the Harvard house where I lived as a tutor; it included Claudio Spies, who actually knew Stravinsky pretty well. Through him and his friends I began to learn a great deal about Stravinsky (I first heard a recording of the *Symphony in Three Movements* with Claudio and another composer, Paul Desmarais, who was thrilled by the Harry James chord at the end), just as I had earlier learned a great deal in a short time about Balanchine. It was therefore inevitable that the relationship between these two important figures should be the source of the almost personal satisfaction I was prone to take about art I was interested in: I felt implicated, involved, aimed at; when the collaboration was written about in the newspaper I felt as if I myself were being discussed.

Stravinsky and Balanchine (photo by Fred Plaut; courtesy the Fred and Rose Plaut Archives, Yale University Music Library)

When I say that my reservations about *Orpheus* represented a "rethinking" of the Stravinsky-Balanchine relationship, I mean nothing more than that my failure to find the ballet *Orpheus* as interesting or beautiful as the score gave me something to think about. But in fact I didn't think about it right away, and it was not until the mid-fifties that I came back to the issue, largely because of Balanchine's decision to drop my favorite *Baiser de la Fée* from the repertory because he could not come up with the right ending for it. This gave rise to reflection on my part about Balanchine's attitude toward the music, thinking that received extra momentum from the concurrent decision to drop *Card Game*, which was not a great favorite of mine as a ballet but whose music I loved. The decision to drop it, therefore, started me thinking about how it came to be made and what it represented of Balanchine's tastes and interests.

The creation of *Agon* in 1957 brought the harmony and positive value of the Balanchine-Stravinsky relationship back into focus, and this state of affairs continued through the collaborations of the sixties, culminating in the Stravinsky festival of 1972. I missed this great event because it was planned immediately after Stravinsky's death (that's part of its glamour, of course) and announced after I had already signed on to teach in a summer workshop. Missing the festival teased me, for it gave me the sense of not being fully inside my own almost collaborative relationship with Balanchine, and I responded by returning fully to my sense of the major role played by the Balanchine-Stravinsky relationship in Balanchine's art. But events immediately following the festival made me begin seriously the rethinking that had in the preceding thirty years taken so desultory a course.

My thoughts about the collaboration are another part of my following of Balanchine's career that did not come in regular chronological sequence, so I must abandon chronological structure in order to present them. Many of my discoveries about the relationship came long after *Orpheus*, but my direction of thinking about the relationship began with that ballet.

*Apollo, Card Game, Le Baiser de la Fée, Danses Concertantes, Orpheus, Firebird, Agon, Monumentum, Movements,* "Rubies," *Stravinsky Violin Concerto, Symphony in Three Movements, Duo Concertant:* the Balanchine-Stravinsky collaboration has been a great enterprise, and I don't propose serious questioning of the value of their body of work and unique artistic relationship. But a couple of events initiated my realization that the relationship was more complicated and peculiar than it had once seemed to me and than it is officially credited with being. First came Balanchine's astonishing depredation of *Apollo* when he revived it for Mikhail Baryshnikov in 1979. The second was a private event: my own surprise and disappointment when the City Ballet danced *Agon, Stravinsky Violin Concerto,* "Rubies," and *Symphony in Three Movements* almost exclusively on the seven programs of their 1981 Boston season. I was originally surprised at the programming, then disappointed by the experience, then seriously interested in the fact that I had felt surprise and disappointment. The programs gave so false an idea of the richness of City Ballet repertory that I suddenly came to a new realization of my sense of the place of Balanchine-Stravinsky in my understanding of the New York City Ballet—and my sense of the difference between my view and what was now, so to speak, enunciated as the official company view. And I have found that when one asks, in a frank and friendly way, "What was the relationship between Stravinsky and Balanchine really like?" one comes up with some odd facts, a few doubts, many gaps—and the material for irresistible speculation.

The Balanchine-Stravinsky canon with which I began is of course merely *my* list, with my own debatable exclusions and my even more debatable inclusions. And Balanchine, for his part, certainly seems to have decanonized *Card Game* and *Danses Concertantes* when he decided not to keep them in the repertory of the City Ballet. Yet these are works of great historical importance, and many perceptive critics have admired them: they are part of the record, if not of the canon. *Card Game* was the first Stravinsky score commissioned either by or for Balanchine. Eric Walter White writes that "when Stravinsky was in America in 1935, Edward Warburg and Lincoln Kirstein suggested he should write a ballet score for the recently formed American Ballet, with which George Balanchine was associated as choreographer." Balanchine set the score in 1937 as *The Card Party,* for the American Ballet, and it premiered at Balanchine's first Stravinsky festival presented that year at the Metropolitan Opera House.

As *Poker Game,* he mounted it for the Ballet Russe de Monte Carlo in 1940, and it remained in the repertory when Balanchine joined that company in 1944; he mounted it again as *Card Game* in 1951 for the New York City Ballet. The ballet remained part of the repertory until the mid-fifties. Then it was dropped completely; Balanchine did not revive or rework it during either the 1972 or the 1982 Stravinsky festivals. He seems to have lost interest even in the score itself, since he did not assign it to one of his disciples, though the Stravinsky scenario might conceivably have been abandoned—if it is acceptable to mount *L'Histoire du Soldat* without a soldier, a fiddle, or a devil, as Peter Martins did in 1981 with Balanchine's approval, why not a *Card Game* without a card game?

I am not sure I understand Balanchine's loss of interest, but I do know it has something to do with the following elements. First, the value of the ballet he had made. I remember the version danced by the Monte Carlo company and the City Ballet with pleasure (especially the dancing of Janet Reed) but not as having had much impact. And when I also remember that the score had been one of my Stravinsky favorites before I saw the ballet, I now recognize a discrepancy I wasn't conscious of back then. The problem was not that something had turned out wrong in the ballet but that nothing had turned out interestingly right; and when you look at the conditions of its making that are on record, you can guess why.

After the work was commissioned, the first report available refers to Stravinsky's impatience at Balanchine's failure to send specific requirements about theme, structure, or length for the new "classical ballet," as it was called. The record goes blank for a while, and the next thing we know is that Stravinsky himself has decided upon the poker game for his scenario. It seems certain that Balanchine was not consulted in this decision and that he did not like it: he told Dale Harris in 1982 that he would "have liked to stage it not with cards but with gangsters" (not that one exactly believes *that*). Kirstein calls the creation of the ballet itself "a complete collaboration," but his own account belies the word. Balanchine had set the first two "deals" before Stravinsky arrived at rehearsal, and what happened then, according to Kirstein, doesn't sound like collaboration to me: Stravinsky "expressed an enthusiasm, an interest, and a criticism as courtly as it was terrifying."

The facts of the case seem to be that when Stravinsky vetoed major elements of Balanchine's choreography, Balanchine simply gave in. There is a photograph of the rehearsals that bears this out. Stravinsky dominates rather upsettingly: he is leaning forward impatiently with his hands clasped in front of him, looking like an irritable French millionaire whose time is worth a lot of money. Balanchine, close to the camera and eying it uneasily, nervous at the thought that this moment is being recorded, looks affectingly young and tense and powerless.

This depressing picture and the recorded facts lead me to believe that Balanchine's wonderful first commission from the revered Stravinsky was a tense chore rather than a delight and that it never engaged his imagination. A ballet about playing cards fits the aggressive polemicism of Stravinsky's anti-Wagnerian neoclassicism, but it has little to do with Balanchine's kind. The absence of a pas de deux in the scenario—to name only one key element—meant for Balanchine the absence of an emotional center, and Stravinsky's motor rhythms may have been too much of a good thing for dancing. The score's wit is brilliant but a little relentless. Wonderful as it is, this music lacks the variety of dance impulse and ambiguity of dramatic suggestion that tap Balanchine's deepest vein of dance imagery. At fifty-three, Stravinsky was the greatest composer in the world, and the idea of working with him in a ballet would therefore have to be the best idea in the world. But by the time the score arrived, it was fully formed theatrically, in a mode that may not have been congenial to Balanchine's instincts. He did what he could, and he did a good job, as he always does; he loyally kept the ballet in the repertory for a long time. But nothing in what I have experienced or read about it has convinced me that Balanchine was ever, in a deep way, interested in *Card Game*.

The *Danses Concertantes* case is more puzzling—and for me particularly tantalizing, since, although it was performed many times by the 1944 Monte Carlo company, I never happened to see it. It was not programmed for the weekends I managed to come to New York, and my memory has it that it wasn't performed during the Boston seasons. Nor did I make a special effort to see it, because I was sure so brilliant a masterpiece was bound to be around for a long time. It wasn't. That it was a masterpiece I have no doubt, B. H. Haggin and Edwin Denby being such reliable reporters, and their reports still carrying so much conviction. Why, then, did Balanchine wait so long to revive it for the City Ballet?

In fact, he never did revive the 1944 version, since what was shown under the same title in the 1972 festival seemed to Denby and Haggin entirely different from, and less than, what they had admired in 1944. The 1972 version, which others besides myself consider negligible and charmless, was soon dropped from the repertory, and in the 1982 festival no attempt was made to revive either of the versions or to make a new one. Again, Balanchine seems to have rejected the score completely.

Behind this odd history of performance lies a correspondingly odd history of conception. Balanchine told Harris that Stravinsky wrote the score for him: "I asked him if he could write me something for a ballet, something simple. I suggested a theme and variations, and he wrote a beautiful little piece for me to use with the Ballet Russe de Monte Carlo—*Danses Concertantes*. Today people remember the ballet as something special, but in those days it wasn't popular." This account is difficult—but, I suppose, not impossible—to square with Eric Walter White's report in his definitive *Stravinsky* that the score was commissioned by the Werner Janssen Orchestra of Los Angeles, written in 1941–42, and choreographed by Balanchine only after he joined the Monte Carlo company in 1944. But Balanchine's account is completely at odds with the spirit and the tone of Stravinsky's "program note," which is reprinted in *Themes and Episodes:*

> In spite of choreographic titles such as Pas d'Action and Pas de Deux, the *Danses Concertantes* were not intended for ballet performance or composed with dance action in mind. They may be compared in this respect with the waltzes of Chopin or Schumann's *Carnaval* which, in my opinion, are also unsuited to the theater. This is not to say that the *Danses* are unacceptable as ballet music, but only that I do not like or think of them as such; and I must confess that though I liked the decors, by Eugene Berman, the ballet is not among my Balanchine favorites.

This is the tip of some iceberg, but there is no telling what kind. What music is and what music is not suited for dance seems to have been a matter on which Stravinsky and Balanchine did not see eye to eye for many years, as we shall discover. But this case does not seem to have been an instance of rational disagreement. Stravinsky's decision not to think of *Danses Concertantes* as music for dance is completely unreasonable and completely unreasoned. And the unspecified dislike of Balanchine's choreography sounds irrational, too—pique rather than substantive criticism. Still, we get the message: Stravinsky did not want this score choreographed, for whatever reason and despite the fact that he must have agreed to the arrangement in 1944. And his disapproval must have mattered to Balanchine, whose accommodation to that disapproval may be what we see in the decision not to revive the 1944 ballet for the City Ballet and in the halfheartedness of the 1972 version. The puzzle lies in the fact that the score, for Balanchine and for me, is one of Stravinsky's most enchanting and enchantingly danceable: Balanchine's turn away from it seems self-defeating. Perhaps we are seeing the hurt, even the anger, of his reaction to Stravinsky's disapproval, however silent he had been. Instead of saying anything about it, he blots the score out of his mind. A kind of revenge, doubtless—not heroic behavior, but well within the range of ordinary human response to disappointment and hurt.

The revenge visited on *Firebird* is far from ordinary; it is, in fact, close to perverse, for instead of dropping the 1949 version from the repertory, Balanchine trashed it. I think that at least to some extent he did this knowingly, wanting his audience to see what he was doing. Those who know only the weird botch that was on view at the New York City Ballet in one malformation or another between 1970 and Balanchine's death in 1983 will hardly believe that the 1949 *Firebird* was masterfully thought through and worked out; but so it seemed to me and to almost everyone. Mastery was truly the keynote: confident, accurate calculation in design; rich, full workmanship in execution. Working on the largest scale, Balanchine filled your eye and mind with bold, simple dance imagery which was so deeply imagined that it wore wonderfully well: you went back again and again. The Marc Chagall sets were treated fondly. They were richly lit for maximum theatrical effect, so that the golden-red figure of Maria Tallchief or Violette Verdy against the sumptuous mystery of the dark forest appeared to be exactly what the Firebird ought to look like, exactly where it belonged.

Formally the 1949 ballet was not a reworking of the Michel Fokine original but a new structure to match the ballet suite that Stravinsky had arranged in 1945, an abridged version of the 1910 score that retains enough of the original music to tell the story in a compressed series of contrasting actions. Both composer and choreographer had tightened up the lax, linear structure of the original without sacrificing narrative, charm, or theatricality. If perhaps they approached their assignment without the eagerness of fresh inspiration, you nonetheless felt the excitement of their professional mastery. To me it seemed that Balanchine, in particular, loved his craft as he went about balancing the two motives he was satisfying: to capitalize on the status of "Stravinsky's *Firebird*" as "Russian ballet" in the eyes and pocketbooks of the popular audience and to fashion a new ballet that would truly belong in the repertory he was creating for his new company.

All of which is to say that the most exciting element in the 1949 *Firebird* was its *formal* interest. It was a very sophisticated work structurally. Conceivably, it was also a new formal mode that Balanchine sought in the changes he made in 1970 and afterward: he relit Chagall's revised sets harshly to cleanse the production of outmoded illusionism, glamour,

Maria Tallchief and Francisco Moncion in *Firebird*, ca. 1950 (photo courtesy Estate of George Platt Lynes, the Dance Collection, New York Public Library for the Performing Arts, Astor, Lenox, and Tilden Foundations; choreography by George Balanchine ©The George Balanchine Trust)

and mystery; he recostumed the now brightly lit Firebird with an elaborate apparatus to define the symbolic nature of the role. But these changes, which utterly wrecked the formal coherence of the 1949 version, produced not a better coherence but rather a perverse sense of deliberate incoherence. Balanchine destroyed the rich theatrical illusion he had created, and doubtless that was his intention. But instead of a new mode—a brilliant two-dimensionality, perhaps—his destructiveness created merely an image of itself, a sense of a man trashing his own work. I see this in the way a few images and motifs from the luxuriously sensuous but accurately asexual pas de deux for the Prince and the Firebird are still visible but are no longer in a connected coherent form: perhaps they are meant to be Cubist, but the way these *disjecta membra* drift about is a testimony to the destructive motive, the fury, that scattered them. What propels this fury and where it comes from are questions to which I have no clear-cut answers. I can understand what issues are involved: Balanchine's refusal, once the New York City Ballet was firmly established, to court the public with an old war-horse that retained little interest for him; his dislike of narrative ballet, however brilliantly modernized; his increasing restiveness inside forms and scenarios not his own; his growing distaste for conventional theatrical illusion. But when you add all these up you still fall short of the anger in the current *Firebird*. We shall be able to take a better reading on this violent motive later on in this exploration, after more of the evidence is in front of us.

The history of Balanchine's *Baiser de la Fée* is similar to that of *Card Game*, but it has a happy ending. As with *Card Game*—and on the same occasion!—Balanchine in 1937 had to work around the fact that Stravinsky had built his own scenario inextricably into the musical structure. Again, as subsequent events made clear, it was a scenario that Balanchine was not happy with; he made several attempts from 1940 until the mid-fifties to make an effective theater work out of a structure and mode that were not to his taste. In fact, for about fifteen years he dropped *Baiser*, as he had *Card Game*. Finally, in 1972—as with *Firebird*, but with no hint of travesty—he edited the score, reworked the scenario, and rechoreographed the dances to make an entirely different kind of work that, remarkably, captured the essential tone of the original.

I hadn't been bothered by the earlier revisions, since I could understand Balanchine's worry over whether his subtle meaning was coming across in the theater. And for the same reason I was not bothered (although I was disappointed) when he dropped *Baiser* completely from the repertory in the early fifties. He had given up the attempt to make a strong ending, but his action did not seem perverse or self-destructive—it was a responsible artistic choice, with which I happened to disagree. But the version Balanchine completed in

1974, which apparently satisfied him, was ironically enormously more problematic as a piece of theater than the earlier, complete ballet. The problems were now, of course, of Balanchine's own choosing; and the mixture of modes in *Divertimento from "Le Baiser de la Fée"* was his own experiment.

I have already described my initial reservations and misgivings about Helgi Tomasson's solo in the 1972 version. I disapproved of Balanchine's having set the variation to an earlier passage in the score in which (in the original scenario) the Fairy, disguised as a gypsy, begins her recapture of the bridegroom. In 1973 I thought the relationship between Balanchine and Stravinsky ought to be, indeed was, one of mutual respect, which Balanchine's tampering with the score seemed to have violated. The changes differed from other bold musical disobediences I had admired, for those testified to the assurance and spontaneity of Balanchine's musicianship: the decision not to use the first movements of Mendelssohn's *Scotch Symphony* or Tchaikovsky's Third Symphony in setting *Scotch Symphony* and "Diamonds," the transposition of the last two movements of Tchaikovsky's Serenade for Strings in *Serenade*. These did no damage to the musical structures, unlike Balanchine's handling of the music for the male variation, which seemed to do exactly that.

By 1974 I had grown accustomed to the solo and therefore lost my sense that Balanchine had violated Stravinsky's structure, but I still wasn't ready for the new ending of *Baiser* that made it Balanchine's own ballet. And yet that ending expressed a deep, intuitive loyalty to Stravinsky, for it retained what was most precious in Stravinsky's original scenario—the disconcerting gap between the sunlit world of ordinary human experience and the dark world of romantic destiny. Stravinsky's account in his *Autobiography* of the discordance he had in mind strikes rather a twenties-ish Parisian note to my ears: "I pictured all the fantasy roles as danced in white ballet skirts, and the rustic scenes as taking place in a Swiss landscape, with some of the performers dressed in the manner of early tourists and mingling with the friendly villagers in the good old theatrical tradition." Balanchine collapsed Stravinsky's two layers of reality into an ironic unity, and with the simplest, though oddest, means. In the new Berceuse of the Eternal Dwellings, the village girls, still in their bright peasant dresses, file onstage in slow solemn bourrées, heads stiffly up, and interpose themselves between the young man and his fiancée, separating them for eternity it seems. Here is an extraordinary transmutation of Stravinsky's vision: the village girls have become the fantasy figures, and their peasant dresses stand for white ballet skirts. The powerful originality of Balanchine's change lies in the way it creates, and holds steady, a modernist "illusion": you are moved, but at the same time you are conscious of seeing a peculiar "effect"—Stacy Caddell, Delia Peters, Marjorie Spohn, and other old friends, in crisp little peasant dresses, turning into agents of doom. Balanchine changed Stravinsky's original scenario, but he did not travesty the original meaning or its power and beauty; he finally used Stravinsky's wonderful score and theme in a mode and a structure that suited him.

The decapitation of *Apollo* would always have seemed ugly, but coming after the sensitive, fruitful (if equally drastic) pruning of *Baiser,* it seems almost inconceivable. But this violent act shows how absolutely Balanchine wanted his forms to be his own. *Apollo* is the key and central work in the Balanchine-Stravinsky canon, one would heretofore have said—and most of us will continue to say—the first important work in their relationship, the spring and fount of modern ballet classicism, the locus of the battle of the ballets, with John Martin sneering at its cheap Parisian triviality on one side, Denby and Haggin marveling at its wit, grace, and spiritual depth on the other. For Balanchine the score "was the turning point of my life . . . a revelation. It seemed to tell me that I could dare not to use everything, that I, too, could eliminate." For Stravinsky, Balanchine "had arranged the dances exactly as I had wished. . . . His beautiful choreography had clearly expressed my meaning." By 1960 the preeminence of *Apollo* was absolute. Then, following the 1972 Stravinsky festival Balanchine dropped the ballet from the New York City Ballet repertory—forever, rumor said.

*Apollo* had long been a baffling example to consult in attempting to figure out Balanchine's attitude toward his own works and particular performances of them. It was hard to believe that he could have looked with pleasure at Jacques d'Amboise's pompous, coarse performances during the sixties; perhaps he *didn't* care. He was always asking, "Who wants to see last year's butterflies?" Yet when d'Amboise was injured during the company's 1968 European tour, a substitute had to be found: the young Peter Martins. So Balanchine *did* care about *Apollo.*

Then came the 1978 revival for Mikhail Baryshnikov and the shock of discovering what Balanchine had cut from his own ballet and—more to the ethical point—from Stravinsky's score. Gone was the opening narrative section: the orchestral prologue, Apollo's birth from Leto, his first steps, the bringing of the lute, and most of his first variation; the curtain rose after a few bars of this music to show Apollo ready to go into that windup that produces the muses. With no Leto there needed to be no pillar on which she gave birth, and thus no stairway to Parnassus. And so at the end, Apollo and the muses did not mount to Parnassus but instead moved around a stage which now represented no illusioned space. This makes a tremendous difference. For Stravinsky and for me the ending of *Apollo* is tragic. When Apollo and the muses leave, they leave us behind in our mortality. This is what the music seems to me to say in its reiterated cry of lamentation dying away at the end, and it is what

Edward Villella and Patricia McBride in *Apollo,* ca. 1965 (photo by Fred Fehl; courtesy the New York City Ballet; choreography by George Balanchine ©The George Balanchine Trust)

the old version of the ballet used to say, simply and effectively, as the four immortals waited motionlessly on the staircase for their chariot.

But this is not what the new version says. Now, to that same music, Apollo and the muses open up into one of the ballet's famous images, stolen from its original beautiful position earlier on—the fanning-out of the sun's rays. *Apollo* now ends with a kind of Apollo-logo; it is brilliant, but the last thing it suggests is loss. Silhouetted against golden backlighting, this image advances into the theater more powerfully than anything that has gone before, and it is held before us as an achieved, completed, unchanging summation. It is a positive consummation, perhaps appropriate to the connection between Apollo and the sun, but it is not a connection the scenario or the music is interested in. The tragic note is missing.

Shortly afterward Balanchine restored *Apollo's* first variation entire but none of the music that precedes it, so that he did not restore the symmetry of Stravinsky's wonderful structure—that questioning first musical sentence which is poignantly answered by the ambiguous apotheosis of the ending. If one wonders how Balanchine could have damaged a score from which he learned "discipline and restraint . . . sustained oneness of feeling"—well, *that* idea of form was last year's butterfly. Balanchine said, "It's my ballet and I can do what I want to it."

The conclusion to be drawn from the history of the Stravinsky-Balanchine ballets before *Orpheus* is that Balanchine's admiration for Stravinsky's music did not automatically lead to his finding every Stravinsky score congenial for his dances. Put in that calm way, this should not be a surprising conclusion. If it does surprise, that is largely Balanchine's fault, because it is mainly he who has encouraged the opposite sense of things by his claim that all Stravinsky's music can be danced and by his decision to hold three Stravinsky festivals. He is the one who has suggested that any good choreographer can make a good ballet if he sets a Stravinsky score.

But why should that be so? What must be true instead is that being inspired by a piece of music to make a meaningful ballet depends on more complex and more personal factors than simply the music's suitability for dance. This has always been the case with Balanchine himself. Music written for the ballet might not necessarily be inspiring or congenial to a choreographer, even one who admires the composer immensely. The more you think about it, the less surprising it is.

The most active and sympathetic collaboration can have its hazards. Composer-choreographer collaboration solves some problems, but it is radically unlike the process that produced most of Balanchine's greatest works. In the annus mirabilis of 1941, when Balanchine composed *Balustrade, Concerto Barocco,* and *Ballet Imperial* in about six months, what took place in each case, surely, was a particular relationship with a personally meaningful piece of music. To put it as simply as possible, one thinks of Balanchine in 1941 as having somewhere in his mind been dealing for some time with the Stravinsky Violin Concerto, the Bach Double Violin Concerto, and the Tchaikovsky Second Piano Concerto, and as having had some concrete sense of why he wanted to set those particular pieces. Even the most intimate and actively detailed collaboration is unlikely to yield this natural gestation of a ballet that comes from a long attachment to the music. Should it do so, one would have to call the choreographer fantastically lucky to have found the right collaborator. This is exactly the familiar view of the Balanchine-Stravinsky collaboration; as is obvious by now, I think the truth is more complicated.

What we know about the collaboration that produced *Orpheus* is more entertaining than helpful. Bernard Taper's anecdotes (of Balanchine suggesting thirty-one seconds of music and Stravinsky asking him whether he could settle for thirty-two, and so on) certainly catch the precision and hardheadedness of the art of these artists, and that is important. But they reveal nothing of how the basic style, rhythm, and pulse of *Orpheus* were established. In these respects *Orpheus* differs so strikingly from other Balanchine ballets that one can hardly see his hand in the choices. For me they were not happy choices. In spite of every indication that Balanchine worked contentedly with Stravinsky on this occasion, I have never felt, as I look at the results, that he worked really well or freely, truly in his own way. Perhaps it should be considered a strength that the pulse of *Orpheus*, the way it moves through Stravinsky's time and Noguchi's space, is unlike that of any other Balanchine ballet—why should all his ballets look alike? But that is not how I see it.

*Orpheus* looks like a work in translation. Let me make an extreme comparison: compare the pas de deux from *Orpheus* in which Orpheus yields to the seduction of Eurydice with the pas de deux to the flute solo that occurs near the beginning of *Chaconne*. Of course, the dancers in *Chaconne* do not represent Orpheus and Eurydice, and the music is called "Dance of the Blessed Spirits," so the parallel is far from exact—I might seem simply to be capitalizing on the apparent coincidence that *Chaconne* is danced to music from Gluck's *Orpheus and Eurydice*. But this is not a coincidence. Here we see Balanchine, long an admirer of the Orpheus subject, treating it in two different ways. In the Stravinsky-Noguchi collaboration he is setting a "story," and he is working with new music and a highly stylized stage setting—in the pas de deux, he uses only the narrow band of the forestage in front of a billowing silken curtain. In the pas de deux from *Chaconne* he sets music he had known for fifty years, using the full stage and organizing its space entirely according to his own wishes. The difference in freedom between the two dances is absolute: the *Chaconne* pas de deux is deeply and personally imagined.

*Agon* at last—the subject of those marvelous rehearsal photographs, a work about whose conception we have ample information, a work created by what finally demands to be called collaboration. The letters between Stravinsky and Kirstein (collected in the first volume of *Stravinsky: Selected Correspondence*) have given fresh information on the artistic process. It was apparently originally Kirstein's idea to ask Stravinsky for a "third act" to follow *Apollo* and *Orpheus* on an all-Greek program. At any rate, we see Kirstein expressing the idea in 1948, the day after the premiere of *Orpheus*, and the terms in which he describes his conception are those of theme and scenario—terms with which, as we have seen, Balanchine never felt happy. Stravinsky appears interested but busy; there follow five years

Balanchine and Stravinsky watch Diana Adams and Arthur Mitchell at the making of *Agon*, 1957 (photo ©1994 Martha Swope)

of brainstorming and dickering over both financial and artistic arrangements. In 1953 the commission is formally extended and accepted, and the real collaborative thinking about the subject begins, whereupon *immediately* the kind of subject Kirstein had in mind (Apollo Architectons, Amphion the builder, Aesculapius, or some such) is rejected by both Stravinsky and Balanchine. Stravinsky shrewdly guesses that such a subject would lead to too much "slow motion" for one evening, but Balanchine's objections are basic and formal: "What he wants (as usual) is a ballet-ivanich," Kirstein complains, meaning by that phrase, I take it, a suite of dances organized à la Petipa.

And "a ballet-ivanich" is, in a way, what got made. In trying to dress up the idea, obviously unattractive to himself, Kirstein soars to a rhapsody of improvisation, in which he suggests that both he and Balanchine would like "a ballet . . . to end all ballets, mad dancing, variations, pas d'action . . . a series of historic dances. . . . The dances which began quite simply in the sixteenth century took fire in the twentieth and exploded. It would be in the form of a suite de danses, or variations, numbers of as great variety as you pleased." *Agon* is indeed a ballet in which Renaissance dance forms are brought up to the minute under great pressure; Kirstein's idea truly bore fruit. Kirstein had sent along a copy of the 1623 *Apologie de la danse* by a certain de Lause to show what he meant, and since Robert Craft reports that Stravinsky read it carefully, we can confidently say that the collaboration that produced *Agon* included Kirstein. Stravinsky's immediate reaction to Kirstein's rhapsody was a dignified little lecture: "The idea you and George have of doing a 'ballet to end all ballet'—well, limits are precisely what I need and am looking for above all in everything I compose. The limits generate the form." Later he and Balanchine met repeatedly to work out every detail of the timing and grouping, and the result is the masterpiece we all put somewhere near the center of the Balanchine-Stravinsky relationship, if not absolutely right in the center.

There is, however, more to say about the circumstances of the production of *Agon*, for in describing what he envisions as Balanchine's treatment of his promised "concerto for dance," Stravinsky produced one of the most important statements about the Balanchine-Stravinsky collaboration: "George will create a matching choreographic construction. He is a master at this, and has done beautifully with Bizet, Tchaikovsky, Bach, Mozart in music not composed for the dance. So, we can well imagine how successful he will be if given something specially composed for the ballet."

In this key passage Stravinsky takes a strong position on the central issue of the Balanchine-Stravinsky relationship: the proper relation between music and dance. It concerns the very nature of choreography itself, and what I see in Stravinsky's statement is a view of the nature, the function, the power, and the stature of choreography that is quite unlike Balanchine's view, and much smaller. Until the outbursts of the 1970 *Firebird* and the 1979 *Apollo*, Balanchine had been expressing his own opinion more quietly. As he gradually began to feel uneasy about or strapped by structures Stravinsky had built into certain scores that had been "specially composed for the ballet," he decided either to drop those scores or to change them radically in order to fashion ballets that were truly his own. For he was always engaged in the larger project of discovering the nature and extent of his own genius and the direction in which he wanted that genius to move. Beginning with *Serenade* in 1934 and continuing with *Balustrade, Concerto Barocco,* and *Ballet Imperial* in 1941 and *The Four*

*Temperaments* in 1946 (although the fact that he commissioned the score alters the circumstances slightly), continuing with *Le Palais de Cristal* in 1947 (which became *Symphony in C* in 1948), and continuing steadily from that point on until his death, Balanchine developed and infused with genius a conception of choreography and its relation to music quite different from Stravinsky's.

To my ears Stravinsky shows himself uneasy about works that are choreographed to music not written specifically for ballet in his implication that what Balanchine has been doing with Bizet and Bach has been a kind of *pis-aller.* He takes it for granted that the choreographic job of "matching" dance to music can be done more successfully—more easily and, by unmistakable implication, *with better results*—when the music has been written especially for the ballet. How indeed could the world's greatest and most experienced composer of ballet music not believe this? But unless I am mistaken, Balanchine did not believe it, as his dealings with the composers Stravinsky cites demonstrate by the extraordinary power and beauty of the results. My guess is that Balanchine held the opposite view—that the best music to use for dance was music that was *not* composed especially for ballet. It is not a clear-cut business, to be sure, and there are exceptions to be named: *The Four Temperaments, Apollo* and *The Prodigal Son, Danses Concertantes.* But I don't think these exceptions really matter.

I am arguing, then, that there developed a quiet disagreement between Balanchine and Stravinsky about the relationship between music and dance, if only the simple one that Stravinsky thought it correct, and more fruitful, for the music to come first as a kind of assignment to the choreographer, while Balanchine preferred to hunt up his own music and do what he wanted with it. And I am arguing, too, that this disagreement brought with it another quiet disagreement, about the nature and dimension of Balanchine's talent. Stravinsky calls him a "master," meaning surely to praise him highly; but Balanchine knew he was something more than what Stravinsky meant.

The conflict I am hinting at ended well, although the savagery of Balanchine's attacks on *Firebird* and *Apollo* seems to represent later flare-ups. Stravinsky's views on Balanchine's genius underwent a development, of which the 1953 statement presents an early phase of mixed respect and reservation. But toward the end of the collaboration Stravinsky made the discovery of Balanchine's true genius, and he expressed it with thrilling accuracy of perception, which must have been an extraordinary experience for Balanchine.

How Stravinsky came to his new understanding of Balanchine is not clear-cut either. In 1951, there was an instructive and amusing exchange between Kirstein and Stravinsky about the title for what was eventually called *The Cage.* Stravinsky had already agreed that the

*Basler Concerto*—the String Concerto in D—could be used for a ballet at the New York City Ballet, and Kirstein requested a title change in a telegram dated April 18: "WOULD YOU AUTHORIZE USE BASLER CONCERTO BALLET TITLE AS ARIOSO." Stravinsky refused (in a letter Kirstein received on the nineteenth—those were the days!) on the grounds that the new title would be inappropriate for the whole ballet, since it referred to only one movement of the concerto. The letter is unironic in tone, but the extreme carefulness of his argument suggests that Stravinsky believed himself to be addressing a musical imbecile. Apparently he is not sure who the intended choreographer is, and there is some diplomatic pressure toward the end of the letter to try to straighten this out: "Please drop me a line about your Basler Concerto project. I hope Balanchine is in it and I will be very happy, of course, if he stages the whole piece; besides, he was the first one to whom I played this work and his first reaction was to stage it as a ballet. I remember also his special enthusiasm for the first movement."

Balanchine, of course, was not "in it," and one can imagine the hurried conference that lay behind Kirstein's next telegram, dated April 19: "BALANCHINE AND I REQUEST USE OF COMPLETE BASLER CONCERTO FOR JEROME ROBBINS'S EXCELLENT IDEA AND CHO-REOGRAPHY THE STORY OF HIPPOLYTA AND THE AMAZONS. UNDERSTAND PER-FECTLY YOUR OBJECTION TO ARIOSO. MAY WE CALL BALLET HIPPOLYTA OR THE AMAZONS?" In his response Stravinsky called Robbins's idea "very good," but he made two absolute conditions: "The music should be kept entirely as is, i.e., no changes, no alter-ations. Moreover you must mention in the program . . . that the music is that of Stravinsky's String Concerto in D."

On 25 June 1951 Kirstein reported the "conspicuous success" of Robbins's ballet; whether Stravinsky ever approved the title *The Cage* is not clear. That he did not approve of the ballet came out two years later, when Kirstein requested his approval for Robbins "to do the Symphony in Three Movements as a ballet: he wants to call it 'Procession.' It would be a dramatic continuous procession embodying a variety of marches—bridal, funeral, battle, etc." Stravinsky's answer makes an extremely important statement, though not one that is easy to interpret:

> Let me tell you frankly how I feel about the Symphony in Three Movements as a ballet. I am against it. As a symphonic composer as well as a ballet composer, I al-ways feel uneasy at the idea of using my straight symphonic forms on the stage. I let the experiment be tried with the "Basler Concerto" and, to tell you the truth (*confi-dentially*), I feel somewhat unhappy and uncomfortable about it. Not that Jerome

Robbins has not done well. On the contrary, I think he is a very talented man and he is still proving it in *The Cage*. But it is simply a matter of "plastic" incompatibility. This one experience has only confirmed me in my opinion and cautiousness.

It seems clear that there had been a simple misunderstanding in 1951, that Stravinsky had assumed that Balanchine was to set the *Basler Concerto* when he gave the New York City Ballet permission to use the score, and that there was no courteous way of refusing when the choreographer turned out to be Robbins. Stravinsky did then feel uneasy; I think he was telling the strict truth when he said that he "always" felt "uneasy at the idea of using [his] straight symphonic forms on the stage"—even with Balanchine, with whom he felt a compatible plastic sense, but who still might create a dance that meant something Stravinsky had not meant in his music. But I take it that when he saw *The Cage* he thought that Robbins had made a ballet with a *wrong* meaning. He may have disliked having the intensity of his allegros in the *Basler Concerto* distorted, overread, and overemphasized to imply the menace and horror of Robbins's scenario for *The Cage,* and he may have foreseen a similar overemphasis in what Robbins proposed for the different marches in "Procession"—not to mention his uneasiness as a musician at learning that Robbins actually heard the *Symphony in Three Movements* as a series of marches.

When Stravinsky said in 1951 that he would be "very happy" if Balanchine were to set the *Basler Concerto,* I think he meant it, but he was at the same time taking an essentially neutral position about whether ballets should be choreographed to straight symphonic forms. And I think, too, that his way of praising Balanchine is also neutral—that is, Stravinsky was saying that Balanchine's choreography would "match" his music "beautifully" because he was a "master" at doing this, but I think that is all he was saying. He probably thought there couldn't *be* anything more, or better, to say; it would never have occurred to him that Balanchine might do something more positive with the music, that he could "use" it to shape a theatrical experience that would in some way add to the music and develop it or—to use the exact word Stravinsky was to find many years later—"explore" it.

In short, Stravinsky in 1951 still had what might be called a pre-Balanchine sense of the role and power of choreography, in which it was seen as essentially an art of execution, like playing a musical instrument. The choreographer—who after all had until recently been called not by that grand name but simply *balletmaster*—was an experienced "dancist," an executant in the medium of dance. He might be a professionally trained musician like Balanchine, in which case the composer could feel thoroughly comfortable with him. He might be a "brilliant" executant, however; and that was likely to mean the awful thing Stravinsky had in mind when he fulminated against virtuoso conductors all his life: such an executant would want to express his own meanings instead of the composer's. This type was to be avoided if possible. Robbins appeared to be turning into this kind of choreographer— and a particularly aggressive and popularly effective one at that. He, therefore, must to be carefully avoided. For in the last analysis, what a composer wished to do with a choreographer was to say, "Here, have that danced, please."

*Balletmaster* gave a fairly accurate representation not only of the esteem in which the choreographic function was held in the twenties and thirties but also of the way the function was carried out. The scenarios for the great, precedent-setting Diaghilev ballets, for example, were rarely worked out by the balletmaster. Instead, an already completed scenario was handed over to the balletmaster to be set in a process whereby the events and effects called for in the scenario would be—more or less well, more or less brilliantly or appropriately— "played" on the instrument of "dancing." This procedure extended even to subtler issues of style, so that when Stravinsky conceived of *Apollo* and *Baiser* as intended for "classical ballet," he expected the balletmaster to have *that* "instrument" well in hand and to be able to play on it whatever music he was asked to play.

All of this seems obvious to me, but I see it in particular in the lack of specificity with which Stravinsky critiques the choreography of his ballets. Compare what he says in the *Autobiography* about Balanchine's *Apollo* with what Balanchine said about Stravinsky's *Apollo*. Here again is Balanchine's tribute: "It seemed to tell me that I could dare not to use everything, that I, too, could eliminate." Balanchine's is a far more exact perception than Stravinsky's: "Balanchine had arranged the dances exactly as I had wished—that is to say, in accordance with the classical groups, movements, and lines of great dignity and plastic elegance . . . his beautiful choreography clearly expressed my meaning." The praise is perfectly genuine and not insubstantial, but quite lacking in bite and specificity and conscious of only one meaning to be considered: the composer's. This is not personal egotism, this talk of "I" and "my," but merely a matter of the natural hierarchy of the ballet, in which the composer establishes the meaning.

In the same year, 1935 (in a letter to Balanchine, presumably about preparations for the 1937 Stravinsky program of the American Ballet, quoted in *Stravinsky in Pictures and Documents*), Stravinsky again praises Balanchine's choreography with convincing sincerity, but there is an additional prudent and monitory note. Expressing his "joy . . . and complete confidence" in Balanchine, he goes on to remark that his "memories of our collaboration during the staging of *Apollo* for Diaghilev in 1928 are among the most satisfying in my artistic life." Then comes the more urgent motive: "Knowing what a good musician you are, I count on you to observe the metronomic tempi." Generalized appreciation rather than specific attention recurs in the praise of *Card Game*. (There is no record of Stravinsky's response to Balanchine's *Baiser,* and his disapproval of Nijinska's version of this music is unspecific.)

Coming back to his 1953 definition of Balanchine's art, the phrase "a matching choreographic construction" will perhaps now be more resonant. It is not a bad phrase, certainly not incorrect, but with its neutrality, its—deliberate?—note of the mechanical, it does not make the heart leap up. *Construction* is a good word in the Stravinsky lexicon, to be sure, and Balanchine is a "master" craftsman. But although Stravinsky spoke of himself often in such terms, which fit his anti-Wagnerian bias, there is ample evidence that he considered himself something greater than a mere master craftsman.

All these readings are relative, and my interpretation of the tone and spirit of Stravinsky's 1953 praise depends on the different tone and spirit of a program note written between 1961 and 1963 and published in *Dialogues and a Diary:* "Balanchine composed the choreography [for *Balustrade,* the 1941 setting of the Violin Concerto] as he listened to my recording, and I could actually observe him conceiving gesture, movement, combination, composition. The result was a series of dialogues perfectly complementary to and co-ordinated with the dialogues of the music." Stravinsky here communicates personal involvement in an exciting experience. And this may, of course, have been the way he always responded to Balanchine's choreography as it was being made "actual" in rehearsal.

Yet my hunch is that something had changed, that the way of recording the experience is very different from what it would have been in 1941. Between 1941 and and the time this program note was written, something had occurred to amplify and perhaps clarify the excitement of the earlier experience: Stravinsky had again seen Balanchine "actually" at work in the rehearsal sessions for *Agon* that are so vividly captured in the photographs; and I think we are seeing the effect of *Agon* in this account of the creation of *Balustrade*—and, most important, in the account of the ballet itself. Compared with "a matching choreographic construction," the new phrase "a series of dialogues perfectly complementary to and co-ordinated with the dialogues of the music" is more specific and "actual"; more has been seen, and it has been seen more exactly. If the infelicity of "complementary to and co-ordinated with" still betrays a certain mechanical spirit, anyone who has tried to describe the relation of music to dance in Balanchine in exact rather than rhapsodic terms will sympathize with Stravinsky's effort.

And it is, in fact, Stravinsky himself who has written the most brilliantly exact and excited account of that relationship. It was published under the title "Eye Music" in *Themes and Episodes,* but it did not absorb me until I encountered it in Nancy Lassalle's program book for the 1982 Stravinsky festival. I do not exaggerate when I say that rediscovering the passage was for me the high point of that festival.

There, Stravinsky writes:

> To see Balanchine's choreography of the *Movements* is to hear the music with one's eyes; and this visual hearing has been a greater revelation to me, I think, than to anyone else. The choreography emphasizes relationships of which I had hardly been aware—in the same way—and the performance was like a tour of a building for which I had drawn the plans but never explored the result. Balanchine approached the music by identifying some of the more familiar marks of my style, and as I heard him fasten on my tiniest repeated rhythm or sustaining group, I knew he had joined the work to the corpus of my music, and at the same time probably reducing the time lag of its general acceptability by as much as a decade. I owe him even more for another aspect of the revelation: his discovery of the music's essential lyricism. I gather that his dramatic point is a love parable—in which ballet is it not?—but the coda had a suggestion of myth that reminded me of the ending of *Apollo.* . . . But are the *Movements* ballet music? Barbarous locution to Balanchine! What he needs is not a pas de deux but a motor impulse.

At this point in my argument that passage can be trusted to speak for itself, although the better reason for trust is its own absolute clarity of expression. Stravinsky calls Balanchine's choreography a "revelation," but his own building metaphor is a revelation, too—a stroke of critical genius. And the note of excited discovery throughout the passage moves me more deeply than I can easily say: it is analogous to having been present when Haydn told Leopold Mozart that his son was the greatest musical genius who had ever lived. Generosity on this scale, with this spontaneous energy, at Stravinsky's age: has there ever been an equal?

You can find it in another medium, a series of photographs by Arnold Newman of Stravinsky and Balanchine working together in 1966 that is reproduced in *Bravo Stravinsky.* In these action shots Balanchine is showing Stravinsky how he would choreograph the *Requiem Canticles,* which the two of them have just listened to on a recording. Both are seated, Balanchine vividly demonstrating, Stravinsky intensely looking and listening, and, at the end, laughing. Craft makes a wonderfully apt point about the relationship shown:

"Like the choreographer, the composer is a born gesticulator, but when the two are together Stravinsky always defers to the professional."

Well, things had changed since 1937 and the *Card Game* rehearsal photograph. In these photographs Stravinsky, even without gesticulation, is fantastically alive, and we know from "Eye Music" what he is experiencing. At first he focuses what appears to me to be a rather nervous attention on what Balanchine is so brilliantly "performing," then he begins to smile; worry returns and then is dissipated in an enormous laugh, which unmistakably expresses the excitement of understanding. Through Balanchine's instrumentality, he has been hearing his own music with his eyes. What Balanchine has shown him is not what he showed with *Apollo,* "exactly what I wished," but a revelation.

# SIX / *Balanchine Institutionalized*

Looking back, some years after Balanchine's death—a painfully clarifying vantage point—it is hard to see how anyone could have predicted in 1948 that Balanchine would have the powers he proved to have. He had already demonstrated his creative genius as a choreographer, if only to a few, but only the combination of this genius with other powers made the achievement of the New York City Ballet possible. Although that basic creative genius was unmistakable in individual ballets, the fecundity of imagination that would create a whole repertory single-handedly was not yet visible. To be sure, Balanchine had done the job Diaghilev hired him to do—that of combination balletmaster and choreographer in residence—with a degree of success that showed a facility of imagination and an easy professionalism. And after the Diaghilev company disbanded he had shown how quickly he could adapt to new circumstances. There are many anecdotes about his entering the unfamiliar world of the Broadway musical and immediately convincing everyone in it that he knew what he was doing, that he was somebody to be listened to. The variety of assignments he took on during the thirties was notable, although not, in fact, noted, except by those few who grasped his stature; and the calm ease and assurance, not to speak of the success, with which he did them became subjects for a few anecdotes but earned little other attention.

A key instance of Balanchine's fertility came in 1941: when Lincoln Kirstein, through his influence with Nelson Rockefeller, was given the chance to form the American Ballet Caravan in order to tour South America as part of a State Department goodwill campaign,

Balanchine not only reassembled and rehearsed his dancers expeditiously, but he composed in six weeks, as the novelties expected for such an occasion, *Concerto Barocco* and *Ballet Imperial*. The truly astonishing aspect of this achievement is not so much that these are two of Balanchine's greatest works as that in them he created the plotless ballet that became his signature. *Serenade* in 1934 had been plotless, and set to concert rather than ballet music, but there is a big difference between using so immediately and appealingly danceable a score as the Tchaikovsky Serenade for Strings, Op. 48, and choreographing Tchaikovsky's larger and more rhetorical Piano Concerto No. 2 for a large ballet, not to speak of the kind of daring it took to set a ballet to the Bach Concerto in D Minor for Two Violins. But I don't recall any awareness then or later of this achievement as the sign of the unprecedented fertility it was.

The other power that made possible the success of the New York City Ballet, which could not have been guessed at the time, was Balanchine's ability to command the respect, loyalty, and love of the many immensely capable people whose willing services are needed to keep such an enterprise working. I had often admired the fact that Balanchine seemed to run the whole show himself, since Kirstein apparently played only a small role in the artistic decisions. And I had often wondered how Balanchine pulled it off. Only after his death and Peter Martins's assumption of the directorship did I understand.

However one might have conceived of the job of director of the company, it changed dramatically after Balanchine's death, when Martins suddenly found himself having to spend much of his time in the office, involved in administration, fund-raising, and publicity, and had relatively little time for the dancers and the ballets. When I learned of this, I realized how many people Balanchine had counted on to make complex preparations for decisions he could then make in a few moments. Martins, in the absence of those people (for he could not command their service or even perhaps their interest in the way Balanchine could), had to do a great deal himself.

It is easy to see that a glamorous, mysterious Russian from the golden days like Balanchine could make an unprepared for, fifteen-minute appearance at a fund-raiser, utter a couple of charmingly inscrutable opinions, and leave people feeling they had had a meaningful experience with the great man; it is just as easy to see how impossible it would be for Martins to attempt the same thing. He must, at the beginning at least, have had to prepare for such appearances in some way, and the time he spent in doing so left him less time and energy for his dancers, not to mention the ballets. Balanchine himself apparently was unconscious of the loyalty he commanded and of how necessary it was to the company;

if he thought about it at all when he chose Martins as his successor he may have assumed that it automatically came with the job.

Needless to say, I was unaware of Balanchine's as-yet-undisclosed powers during the first years of the New York City Ballet. From 1948 to 1957 it was with great pleasure but without the sense that I watching a great new enterprise that I came down from Boston for as many of the company's performances as I could manage. I have nostalgia for some ballets that have disappeared—for instance, the Haieff *Divertimento,* the first ballet with a distinctly erotic perfume I had encountered, which featured the rare, exotic pairing of Maria Tallchief and Francisco Moncion (it did not come to life for me in the revival during the 1993 Balanchine celebration); *Jones Beach,* an appealing trifle which probably did not deserve to last but which I admired for its show-business flair; and the enchanting and elegant *Roma,* to Bizet's lovely score, which was mysteriously dropped even before Tanaquil Le Clercq's illness, although it was one of her best roles. I missed a couple of Balanchine's innovative ballets of the period, *Metamorphoses* and *Opus 34,* and now it seems to me I did so deliberately, confessing at that early date my relatively small interest in the experimental part of his output that has become perhaps his most famous work. My failure to attend these well-publicized events also shows that I was not quite the dedicated follower of Balanchine's career that I had claimed to be in my *Foreground* piece.

Indeed, I was still so much the competitive follower of the arts I had been in high school that it was only when an occasion for competition arose that I actually caught a glimpse of what Balanchine had achieved in founding his new company. What I remember most vividly, and even with the most pleasure, about the New York City Ballet in its first decade is *reading* about it at a dramatic moment in its early life. In 1950, Kirstein and Balanchine took the brilliant risk of convincing David Webster to invite the company to offer a season at Covent Garden, throwing down an international gauntlet at a boldly early point in the company's career. I kept the closest track of the by-now legendary success of that Covent Garden season, and with my characteristic emotions. I was again competitively following a reputation—not Willa Cather's or Mozart's, but Balanchine's and that of the New York City Ballet—and again staking my own claim to worth on the artistic enterprise I was following. I was filled with my habitual scorn for the unfavorable reviews of my ballet company in the London newspapers and magazines and with a warm approval close to love for the favorable reviews.

This was a tense moment in my life in another respect. I had applied for a Fulbright scholarship to study Dickens under Geoffrey Tillotson at Birkbeck College in London University and had received a letter telling me that I was likely to be awarded one, but the confirming letter was irritatingly, then alarmingly, delayed, and I was on tenterhooks all spring and almost all summer. (I've since surmised that the delay was due to some trouble in my getting security clearance because of the leftist sympathies of some of my *Foreground* friends, although I've never bothered to check, as one can these days, through the Freedom of Information Act.) While waiting, all pretense of work on my Ph.D. yielded to two obsessions. Practically every night I played poker and a ridiculous, puerile, fascinating game called Red Dog with fellow graduate students. These included another compulsive gambler, Dave Aivaz, who was my opponent in the final two-man Red Dog debauch that stretched into the small hours, during which I might lose what were for me dramatically large amounts of money one night, then win them back the next—I ended up a fairly serious loser. And during almost every afternoon I sat in the periodicals room of Harvard's Widener Library reading about the City Ballet season in London. I was proving myself and my identity in two modes and two places, testing my luck (and, I suppose, my adulthood) at the poker table and my authority as a follower and critic of the arts at the library, tracking the fate of my ballet company in the London newspapers and magazines.

What I was most inflamed by in these reviews was the parochial certainty of taste with which the reviewers approached this American phenomenon—which is saying nothing more, of course, than that the reviewers were British. There were favorable notices by one leading critic, Richard Buckle, who had a sassy, free, international spirit, somewhat rebellious on principle against the veneration of Ninette de Valois and the nannyish good taste that the Sadler's Wells represented; Buckle had seen the Diaghilev company when Balanchine was balletmaster and remembered the masterpieces of those days. Clive Barnes was writing seriously and with substance in 1950 for the *Spectator,* and the excited welcome he extended to the new company turned out to be an important sign of change in the British scene. But most of the critics, understandably enough, were writing from inside a tradition where Balanchine's style, his technique, his ballets, seemed just what one would expect from the man who could say, "In England, if you're awake, it's already vulgar." So there was nothing surprising in their calling the New York City Ballet "athletic," deficient in temperament, personality, and style—perhaps, it was said, the company was too immature for imaginative and romantic ballets. I formulated rebuttals in an intoxication of fury. And there was a marvelous reward in store: late in the ballet's London season, a few critics discovered that in the space of little more than three weeks these coldly athletic American dancers had acquired, apparently from the English air itself, a beautiful new sensitivity and poetry.

More worrisome was the judgment on the part of several British critics that Balanchine followed the structure of the music in his plotless ballets too literally, and therefore un-musically; since my musical friends and I all thought Balanchine a marvel of musicality in exactly this respect, the charge was puzzling and remains so. But because the plotless ballets present so original an organic relation with music that they can be said to have created a new art form, it is conceivable that the English, a musical people with a great tradition of musical performance, were less ready for this new form *because* their love of concert music in the concert hall was so genuine, and so inward.

I could easily counter the British pity for the company's lack of decor by a snide preference for ballets dressed in practice clothes ("we're interested in dancing, not back-drops"); as for the criticism of the few ballets that did have sets, one could call on the celebrated English ineptness for the visual arts in argument—"compared with what?" Not that I myself yet understood the visual power of the brilliant dimensional lighting Bal-anchine was gradually working toward, lighting that makes his undecorated ballets such original visual experiences. I had nothing but scorn for the critics whose "a place for everything and everything in its place" attitude and tone could find room on a ballet program for *one* abstract ballet (hadn't Mr. Ashton made that wonderful *Symphonic Varia-tions?*) but not for three or, as used to be the case in those wonderful days, four.

Many of my reactions were heat without light, derived from the pleasure of fighting rather than from insight, but I did learn something from trying to answer the loudest outcry of all, the one over what Balanchine had done to *Firebird*. I had never seen the Fokine version of this ballet (which I enjoyed when I finally saw the Royal Ballet performance of it), but I had loved Balanchine's version when he had mounted it in 1949. At the center was his magnificently theatrical conception of the Firebird as it was realized in Tallchief's dancing—sharp, exotic, sensuous, tender—and I had recognized the relaxed ease of a master's hand in the folk-dance style of the dances for the Princess and her ladies. But my sense of the structural mastery of the piece remained inchoate until the British complaints ("Where are the golden apples of yesteryear? What's happened to the *story?*") led me to grasp what Balanchine had achieved in making the ballet a suite of dances rather than a linear narrative. Thanks to British nostalgia for the old version, I saw more clearly the positive form Balanchine's growing antipathy to ordinary ballet narrative had taken, and this amounted to a real advance in my understanding of his style and his sense of dance structure.

Only later did I realize that Stravinsky himself may have led Balanchine away from the familiar linear structure. In 1945, doubtless for reasons having to do with protection of copyright, Stravinsky had fashioned a new *Firebird* suite, calling it now a "Ballet Suite," and it is probable that Balanchine would have wanted to use the new suite instead of the

Balanchine and Edward Villella rehearse *Swan Lake,* ca. 1962 (photo ©1994 Martha Swope; choreography by George Balanchine ©The George Balanchine Trust)

complete 1910 version, now out of copyright, if only in order to give his old friend and compatriot some of the money he was always interested in.

The British dislike of *Firebird,* which had been useful in bringing to sharper focus my own understanding of the new structure Balanchine had created, helped me again in 1951, after I had returned from England, when Balanchine mounted act 2 of *Swan Lake.* The new *Swan Lake,* like *Firebird,* aims at sustaining drama and atmosphere in what is structurally a suite of dances; and I now think that I came to understand this principle of structure fully only when my experience of *Swan Lake* had been added to my experience of *Firebird.* Indeed, I was so convinced by the structure of the new *Swan Lake* that I took issue with Balanchine's own later decision to cut the superb "jumping" pas de trois he had made for Patricia Wilde in 1951. (I still take pleasure in remembering her splendidly full-bodied energy in that role and recall with pleasure too Carolyn George's piquant and alert performances a bit later, long before her days as one of the company's house photographers and mother of the d'Amboise brood.) I had been completely in favor of the decision to cut the surefire pas de quatre of the cygnets; although Balanchine was making a suite of dances, he wanted to maintain a consistent tone, and I guessed he had decided that, despite the exquisite workmanship of Tchaikovsky's score, the perky charm of the mechanical dance of the baby swans endangered the mood and the dramatic atmosphere he wanted. For a powerful though indeterminate dramatic implication informs even so abstract a dance as the beautiful pas de neuf Balanchine created for the too-seldom-remembered, beautiful Yvonne Mounsey, which has become a permanent part of the City Ballet *Swan Lake*. Balanchine must have thought the jumping pas de trois also interfered with his larger intentions, but my understanding of those intentions seemed clear enough for me to disagree confidently and to argue that this dance had a fullness that did not threaten the mood of the rest of the ballet.

My understanding of Balanchine's method in reworking *Firebird* was still a blend of awareness and combative argumentativeness in 1950: I did indeed grasp some of it and was able to see that on the stage, but a lot of it I was just "saying" to myself as I defended my favorite against attack. And this is true of what appeared to be another important development in my understanding of Balanchine, which came the next year when I was enjoying the Fulbright that had at last come through. Before the New York City Ballet's London visit, in the spring of 1950, Balanchine had mounted *Ballet Imperial* for the Sadler's Wells company, and I saw them dance it in London a year later. It was a ballet I had come to know well during the Monte Carlo seasons, but the English performances put into relief important aspects of Balanchine's technique and style—and their difficulty. The English company danced this ballet too softly and mildly, and, as I remember, too slowly, as well, although this last seems unlikely, since tempi are easier to maintain than other aspects of style. Feeling sure that Balanchine had taught them to dance it correctly the year before, I was free to be outraged by their desecration of a masterpiece. My grasp of Balanchine's methods developed only later to the point where I could guess that when he mounted *Ballet Imperial* for Sadler's Wells, his practicality would have led him to adjust the ballet to what the company could handle, so that from the beginning the ballet would have looked and felt at least somewhat different from the way it looked and felt when danced by the Monte Carlo company, which he had been able as balletmaster to work up to his standards. And yet I was probably not entirely wrong in believing that in those months between the first performances and those that I saw, the habitual Sadler's Wells "good taste" had to some extent asserted itself: the dancers had lost edge, variety of attack, and the wide dynamic range of Balanchine's more highly inflected and larger classical style, which they needed to have learned briefly even to dance *Ballet Imperial*.

My experiences with *Ballet Imperial* afterward put the English experience in a different perspective, for this ballet also turned out to be problematic in later versions supervised by Balanchine himself. It had been one of my favorites during the Monte Carlo seasons, but I didn't take to it at all when Balanchine revived it in 1964 for Suzanne Farrell, nor in Patricia McBride's performances, nor even in Violette Verdy's, although Bernard Haggin was so keen about Verdy's that I may have missed something. But I don't think my response here was one of mood or temporary indisposition. I am positive that the great ebb and flow of energy had gone, leaving behind a painfully heightened audibility of Tchaikovsky's rhetoric, particularly in the loud cadenzas, with their mechanical sequences and thunderously cascading scales, to which the ballerina must execute her cruelly difficult bravura feats. In 1964 it seemed that neither dancer, pianist, nor audience would ever get a reprieve—an effect intensified by the banging of whoever the house pianist was, and one that is still not entirely unknown. Because the company had moved to Lincoln Center, there were hatefully overblown new sets of St. Petersburg commissioned from Rouben Ter-Arutunian: one of the gigantism effects thought appropriate to the new huge stage in the first years, just as were the same artist's giant Sequoias in the new *Nutcracker* and Peter Harvey's Brobdignagian swags in *Brahms-Schoenberg Quartet*. After a few seasons, the Ter-Arutunian sets were replaced by the standard City Ballet blue drop, but someone had come up with uniquely bilious nylon rags for costumes. The great work seemed doomed, under an unlucky star. Then in 1974 the ballet's name was changed to *Tchaikovsky Piano Concerto No. 2*, the bilious rags were replaced by attractive light-blue chiffon dresses, Merrill Ashley swept through the piece on her exhilarating dance impulse, and *Ballet Imperial* was born again. After Farrell rejoined the company in 1975 she danced a few marvelous performances, although this never became one of her regular roles. It has since been danced wonderfully not only by Ashley but also by Kyra Nichols and Heather Watts and has become an utterly unproblematic part of the repertory. It is possible that Balanchine himself came to understand only gradually how to steady the oddly precarious balance of this great work.

The Sadler's Wells *Ballet Imperial* also gave me my first sense of the poignant ephemerality of ballet. I had known that entire ballets could be lost—as *Cotillon* had been lost—and I suppose that is the worst kind of ephemerality, but what I saw happen to *Ballet Imperial* seemed almost more disturbingly final. For the precious thing that had vanished—the ballet's special life—had left behind a zombie version of itself. I felt something akin to this when I saw the *Symphonie Concertante* that Baryshnikov revived in 1983 for the American Ballet Theatre with such good intentions.

I had missed the premiere of *Symphonie Concertante* at Ballet Society, and I saw the ballet only a few times at the New York City Ballet in the fifties, but my underexposure to it

Tanaquil Le Clercq and Francisco Moncion in *La Valse*, 1951 (photo by Walter E. Owen; courtesy the New York City Ballet; choreography by George Balanchine ©The George Balanchine Trust)

Maria Tallchief, ca. 1950 (photo by Walter E. Owen; courtesy the Dance Collection, New York Public Library for the Performing Arts, Astor, Lenox, and Tilden Foundations)

was really deliberate. Haggin admired the piece immensely, and I was accustomed to believing without rancor that whatever he liked I would eventually come to like; but something kept me from feeling this way about this ballet, and I think I stayed away from it in order to avoid debate with Haggin about its merits. For him it was on a level with *Concerto Barocco*, and I imagine also on a level with *Divertimento No. 15*, but that was far from the case with me. I liked the slow movement, yet the pas de trois format could not match the depth of emotion in Mozart's music, as I have already explained.

I did appreciate the exciting difference between the dance styles of Tallchief and Le Clercq in *Symphonie Concertante*, although for some reason that experience did not carry through to illuminate the same qualities for me in other roles. I barely noticed either Tallchief or Le Clercq in the revival in 1950 of a ballet I knew much better from my Monte Carlo days, *Le Baiser de la Fée*. Tallchief danced the Fairy in both versions, and I believe I remember both equally well, but Danilova's bride was so beautiful and so strong a memory (I saw the ballet a surprising number of times—it was danced repeatedly in Boston) that Le Clercq's performance never quite registered; this was for Haggin one of the great moments in her career, and again I missed it.

Balanchine's setting of *Divertimento No. 15*, Mozart's Divertimento No. 15 for strings and two horns, K.287, marked a gratifying bridge between Balanchine's musical tastes and my own. Toscanini's performances of this score had been among my touchstones for accurate musical style, and in the late forties Haggin told me the anecdote he later recorded in *Conversations with Toscanini:* Toscanini had been listening to a Serge Koussevitsky Tanglewood performance of the music on the radio and had exploded with contempt when Koussevitsky had not recognized the six-four chord in the adagio as the signal for a cadenza. "Ignorante!" he exclaimed, and decided to conduct the piece himself to show how it should be done. This is a marvelously exact instance of what Haggin eternally sought and sometimes found—incontrovertibly "factual" evidence to support issues of judgment and taste, but what moves me especially is how deep and loving the musical style of Toscanini's performance actually is. The fact that Toscanini was not generally fond of Mozart made the rightness of his performance the more beautiful. I wondered whether Toscanini had known the music before he heard the ignorant performance that made him want to demonstrate his own superior musicianship (I was fascinated by this instance of competition between artists, my own special vice); I wondered how Koussevitsky had come to know the music; I wondered whether either of them had heard the great recorded version with Josef Szigeti, and whether Haggin himself knew this version. The possibility that Balanchine had come to know the music through the Toscanini record made the ballet more personal to me.

The unusual structure of *Divertimento No. 15*—the adagio is danced not by one but by five ballerinas, with three partners—at first seemed to me due to the dimension of the slow movement. I felt that Balanchine was at once confessing and conquering a certain nervousness about having to set the huge arch of melody in the Mozart score. Later I came to see the variation movement as the key to the format: Balanchine spotted this movement as the ideal locus for dance variations to match Mozart's musical variations, and I now recognized how crucial the variation form is to Balanchine's art. I think Balanchine set the first movement in a way that makes us grasp that the ballet is to be danced by five equal ballerinas and three cavaliers; these then appear quite naturally in the variation movement, so that we are prepared to find them in the adagio, too. I even see Balanchine looking ahead to using two ballerinas in the wonderful pas de trois entrance in the last movement. I felt I had achieved real insight into Balanchine's creative habits when I caught sight of the second possibility and abandoned the first.

Balanchine mounted his 1946 *La Sonnambula* at the New York City Ballet in 1960, with Allegra Kent as the Sleepwalker and Jillana as the Coquette. This ballet was apparently one of Balanchine's favorites, so I had to look elsewhere for an explanation of why it took so long to revive it. There is a big difference between its casting requirements and those of *Le Baiser de la Fée,* which he had mounted at the City Ballet in 1950. In the latter, the bride has the adagio pas de deux, which confers top status, but the role of the Fairy is very powerful and more substantial; in *La Sonnambula* the role of the Sleepwalker is infinitely more important than the beautifully written demi-caractère role for the Coquette. The sleepwalker—Danilova's last great Balanchine premiere—has not only the fantastically original and haunting adagio of the eternal bourrée but an illusion piece at the end, when the four men from the world of fantasy place the dead poet in the sleepwalker's frail arms for her to carry to her private domain. It was feasible to cast the senior Tallchief and the junior Le Clercq together in *Le Baiser de la Fée* without making the former feel deprived of her status but impossible to cast them both in *La Sonnambula,* which therefore, in Balanchine's attentive calculations, had to wait until an almost complete change in the roster of dancers made the right casting possible.

These revivals were steps toward creating an adequate repertory for a permanent company, as is clear in the range of styles, moods, and atmospheres they comprehend: even narrative ballet, already separated from Balanchine's name in the popular mind and in the press, is well represented. I was aware of this variety and impressed by it, but I had only a dim sense of the scope of the repertory-building Balanchine was accomplishing at this juncture, between 1948 and 1957. I understood that *Firebird, Swan Lake,* and *The Nutcracker* were aimed at forming a historically representative repertory, as was the setting to Delibes's *Sylvia*, the *Sylvia Pas de Deux* in 1950, and I was annoyed as usual by John Martin's tantrum about Balanchine's wasting energy on an old war-horse like the "unnecessary" *Swan Lake*, energy that might better be spent on creative new repertory. (Martin had by now come around to seeing Balanchine's genius, although he saved face amusingly. Like the English critics, with their fantasy that the spiritualizing atmosphere of England had "softened" the company, Martin ascribed his illumination about Balanchine to the fresh dramatic nuance brought by the importation of Diana Adams, Nora Kaye, and Hugh Laing from Martin's favorite company, Ballet Theatre. At the time, I was still fixed in my unsympathetic view of Martin, which I didn't change until frequent contact with the actual words he wrote in the fifties opened my eyes to his distinction.)

I did not yet understand Balanchine's subtler repertorial intentions in making such ballets as *Scotch Symphony* in 1952, *Pas de Dix* in 1955, *Allegro Brillante* in 1956, *Donizetti Variations* in 1960, and *Valse et Variations* (later *Raymonda Variations*) in 1961. At the time of *A Midsummer Night's Dream* in 1962 I began doing serious thinking about his repertory; and when Balanchine's own efforts as a maker of repertory reached their fruition in his return to the music of Delibes, in *Pas de Deux and Divertissement* (1965), *La Source* (1968), and finally *Coppélia* (1974), I realized that throughout his tenure with the New York City Ballet he had been composing a repertory to present all the major ballet traditions of the past: the Tchaikovsky and Glazunov scores continued his ongoing tribute to and extension of Petipa; *Scotch Symphony* and *Donizetti Variations* acknowledged not only Bournonville but perhaps his own brief experience as guest balletmaster of the Royal Danish Ballet in 1930; and the Delibes ballets wiped the grime of overfamiliarity from the masterpieces of French classical ballet and the wonderful music of one of Tchaikovsky's two favorite composers (the other, of course, is Mozart).

From the time of *The Four Temperaments* I was aware of Balanchine's intent and capacity to enrich and modernize ballet style and vocabulary; I saw this continuing not only in *Ivesiana* and the two ballets of the fifties that I didn't see, *Metamorphoses* and *Opus 34*, but also in *Western Symphony* (1954); *Stars and Stripes* (1958); the 1968 revival of the 1936 *Slaughter on Tenth Avenue*, and the zenith of this repertory-building, the complete organic fusion of popular and classical high style, *Who Cares?* (1970), a tribute to Gershwin, America, and his own younger days in theater and film. At first I saw the vast differences between Balanchine's ballets as a reflection of his vast range of taste and interest, but I later appreciated that they were also a sign of his belief in the permanence of his new company and a proof of his ability to create it.

I welcomed the fact that *The Nutcracker* was made to attract a general audience, but I've shared the faint annoyance *The Nutcracker* generates in the minds of out-of-towners during the Christmas season, since it is the only ballet performed during one of the few times we can be in New York for an extended period. But Balanchine was right to try to keep the company out of the red by filling the house at Christmas, and later I caught on to his deeper design of using this ballet to implant his style, technique, taste—and his own personal history—into the eyes and minds and hearts of as many people as possible, especially as many children as possible. And I loved the piece without reservation. It was the first act of *Nutcracker* that led me to judge Balanchine the greatest theatrical artist in my experience. I was endlessly pleased by the continuity and flow of the narrative and by the thousand effortlessly right decisions concerning pacing and emphasis, and I was moved by such evocative theatrical strokes as the wandering bed; above all, I admired the original theatrical illusion Balanchine created. He was asking fresh, natural American young men and women to impersonate the courteous civilization of the nineteenth-century Biedermeier Christmas party: you saw both at once, the American behavior and the style it was mimicking. The transparency with which these dancers played the parts of nineteenth-century German mothers and fathers produced a precise half-illusion that I found utterly original. I began to understand, not merely accept, the command: "Don't act." And it is partly through this mode of illusion that *The Nutcracker* became perhaps the first Balanchine ballet to give highbrows and middlebrows the chance to enjoy the same thing at the same time and almost in the same way.

# SEVEN / *Teaching*

During the 1950s, when the New York City Ballet was establishing itself by forming a growing roster of dancers, a repertory, and an audience, I was finding myself as a college teacher and critical writer and establishing myself as a permanent member of the English Department at Wellesley College. My motivation for becoming a teacher of literature was confirmed by my experiences as a member of Balanchine's audience: as I had no question about the value of what was giving me so much pleasure, I easily transferred that value into the material I was teaching. Following Balanchine was the most important experience of the arts for me in those days, but figuring out how to do my job well took more of my attention.

My teaching took a form that could have been predicted: I emphasized the actuality and the value of the experience of art. I never really tried for a discussion method—not to speak of Socratic results. Rather, I presented myself as a person for whom following an artist's career was virtually a motive for living. As I tried to embody and perform for my students my idea of what it was like to be intensely and passionately interested in the arts, I again expressed the influence of my parents' religion of the personal experience of Christ: I was bearing witness, just as my father had done in Rescue Missions and storefront meetings. I say *the arts* because although I taught English literature almost exclusively until the mid-sixties, when I began to teach film, I was nevertheless as much and as deeply engaged in thinking about film, music, and ballet as I was about literature. I didn't become a specialist in either a period or a genre of literature, although I had read widely in many periods and genres. I kept up with the little magazines and with a few professional journals, but I was never in danger of becoming a learned person.

Here too I'm reminded of my father's wary relations with institutions and with serious scholarship about the Bible. But I easily absorbed from the air around me a great deal of sound knowledge about the literature I taught, and I can claim to have been since the mid-1950s a highly trained and skilled reader of English prose and poetry. I think of myself as a close reader, or a "slow" reader, as they used to say at Amherst: a disciple of I. A. Richards (I became one of his section men at Harvard) and William Empson, T. S. Eliot and F. R. Leavis, John Crowe Ransom, Cleanth Brooks, Robert Penn Warren, and Reuben Brower. I don't like to be categorized systematically as a believer in New Criticism (I was never taken with W. K. Wimsatt's systematic thinking), for I am a committed and fairly well-informed student of literary tradition. I have never presented historical material by itself as background or context, however; I half-cheated and half-Socratized by trying to let it arise as if inevitably from the task of close reading—as if my students simply needed to be reminded of what my experience as a professional reader and student of literature had taught me. And this questionable practice still seems to me the right way to do it.

When I had arrived at Harvard I had tried to pick up clues about how to *talk well* about literature. I took note of the terms people were using, what seemed to them worth pointing out in discussions of a poem or a play, and I gradually developed a blurred and inchoate, but gradually clarifying, sense of what I was supposed to understand and say. And then I discovered Richards's *Practical Criticism* right before I was asked to become one of his section men: I learned all at once an immense amount from the clarity and strength of Richards's expository gifts, as well as from his immense skill, certainty, and finesse as a reader. My sense that *tone* is the key word in close reading comes from my discovery of it in *Practical Criticism,* and I'm pretty sure that my sense of how delicately one must pay attention to context, along with my skill at being alert to shifts in tone and in levels of illusion and convention, come from Richards. And I think that Richards's influence too immediately fitted in, as if it were meant to be, with two other important aspects of my experience, memory, and habitual thinking: B. H. Haggin's emphasis on choices in following an artist's mind at work and the way Balanchine's ballets both ask for and train you in a flexible sense of genre, convention, and level of illusion—the difference I discussed earlier between the brilliant points of invention of imagery in *Apollo* as contrasted with the way the sentence structure of *Concerto Barocco* worked, or the way mimetic gesture relates to abstract conventional ballet-language imagery in all his ballets.

Equally important to my identity as an experiencer of the arts was Shakespeare. My big literary experience in high school had been Miss Gerhardt's teaching of *Macbeth*, but I don't remember any details from the class, and I'm sure that my excitement had nothing to do with the language-oriented approach to Shakespeare that I developed in my first year at Harvard. I didn't take a Shakespeare course there; indeed, I never studied Shakespeare (or, for that matter, any other writer who came to mean anything to me) in graduate school, but Shakespeare's reputation (I was still, of course, very hot on status) helped me to realize one of my axioms in criticism, that Shakespeare's relation to the English language was the great single central fact of the study of English literature. I have the clearest possible memory of my first encounter with Eliot's contrast of Shakespeare's "She looks like sleep, / As she would catch another Antony / In her strong toil of grace" (5.2.345–47) with Dante's simile about the way a tailor looks when he is threading a needle—and the clearest memory, too, of a sense of revelation at the sheer fact and the sheer pleasure of the Shakespearian metaphoric method.

By the time I came to know my closest literary friends at graduate school, Joel Dorius and Beverly Layman (fairly early in my second term), I was already high on talk about metaphor in Shakespeare. I think it was that particular interest—supplemented with music and other cultivated tastes—that led my friends to suggest me as the third section man in the course to be taught by Richards and Theodore Spencer, which I entered in my second year. I was talking with my *Foreground* friends, Jackie Steiner and André du Bouchet, about Berlioz, Delacroix, Debussy, and politics, and at the same time but in a completely different vein, virtually a different avatar, even a different personality perhaps, I was having exciting talks about literature with Joel and Bev. Everything conspired to give my approach to literary study its still-current emphasis on the experience of reading in time as opposed to studying for the meaning of what was read. And there is the clearest possible line between that approach and this book, which I call *Following Balanchine* entirely because of the emphasis the phrase places on the *experience* of art rather than the study of art.

Literature was my main interest, in teaching and writing. I had written my thesis on Dickens's "characterization"—what seems now an amazingly old-fashioned way of naming the first version of a view of Dickens's art that I still think right; in the early sixties I published a completely reworked version of my thesis in a book called *The Dickens Theatre*. I did a lot of book reviewing of literary criticism and fiction. I developed my special, rather obsessive, interest in a few contemporary writers—Anthony Powell, Eudora Welty, Philip Larkin, Elizabeth Taylor, Philip Roth, Samuel Beckett, but most of my interest was in the literature of the past: Jane Austen, George Eliot, Henry James, Tolstoy, D. H. Lawrence, and James Joyce. I rarely went to the theater, and I attended the movies much less frequently than I had done in the forties: not until the advent of Federico Fellini, Ingmar Bergman, Michelangelo Antonioni, the French New Wave directors, and American directors like Stanley Kubrick and Robert Altman did I reimmerse myself in film. Music remained a leading interest and pleasure. My love of it was closely connected with my continuing friendship with Haggin, but it was reinforced as well by the musical interests of many other friends. My continuing strong interest in ballet was also connected with Haggin, who often took me to performances, and with whom I maintained an ongoing conversation.

My interest in music, my early excitement about Shakespeare, and my concentrated interest in Balanchine revealed the pleasure of experiencing flexible modes of art and in the process improved my skill in handling them. By the late fifties and early sixties I had become well practiced in handling shifting modes of illusion and abstraction in art. And my thinking about such art had a powerful influence on my thinking about literature. My subjects at Wellesley were modern drama, the novel, and Shakespeare, and I needed no special effort to see and make relations between them and the process of seeing Balanchine's ballets and talking about them with my friends. From Balanchine's handling of mimetic and nonmimetic art, as well as from his skill and ease in moving from one mode of theatrical illusion to another, I learned flexibility in handling similar issues in the works of Shakespeare, and later in those of Dickens, George Eliot, James, Austen, Tolstoy, Joyce, Lawrence, and other writers of central importance to me. These issues became central to my teaching and writing.

The fit between me and Wellesley College was a nice one. My friend from graduate school, Bev Layman, had preceded me there, and the year after I arrived David Ferry, another English teacher, was hired and immediately became my closest friend and intellectual companion. Along with him, I became interested in the academic and political goings-on of the college and began to demonstrate an involvement with it that amounts to loyalty and commitment, however shy-making these words are when offered earnestly.

Because I was not a discussion leader, the rather withdrawn, reserved, and—not to put too fine a point on it—*shy* Wellesley students worked well for me. My attempt to embody the activity of being interested in the arts carried with it a dogmatic missionary aim of spreading my gospel of judgments about the arts, and my students in the fifties and sixties did not seem to mind this, although occasionally I heard a murmur of one of my nicknames, "God Garis." The words were spoken in irony and with a certain affection, but they contained at least some serious complaint against my unwillingness to pay attention to opinions that differed from mine unless they were grounded in actual details in works of art.

These years preceded the era of student evaluation questionnaires at Wellesley, and I have only my hunch to say that I was a fairly popular teacher. I had high enrollments, even though, in a setting where the grade of "B" was perfectly respectable and there were plenty of "C"s handed out, I was an unusually hard grader—looking back on my grade books, I am astonished that my signs of approval and acceptance were allowed to be so rare by me, my college, and my students.

My tough grading was all the more remarkable because the student body at Wellesley, especially during the late fifties and through the sixties, was an extraordinarily gratifying one to teach. These were the days when the Seven Sisters (Wellesley, Smith, Vassar, Mount Holyoke, Radcliffe, Barnard, and Bryn Mawr Colleges) were the inevitable choice of the privileged and well-educated young women of the eastern seaboard. There were few competitive coeducational schools; the Seven Sisters thus had their pick of the best female students in the country—a situation that changed dramatically at the end of the sixties, when all the equivalent male colleges began accepting women. The social mix of students who choose Wellesley now has not changed significantly since the fifties, although we can no longer attract nearly as great a proportion of the most gifted students.

In the sixties, right before the women's movement began to exert power over the whole country, not least over the women's colleges, most Wellesley students came to college without a commitment to a serious lifelong career outside the home. Few worried about preparing a good transcript in order to be accepted into graduate school. Although the attitude was not explicitly formulated, the students seemed to regard their college careers as four years of freedom from anxious planning for the future, and accordingly many of them approached their courses with amazing concentration and flexibility. The Seven Sisters were important socially in both senses of the word: they trained well-educated and prosperous middle-class young women to take their place in the segment of American social life to which they had for a long time known they were destined, and they trained women for lives of service in the community. But in the 1950s and 1960s, this training involved a conscious dedication to hard intellectual work while in college; taking one's classes seriously and spending time on them; and often allowing oneself to become especially involved with only one or two courses, while being content to do merely passing work for the others.

Another aspect of this period at Wellesley (until our president in the second half of the 1960s initiated cross-registration with MIT) was the fact that Wellesley's relative isolation from Boston—despite many references to the cultural richness of the city in our publicity—made the accomplishment of an active social life away from the campus depend on considerable administrative and executive energy and competence. Some students managed this well, but many decided not to make the effort, with the result that for a large group, college life was centered around course work. The combination of a highly selective admissions policy, the lack of explicit career goals, and the campus-bound nature of the social life produced an atmosphere of intellectual seriousness and freedom such as I have never really heard of elsewhere: I couldn't have found a more rewarding place to teach anywhere in America at the time. It is true that intellectually rebellious, boldly articulate, or socially outgoing students were rare, and that made for a certain submissiveness and blandness in the classroom. But the level of intellectual grasp, the willingness to work hard, the sense that becoming personally involved in the intellectual substance of the course work were what college was all about—these made my teaching remarkably rewarding.

My relations with people have been more problematic. I have put a Bloomsburyish value on asexual personal relationships, which may have thus become overdeveloped emotionally—I have made my life of friendship fairly dramatic. But I have a gift for friendship: I'm still in close contact with friends from my adolescence and my twenties. Traveling with various pairings or groupings of these friends became an important part of my life in the sixties. My life has taken the form of a sort of aestheticism familiar in our culture since the turn of the last century.

I have always looked for the sense of augmented living I find in sharing my response to the arts. When a friend asked me whether my pleasure in discussing Balanchine's ballets and dancers did not lie to a large degree in my satisfaction in shaping my friends' tastes, judgments, and pleasures, I felt at first that I had been rightly rebuked, but the truth is less simple. I have certainly satisfied a need for power over other minds by inspiring my friends to become members of the Balanchine audience. But power over my group has always gone along with friendship and affection, with learning more and seeing better. And here the nature and especially the dimension of what I shall name the Balanchine Enterprise makes a difference: being attached to it gave me and my friends the riches of its sheer size, its multifarious, multitudinous *life*. There was plenty to go around.

EIGHT / *Violette Verdy and Other New Dancers*

Watching Balanchine's ballets had always given me, in the highest degree, what I value most in art, the sense of being in contact with a working mind—participating in the choices a work of art is making, being held in a tension of energy by its momentum and continuity. In 1957 I began to experience this life at the New York City Ballet on a larger scale and with greater impact. I began to feel in contact not just with *this* performance of *that* ballet with *those* dancers but with a large, complex form of life taking shape beyond, behind, and above these particulars—a huge work of art in progress that I named the Balanchine Enterprise.

I date this occurrence in 1957 because changes in my own life in that year coincided with changes in Balanchine's life and work. Connie and Richard Harrier, close friends from Allentown, moved to New York, and I began visiting them once a month or so for ballet weekends. We would often go to five performances in three days; this allowed me to recapitulate the experience of my 1946 immersion in the Monte Carlo season, but with the added pleasure of conversation with my friends immediately after we had all seen the performance together. I began to see the same ballets over and over again, and to discuss them over and over again, and inevitably I began to *see* more. Balanchine centers ballets in the soloists, both for the sake of coherence and because that is how his imagination works, and when you first encounter a ballet you follow his directions—it is hardly possible not to. I am unusually attentive to the center of a work of art in any case. But I am not resistant to seeing new things in ballets, and after 1957 I began to notice more of what was taking place at the background, or in the inner spaces, or at the margin of the ballet; I looked longer and

Violette Verdy in *Allegro Brillante,* ca. 1962 (photo ©1994 Martha Swope; choreography by George Balanchine ©The George Balanchine Trust)

harder at what the secondary dancers were doing, and then at those dancers in themselves, and at their development. Before long I was keeping track of the entire company, and it was probably this dividing of my attention over so many concerns that gave me the sense of encountering the life of a large, multi-featured, multi-faceted work of art in progress. The Balanchine Enterprise was alive also in the sense that it was growing: in sheer numbers; in the levels of ranking of the dancers; in technique—the speed and scale, the elegance and eloquence of the dancing. And after 1957 Balanchine began concentrating increasingly on younger dancers.

As I see it now, the shift began with a catastrophe: Tanaquil Le Clercq, one of the company's leading ballerinas, who was married to Balanchine at the time, contracted polio in late October 1956. During the rest of that year and much of the next, Balanchine worked with her in a regimen of physical therapy that ended unsuccessfully in 1957; she never danced again. The loss of Le Clercq precipitated additions to the roster of dancers, which gradually led to a change in the way Balanchine used those dancers. His disappointment about Le Clercq's therapy was followed by a powerful life-movement of compensation, a surge in the fertility of his choreographic imagination, which had the result for me of making my involvement with the Balanchine Enterprise more deeply and complexly absorbing than before.

Between 1948 and 1957 I had tended to take the dancers at the New York City Ballet for granted. Of course, I loved a great deal of the dancing, and I felt that I understood what was good about it. Because of my need to judge all my experiences in art, I constantly compared dancers with each other, as well as the different performances of a single dancer. I thought the dancers were wonderful artists, but I was concentrating on Balanchine, and I regarded his performers as the instruments of his art, encouraged by the received and not completely erroneous opinion that Balanchine thought the dancers should not be stars, or act, or think about their dancing, or conceive their own independently worked out "performances" but rather gain fulfillment by giving themselves to the roles as he taught them—"just do the steps." Along with this idea, I accepted a settled ranking. Maria Tallchief and Tanaquil Le Clercq were supreme; Diana Adams had a lovely, natural style, as did Yvonne Mounsey; Melissa Hayden and Patricia Wilde were dependable performers who capably imitated high style without quite possessing it (Edwin Denby once noted that elegance was a "mime effect" with Wilde); Francisco Moncion was the only distinguished male dancer (though not a technician); Nicholas Magallanes (also no technician; he specialized in "low leaps") was an invaluable partner, lending to such roles as *Orpheus* an eloquent presence; André Eglevsky's technical virtuosity filled a company need; Jacques d'Amboise was a useful cavalier. These views conveyed a sense of hierarchy that suited my philosophy of both art and life, and the hierarchy at the New York City Ballet seemed right.

Balanchine himself deployed his dancers in a ranking that reflected his judgment of their talent. Most of the premieres went to Tallchief or Le Clercq, defining them as the prima ballerinas, but "experimental" work like *Opus 34* or *Ivesiana* went to Adams, who, along with Hayden and Wilde, also danced the prima roles, but only after they had been around for a couple of seasons. I learned a lot from this system. It suited my own concentration on critical judgment to try to understand why Balanchine did not like Hayden and Wilde as much as Le Clercq, Tallchief, and Adams, and my sense of learning how to judge dancing was particularly keen when I could note and relish the difference between Tallchief's *Firebird* and Wilde's or Hayden's. I was perhaps ungenerous to the latter two, for my sense of the difference between the best and the good was already extreme, as it continues to be, but I feel little regret on this score, since I sensed the deep connection between the way Balanchine followed his own taste in casting and the role hierarchical order played in the choreography itself. Yet the fact that I repeatedly encountered so settled a ranking probably has a lot to do with the fact that I did not concentrate on the dancing during this period.

Tallchief showed herself a prima ballerina assoluta in *Swan Lake, The Nutcracker, Scotch Symphony,* and *Allegro Brillante*—bold, proud, authoritative—and I have a treasury of memories of her *Firebird:* the silky sinuosity of her beautiful legs and knees in the first pas de deux, when she has been caught by the Prince and is stretching voluptuously under his care, the power and speed of her pirouettes as she flashes in bearing a sword to help him fight the Katschei. But for me her central role was in *Pas de Dix,* Balanchine's first ballet suite to the music he loved from Glazunov's *Raymonda,* an evening-length 1898 Petipa ballet that he and Alexandra Danilova had staged for the Monte Carlo. I still see Tallchief riding the beat exuberantly at her entrance in *Pas de Dix;* her exotic variation, with its insolent clap of hands and Czardas arms; and her pirouettes in the second finale down the diagonal line of dancers, punctuated by startling leaps with head and arms flung back— these are so present to me that I have the impression I saw the ballet more often than I could have done. When I wonder why *Pas de Dix* looms so large in my memory, the best answer I can come up with (apart from its brilliance) is that Balanchine expertly crafted it for just such an appeal: as witness the fact that it has two finales.

Of Tanaquil Le Clercq's dancing I have sharp, full memories of the elegantly raucous characters she created in *Bourrée Fantasque* and *Western Symphony*. In addition, her highly bred youthful self-sufficiency was mysteriously allied with Moncion's remoteness in Robbins's *Afternoon of a Faun:* the power of this relationship gave me from the start my sense

Tanaquil Le Clercq in *Western Symphony,* ca. 1955 (photo courtesy the Dance Collection, New York Public Library for the Performing Arts, Astor, Lenox, and Tilden Foundations; choreography by George Balanchine ©The George Balanchine Trust)

that the heart of this revision of Nijinsky's masterpiece, which is also Robbins's, lies not in its representation of dancers' narcissism as much as in the clarity with which it brings out their temperaments. I caught a few glimpses of Le Clercq's genius as a pure dancer: I still use her image as a standard for the chic, swaggering, long-legged variation in *Divertimento No. 15*. But I responded mainly to her temperament. A personal encounter may have had something to do with my failure to take the measure of her genius as a classical ballerina. A group of us, undergraduates and graduate students both, had come down from Cambridge for a weekend of ballet in 1948 or 1949, and because one of us had gone to school at Putney with "Tanny," we went backstage to congratulate her after the performance. I remember how funny and nice she was, but also how ordinarily American: she had no mysterious charismatic aura.

I never realized I was seeing something marvelous when I saw Le Clercq in *La Valse*, as I did several times, but that was probably because I was so much influenced by B. H. Haggin, who despised Ravel and, as I remember, thought Balanchine's *La Valse* also unimportant; although I liked the music well enough, I went along with Haggin's judgment of the ballet and didn't study it closely. My view has changed since. The decor and the opening imagery still remind me of a Bonwit Teller window, but I soon get caught up by the precision with which Balanchine has targeted this chic mode, and then I become fully absorbed in the dance invention that transcends that mode: the last pas de deux in the first section (set to *Valses Nobles et Sentimentales*) and the whole second section (set to the tone poem for which the ballet is named) rise to emotional grandeur, achieving that metamorphosis of near-kitsch into high art that is one of the knacks and glories of modernism in all the arts, as well as one of Balanchine's specialities, as he showed in the marvelous *Vienna Waltzes*.

At some point during my experience with *La Valse* I noticed its structural solidity, which Balanchine achieves, characteristically, by using Ravel's glamorously moody tone poem about "dancing on the brink" as a huge formal coda to the earlier set of waltz variations—a structure he points to by rescheduling the entrances of the dancers in the coda in the order in which they have appeared in the variations. This simple device is so oddly powerful in the codas of *Symphony in C, The Nutcracker, Divertimento No. 15, Coppélia,* and *Who Cares?* among others, that I believe it must be idiomatic to the way I experience ballet in the dimension of time: in any case, it was only when I noticed it in *La Valse* that I really respected the piece, as if structural solidity licensed me to admit it into the canon of Balanchine's high art. Now, when I watch the two short silent film clips of Le Clercq dancing the duets from *La Valse* at Jacob's Pillow, I am ravished by the dance genius I finally recognize, but I am also struck by how much she foreshadowed what was to complete itself in Suzanne Farrell in terms of style and even of physique, although the two bodies seem strikingly different at first glance. So I not only missed the full greatness of Le Clercq's dancing but missed as well what she showed about the direction in which Balanchine was moving, in dance technique, style, and physique.

To confess all, one of my clearest memories of Le Clercq is of making an invidious comparison of her dancing with Tallchief's in the the finale of *The Nutcracker*, when the ballerina performs multiple turns in front of her cavalier: Tallchief threw her arms full out and held them triumphantly steady for a split second, but it seemed to me then that Le Clercq lacked the technique, or persistence, to manage such feats, and she gave the movements only a lick and a promise. But the fact that neither she nor Balanchine thought this kind of technical correctness interesting actually predicted how Balanchine would loosen and enlarge ballet style.

The upshot of my desultory attention to Le Clercq is that I didn't feel the deep sense of personal loss that Haggin and others felt at her tragic illness. This occurred in the same year that Guido Cantelli, Toscanini's protégé and one of the great conductors of the century, died in a plane crash at the age of thirty-six, and for Haggin these were equivalent losses; I am sure he was right, but I simply did not know enough about Le Clercq's dancing to feel her absence in that way. Cantelli's death had a personal implication for me because I had paid particular attention to him as Toscanini's protégé; I had gone with my brother Gene to hear him conduct a thrilling performance of Verdi's *Requiem* with the Boston Symphony in 1954, and through records and tapes I have continued to experience his musical spirit. But with Le Clercq my most intense realization of what we lost when she stopped dancing came, I ruefully confess, on those evenings years later when she was brought to the ballet in her wheelchair to see important moments in younger dancers' careers—most poignantly, of course, even painfully, when she came to see Farrell. She was present at Farrell's first *Swan Lake,* and when Balanchine came down the staircase from his customary vantage point at the back of the first ring, he went not to Le Clercq, from whom he was long estranged, but backstage to Farrell. This seemed to me a great drama and Le Clercq a great heroine, but it is a different order of experience from having appreciated the grandeur of her dancing, which I finally achieved only when I was lucky enough many years later to see a tape of her slow movement from *Concerto Barocco* from the early fifties.

Le Clercq's polio was something I thought about, then, rather than felt personally moved by, but it came to matter a great deal to me anyway, for eventually I regarded it as one of the turning points in Balanchine's career. After his dispiriting failure to help Le Clercq, he came back to the company with new energy: two brilliant new ballets were premiered in less than two weeks, *Square Dance* on November 21, and *Agon* on December 1, 1957. He recaptured at fifty-three the energy he had had at seventeen, in 1921, when after graduating from the ballet school in St. Petersburg he became a full-time dancer at the Maryinsky Theater, a full-time student at the adjacent conservatory of music, and the animating genius of a little group of dancers who were allowed to stay backstage at the Maryinsky after evening performances to try out some of George's ideas. In the early 1920s, this nonstop energy prefigured the career to come; the starburst of *Square Dance* and *Agon* in 1957 prophesied that the Balanchine Enterprise was in grand metamorphosis.

*Agon* came at the very center of the complex and interestingly developing relationship with Stravinsky that produced key works at every juncture of Balanchine's career: I have already discussed how my conception of the Balanchine-Stravinsky project changed over the years. As the new product of the most celebrated collaboration between a composer and a choreographer in ballet history, *Agon* received all kinds of attention. It was Stravinsky's first major score after *The Rake's Progress* and the first to show an interest in serial composition on the part of the composer who had for half a century been the mighty opposite of the second Viennese school of Arnold Schoenberg, Anton Webern, and Alban Berg. There was inevitable and genuine suspense about what Stravinsky's twelve-tone music was going to sound like—it sounded like Stravinsky, happily—and an equivalent suspense about how Balanchine was going to find a choreographic match for Stravinsky's venture. And while *Agon* looked like nobody but Balanchine, it marked a shift in his style, too. As if to sum it all up, Martha Swope's photographs of Balanchine and Stravinsky at the *Agon* rehearsals are major dance documents.

*Square Dance*, too, was a triumph both of publicity and of art, and it stands at the midpoint in another of Balanchine's key developments, his interaction with American popular culture. The interaction had begun in the story he himself spread of having always wanted to come to a country where all the women must look like Ginger Rogers, and he was soon drawn to Broadway and Hollywood in the 1930s, where he mastered the style easily and absorbed many of its elements into his conception of the ideal American ballerina and his amplifications of ballet style and technique. In the thirties and forties it may have looked as if Broadway and Hollywood served him only with the money that kept him going despite bad luck in the world of serious ballet, but the genuineness of his interest in popular dancing had been apparent as early as the show-dancing motifs and accents in *Apollo*—the jazzy show-girl movements of Polyhymnia and Calliope at the beginning of the coda, for an obvious instance. In *Western Symphony* in 1954, this interest became explicit and thematic; it took its most famous form in *Stars and Stripes* in 1958 and reached the level of masterwork in *Square Dance* and above all in *Who Cares?* in 1970.

But the stature of *Square Dance* was diminished for me in its first version by a gimmicky sales pitch. While a small, informally dressed string orchestra played Vivaldi and Corelli on the left side of the stage, the ballet was performed on the right side by dancers dressed in practice clothes: a lead couple and a little corps of four couples—and an emphatic meaning of *Square Dance* in 1957 was that they were American couples. Some of the dancing was reminiscent of the steps and patterns of square dancing, but it continually modulated from this style into brilliantly virtuosic ballet vocabulary. But while Balanchine was with the highest finesse making connections between square dancing and ballet for the eye, a famous American square-dance caller, Elisha B. Keeler (whose voice matched his name), was assaulting the ear with twanging couplets about "Nick" and "Pat," whose feet "go wickety-wack." When Balanchine reworked *Square Dance* in 1976, he discarded the caller, put the orchestra back into the pit, and revealed the ballet as a masterpiece, in which the title itself alerts the viewer to the stylistic comparisons to come. A wonderful dividend of the 1957 *Square Dance* was its leading role for Patricia Wilde, who was revealed late in her career as the brilliant technician of the company: her *gargouillades* were so dazzling that I felt I had to learn this technical word to name what she was doing.

The difficult, bare, and cryptic *Agon,* with its advanced score, turned out to delight the general audience, who perhaps took justifiable pride in applauding such avant-garde austerity; *Square Dance* was popular too, but this was less surprising. The life in these ballets brought Balanchine back to the center of my attention with a force I hadn't felt since discovering *Apollo* in 1945. This time there was a new inflection because in *Agon* I saw for the first time something autobiographical in his choreography. This came fully clear to me only a year later, when the partnering in another new ballet, *Episodes,* reminded me forcibly of the partnering in the pas de deux in *Agon.* I was seeing a new kind of collaboration between men and women: an intensely careful, watchful, tender, and grave working together to achieve tense and perilous extensions and balances. From one point of view, the *Agon* pas de deux was just another Balanchine revision of classical pas de deux, but to me it seemed to stem from and reflect, though not quite to imitate, his work with Le Clercq in physical therapy—not that the dance mimics the movements of physical therapy but that in both cases the man and woman seem required by some urgent necessity to move quietly, cautiously, with all the skill and courage they can muster, and in a mood of held-breath crisis.

My sense of this connection still holds, although I've been leery about expressing so autobiographical a reading of a classical pas de deux, since the dance is, of course, a major and central Balanchine ballet invention, with many other aspects to it. I can hardly remember with whom I've shared my reading, and I never received enthusiastic agreement—I do recall being heard out patiently. But it marks an important juncture in my following of Balanchine's career, because it is the first connection I ever made between Balanchine's private life and his art. I had not attempted such connections with the lives of many artists; in fact, in 1957 this was the kind of thinking one didn't do on principle, a notion that derived from T. S. Eliot's dicta about the impersonality of the artist and that was echoed in the writing of virtually every literary critic I cared about (except William Empson, who was always free from dogma). But from then on my following of Balanchine's career developed this approach extensively, and later it was fully warranted by the autobiographical elements in some of the ballets he made for Farrell—*Meditation, Don Quixote,* and *Robert Schumann's "Davidsbündlertänze."*

*Agon* and *Square Dance* made me think about Balanchine's way of using and caring for his dancers just when, as it happened, he was about to enter a new relationship with the rapidly changing company. The roles he made for Hayden in *Agon* and for Wilde in *Square Dance* are the splendid finale to his old relationship with his company. I had loved Wilde in some of the roles Balanchine tailored for her, such as the Scottish girl in the first movement of *Scotch Symphony* and in the soon-to-be-cut jumping pas de trois of *Swan Lake,* but for me she had only a slightly strenuous efficiency in *Firebird, Allegro Brillante,* and other lead ballerina roles. And audiences had loved Hayden; they did not even, as far as one could tell from the applause, make any distinction between her performance and that of Tallchief in *Firebird.* If it was unsurprising that Balanchine gave these two dancers richly and personally imagined roles late in their careers in *Agon* and *Square Dance,* it was also unsurprising that it was Adams who won the truly central "experimental" role in *Agon,* in the pas de deux. The new roles for Hayden and Wilde showed that Balanchine thought their dancing needed refreshing, and this was wonderfully accomplished by both choreographer and dancer; but it differed widely from what happened when he worked with Tallchief at the beginning of the fifties to enrich her sharp, brilliant style with the rich legato she achieved in *Swan Lake.* With Tallchief he was developing the range of a major dancer in her prime, and the payoff came immediately, in the lyrical role he made for her in *Scotch Symphony.* The new roles for Hayden and Wilde, on the other hand, were valedictions to what Balanchine chiefly valued in their dancing: Hayden's cool wit, Wilde's full-bodied strength.

As I thought about Balanchine's way of using dancers after Le Clercq's retirement and in those last important roles for Hayden and Wilde, I was struck by the thinning-out at the top of the roster. Although new aspects of Hayden and Wilde were, in fact, revealed, these good and faithful artists were not major dancers with a wide range of potential. Tallchief, Le Clercq, and Adams had been more than equal to the prima-ballerina demands Balanchine had made on them for a decade, but Le Clercq was gone, and Tallchief left the company next, in 1958 (returning with diminished powers for a brief period in the mid-sixties). Only Adams remained. So there was a definite need.

What then began to happen with thrilling rapidity was that Balanchine demonstrated his own awareness of the need by meeting it. First he brought forward a couple of remarkable younger dancers who were already in the company. The superb Jillana had been a principal since 1953, but I didn't discover her as an important dancer until 1960, when Balanchine's casting of her in *La Sonnambula* (the revival of the 1946 *Night Shadow*) and *Liebeslieder Walzer* showed me her ravishingly warm and full presence. Her performances in more abstract classic roles never revealed to me a very interesting dance identity, but when I was trying to make a point about dance-acting in Balanchine's ballets for a piece about the New York City Ballet dancers in *Partisan Review* in 1966, I chose her as my example:

> We don't think of our Jillana as a "great dance-actress" but she has that effect (which is all that matters) when she dances the Coquette in *La Sonnambula* at Lincoln Center, because she performs all her special contraposto dance movements with bold inflection. This gets her immediately inside the role and then the acting seems to take care of itself: Jillana's malicious gestures as she spies on the lovers or as she whispers to the host have exactly the witty boldness of semi-parody that *is* the characterization.

A major genius of dance whom Balanchine had already singled out for attention before the loss of Le Clercq was Allegra Kent, unrivaled in my experience both for her extraordinary pliancy and for her moving blend of what Suki Schorer calls vulnerability with a highly independent inflection of the Balanchine style and technique that nevertheless remained within its norms. She came and went near the center of my attention for almost twenty years, but I think the variability of my interest in her differed from my mixed record with Le Clercq in that it had less to do with my own lack of perception than with the elusiveness of Kent's own special quality, together with those aspects of her independence that showed up in her failure at perfect balances and other feats appropriate to her prima ballerina rank.

In a literal sense Kent disappeared from attention more often than other dancers when she absented herself for the pregnancies Balanchine was notorious for discouraging. But

Allegra Kent and Jacques d'Amboise in *Afternoon of a Faun*, 1968 (photo ©1994 Martha Swope; choreography by Jerome Robbins ©1968 the choreographer)

despite her faint insubordination, Balanchine maintained a strong interest in her for many years. As early as 1956, in *Divertimento No. 15*, he had given her the heart, the middle double stanza, of the ballet's huge slow movement to show her power in classical adagio; then as she was carried off the stage after this demonstration of authority, the choreography released her almost unbelievable fluidity, as her body flowed back over her cavalier's arms like a vine. (This fluidity has a magically kinetic effect in Martha Swope's still photographs of Kent and d'Amboise in *The Afternoon of a Faun* from 1968.) While Balanchine was moving her up rapidly through leading roles of the regular repertory in the late fifties—the slow movement of *Symphony in C, Swan Lake*, the Sugar Plum Fairy in *The Nutcracker*—he investigated and developed her range in new roles. She was deliciously witty and observant in the affectionate parody of American behavior in the "First Campaign" of *Stars and Stripes* and later, in the final grand pas de deux of that ballet. At the end of 1958, Balanchine confidently matched her dance power with the stage presence of the great Lotte Lenya in the dancing-singing double role at the center of his revival of the Weill-Brecht *Seven Deadly Sins*. By 1959 she was available to help Violette Verdy explain his new difficult style in *Episodes*, and he created one of her most idiomatic roles for her in *Bugaku* in 1963, just before Farrell appeared on the scene.

Balanchine was more interested in women dancers than in men dancers, but his practicality as a man of the theater led him to invite the Danish Erik Bruhn to join the company after Eglevsky left in 1958. I saw Bruhn's marvelous performances in *La Sonnambula* and *Divertimento No. 15*, and there was to have been an *Apollo*, but the working conditions in Balanchine's company did not match Bruhn's habits and he soon left. (The final indignity may have come when Balanchine allowed d'Amboise to choreograph an essentially nondancing role for the world's purest virtuoso in the flop called *Panamerica:* as I remember it, Bruhn spent most of the ballet chained to the floor in a dungeon.)

And Balanchine's practicality alone would have been enough to make him exploit the talents of the young Edward Villella, who had returned to the company from Maritime College in 1957, although in the long run Villella proved a powerful stimulus to his imagination as well. Villella had shown brilliant verve in *Symphony in C* and *Stars and Stripes*, and in 1960 Balanchine revived *The Prodigal Son* for him, one of the two ballets from the Diaghilev period in which he remained interested. Moncion's beautifully grave, inward performances earlier in the fifties lacked technical virtuosity, and the original conception had also been tailored for a dancer with little technique, Serge Lifar; but Balanchine obviously welcomed the bravura Villella brought to the role, and he reworked it to suit not only Villella's brilliant speed, elevation, and electric energy, but also his open warmth and graceful manliness; the ballet became one of the big draws at City Center. Shortly afterward a lovely refinement delighted me in 1960 when Villella danced the Prince of Lorraine in a pas de trois in *The Figure in the Carpet*. By 1962 all these characteristics had been fully integrated in his dancing, to the point where Balanchine could center the first act of *A Midsummer Night's Dream* in Villella's Oberon.

In 1958 Balanchine recruited a dancer trained in a non-Balanchinean tradition in France, Violette Verdy, and immediately created a rich succession of roles for her, first in one of his most advanced works, *Episodes,* and then in the premiere of a traditional show-piece, *Tchaikovsky Pas de Deux* (1960), a heightened, tightened-up, enriched revision of Petipa style, set to the recently discovered original music for the act 3 grand pas de deux from *Swan Lake*. In the same year she was put in the center of two large-scale works, *The Figure in the Carpet* and *Liebeslieder Walzer*. Balanchine was exhibiting the wide range of this outsider's dance identity, while at the same time refining and modifying it—adjusting her dancing to the company style without destroying her individuality.

Jillana, Kent, Villella, and Verdy were soon joined by a large group of very young ballerinas: Patricia McBride, Suki Schorer, and Gloria Govrin in 1959, Mimi Paul and Patricia Neary in 1960, Marnee Morris and Suzanne Farrell in 1961. These dancers soon commanded much of Balanchine's attention; in the case of Farrell, the attention became a fascination both professional and personal, which by the end of the decade had moved into the high drama of infatuation, insubordination, and catastrophe. Watching the development of these new dancers involved me still more deeply with the company. Everything was burgeoning, the level of dancing of the whole company continually increased, and I felt more exhilarated after each year's performances.

The company's growth from 1956 to 1962 created an exciting sense of competition among the dancers, and it seemed to be a competition to please *us,* which, in the beginning, hurt no one. I say "us" to include not only the Harriers but also Haggin, my mentor from the late 1930s on in the positive and negative arts of competition, who was still an important guide in my experience of ballet. My earliest memory of Allegra Kent, for instance, is not of her actual dancing but of reading about it in Haggin's column in the *Hudson Review* of spring 1958, where he noted that she "quietly held her own in the Minkus *Pas de Trois* with higher-powered Tallchief and André Eglevsky." Haggin's description of the dancers as in some sense pitted against each other was normal to his (and my) preoccupation with separating the best from the worst; comparing the New York City Ballet dancers with one another moved to the center of my attention in the 1960s. The influx of new talent virtually demanded the comparative judgments I loved to make and found so instructive.

A sense of competition must in any case enter the performance of the Minkus *Pas de Trois,* a charming work of high civilization made expressly as an occasion for three dancers to exhibit different ways of demanding and deserving applause. But competition is everywhere in ballet, and you, the viewer, must learn to keep your nervousness about good manners from inhibiting your pleasure in a performer's attractive and exciting self-presentation if you want to participate fully in any performing art. Beginners at the ballet applaud anything that is very high, very fast, very steady, or very often repeated; but the next step in education and taste is often a snooty rejection of these feats. Hardly a fan has not at some point claimed to be bored by Aurora's balances and Odile's thirty-two fouettées. Most of us pass through this phase too and come back to an enjoyment of explicit feats of skill and endurance. Technical competition is more complicated, since a mechanical eye for mere correctness can be a terrible handicap to intelligent taste. Violette Verdy likes to inflect the word *legal* enthusiastically to praise correctness that is fine and eager, not simply well-behaved: she has called Merrill Ashley a "wonderfully legal" dancer. The great Farrell was a notably illegal dancer, a veritable gangster by some standards. James Boswell once teased Dr. Johnson by asking for his opinion of another Samuel Johnson, a circus performer who was famous for riding three horses at the same time, and Dr. Johnson fielded the question by gravely responding that he very much admired his namesake because he showed what human beings could achieve with discipline and concentration. Dancers who dance very quickly or with an unusually clear technique please us for Dr. Johnson's reason, although it is only when they offer their accomplishments with grace and tact that their competitiveness becomes beautiful. But when Haggin enjoyed seeing Kent hold her own on the same stage with the "higher-powered Tallchief," he was also responding idiomatically to the ballet they were dancing and to what must have been the choreographer's conscious intention, for Balanchine would have made a serious mistake in casting Kent in *Pas de Trois* had she not been able to hold her own. And an important pleasure of a ballet like this comes from seeing why and how a dancer as delicate as Kent can win our attention on the same stage as a dancer as famous for bold attack and edge as Tallchief. Such benign competitions gradually taught me how to notice and enjoy different kinds of dance power and dance identity.

In this spirit of eager and fruitful competition I realized with the pleasure of having taken an important step that I was checking Balanchine's judgments of dancers against my

Balanchine rehearses students from the School of American Ballet in Stravinsky's *Choral Variations on Bach's "Vom Himmel Hoch,"* 1972 (photo ©1994 Martha Swope)

own—arguing directly with the management, so to speak. It was partly for this reason that I tried to become familiar with the new dancers in the corps de ballet as soon as they arrived. Some of the new principals had been drawn from the corps; I therefore tried to figure out which newcomers to the corps were going to make it to the top, and also—particularly exciting—which had actually already made it in Balanchine's eyes and were serving in the corps merely for the sake of protocol before their power would be revealed in a new role that would justify their elevation.

I was now consciously but not, I think, pretentiously thinking of the Balanchine Enterprise as the significant public institution it had, in fact, become; thus, each development interested me not only in itself but also for what it was accomplishing for the institution. I watched the parts of the Balanchine Enterprise both separately (the new dancers and ballets were interesting in themselves) and as they worked together and influenced one another. And other members of the audience besides me were aware that different ways of being interested in art were coming together in an exciting unity when we experienced the Balanchine Enterprise. Balanchine's audience consisted of people who enjoyed going to shows, people who loved his art and that of their favorite dancers, people interested in the way Balanchine was shaping an American dance style and an American dance theater: we were conscious citizens of a culture, who enjoyed reviewing the terms in which we were committed to it and the degree to which it was worth the commitment. The Balanchine Enterprise had become one of the central focuses of my life: I looked forward eagerly to each new season in the expectation of encountering new experiences that would be as rich as those I hoped to encounter in my personal and professional life. And it was indeed life I was following in the Balanchine Enterprise: the intricate and coherent self-generating abundance of a highly developed organism accomplishing its purposes.

My attention was still centered on the choreography, but during the late fifties and early sixties I acquired another focus of interest, Violette Verdy, the first dancer I had ever *followed* closely. I first saw her in 1958 when, as a guest star with the American Ballet Theatre, she and Erik Bruhn were receiving strong notices in *Miss Julie,* a new ballet by Birgit Culberg. It must have been to check them out that Haggin decided to look in at the ballet, which was not at all the kind he was ordinarily interested in, and he took me along. Although the ballet itself was poor, we were both struck by Verdy's stage power, the depth of her impersonation, and her authority as a dancer. Yet even these talents did not prepare us for the news that Balanchine had invited her to join his company and that she had accepted.

It was just as adventurous for a dancer trained in another tradition to join Balanchine's company as it was for him to issue the invitation. In 1949, Janet Reed left Ballet Theatre (as it was then called) for the New York City Ballet, followed by Diana Adams and Melissa Hayden in 1950; but Balanchine knew their dancing from having mounted *Waltz Academy* and *Theme and Variations* at Ballet Theatre in the late forties; Patricia Wilde, who also joined the company in 1950, had danced the Balanchine repertory at the Monte Carlo company. All four fitted easily into the New York City Ballet style, and they stayed with the company until the end of their careers. In order to get Adams, Balanchine seems to have been obliged to invite another Ballet Theatre dancer, Hugh Laing, who was her husband at the time. Jerome Robbins came from Ballet Theatre to be associate artistic director of the City Ballet in 1949; it may have been his personal involvement with Nora Kaye in about 1950 that led to the recruitment of this major Ballet Theatre star. Both Laing and Kaye were dance actors who had become famous in the Anthony Tudor ballets that were a staple of Ballet Theatre, and Tudor was immediately asked to work with them at the New York City

Ballet. He created *Lady of the Camelias* for Adams and Laing in 1951 and *La Gloire* for Kaye in 1952, and revived *Lilac Garden* in 1951 for Kaye and Laing (and Tanaquil Le Clercq). In 1951 Robbins made *The Cage* for Kaye; she had a personal triumph, and the ballet is still a company staple. But Kaye and Laing proved inadequate to the Balanchine repertory, and they soon left. Inviting them to join was connected with the experiment of acquiring choreography by outside artists, not only Robbins and Tudor but also Frederick Ashton, Ruthanna Boris, William Dollar, and Lew Christensen, a politically wise step for the beginning company to have taken but not artistically fruitful: apart from a small group of early Robbins ballets, only Ashton's *Les Illuminations* survived for more than a couple of seasons. And even this engaging ballet may have survived mainly because it contained useful roles for the company: for Le Clercq in the section called "Being Beauteous" and for Nicholas Magallanes as the poet.

While this attempt at diversity was going on, Balanchine was already, with such ballets as *Firebird* and *Scotch Symphony*, beginning to make a diversified repertory for the company himself, in his own style, reflecting his own taste and technique. By 1958, when Verdy arrived, much of this repertory had been completed and had established a coherent and easily recognized company style, so that Verdy was joining an enterprise with a clear identity. She was younger than Kaye had been when she joined the company; in fact, she was the same age Adams had been, but at twenty-five she was a fully formed artist. She had been a "baby ballerina" a decade after the Balanchine trio of baby ballerinas (Tamara Toumanova, Irina Baronova, and Tatiana Riabouchinska), having made her debut with the Ballets des Champs-Elysées in 1945, at the age of twelve, and appeared in the film *Ballerina* in 1949; her power in dance drama may have stemmed from her work with the actors Madeleine Renaud and Jean-Louis Barrault. Her style seemed to me to differ from the typical New York City Ballet style as widely as Kaye's had, and it became wonderfully interesting to me to watch how Balanchine would go about using her.

The process in which Verdy's development and assimilation happened was so rich and vivid that I almost had the illusion of taking part in it myself—as if Balanchine, Verdy, and I were in constant collaboration. Naturally, she was first cast in roles from the regular repertory before Balanchine made new parts especially for her, and there was a rare interaction between new and old with Verdy. Like any new dancer, she produced unfamiliar effects in familiar roles, but I found myself confidently isolating and examining these effects in and for themselves. When I saw her in new roles, I looked for qualities I had already discovered in the familiar parts, and I thought I saw then that Balanchine had been watching her as well, with the same interest in her differences from his other dancers—

enjoying her powers and testing their range, quieting the emphasis of her inflections a bit and increasing her continuity, so that in the new roles he could both release and create a deeper and clearer identity. Verdy herself seemed quite consciously involved in this experiment, and although I can't claim to have understood the whole thing fully, I was conscious of the big things going on and happy to be seeing them sharply. During Verdy's first year in the company I remember thinking that I understood the first movement of *Symphony in C* (the role in which Kaye had made her disastrous company debut) better than ever before. Verdy's performance amounted to an essential discovery of the piece—I saw for the first time both the sharpness and the solidity of the energy required, despite the fact that I had seen Tallchief dance it many times. I also remember wondering to what extent what Balanchine and Verdy showed me about her style in her first new role, *Episodes,* enabled me to see better in retrospect what she had been up to in *Symphony in C.* The assimilation of Verdy was a richly alive episode in the Balanchine Enterprise.

What Verdy showed me about the first movement of *Symphony in C* became a permanent part of my conception of Balanchine's work. I had, for instance, followed Suki Schorer's dancing with pleasure from the time I saw her as the Blue Butterfly in *A Midsummer Night's Dream,* and she was the only dancer who made a worthy replacement for Le Clercq in the leggy variation in *Divertimento No. 15:* it seemed a mutual joke of hers and Balanchine's to show how witty an effect her small-scale legginess would make in this swaggering role. And it was partly through what I had learned from Verdy about the first movement of *Symphony in C* that I was able to see with admiration and excitement that Schorer had become a true ballerina in her performances of the same role in the late sixties and early seventies, just, as it happened, before she made the decision to leave dancing to join the faculty of the School of American Ballet as its leading teacher of the Balanchine style.

The premiere of *Episodes* in 1959 surpassed even *Agon* as a news item. In this ballet Balanchine was setting the complete orchestral writing of Webern, to which Stravinsky had drawn his attention, and once-in-a-lifetime invitations had been extended to two leading figures from the alien world of modern dance. Martha Graham composed and danced the opening movement, part 1, to the Passacaglia, Op. 1, and Six Pieces, Op. 6, as a dance-drama about Queen Elizabeth and Mary, Queen of Scots, using major dancers from her own company and her own kind of decor; and Paul Taylor, a leading Graham dancer and the director of his own small company, danced the long solo Balanchine composed for the Variations, Op. 30. The New York City Ballet was represented by old and new members:

Verdy and Jonathan Watts danced the Symphony, Op. 21; Adams and d'Amboise, Five Pieces, Op. 10; Kent and Magallanes, the Concerto, Op. 24; Hayden and Moncion, the orchestration of the Ricercata from Bach's *Musical Offering*. But it was Verdy's clear and pointed articulation of her unusual movements that established the vital connection for me; her musicality helped me to understand, to enjoy, often simply to *follow*, what Balanchine had invented for the Webern music, to which I brought little understanding of my own.

Verdy's musicality was different from what I had come to expect in the Balanchine style: she demonstrated what she was doing by unusually explicit sophisticated inflections—of rubato, of attack and emphasis, and of other ways of articulating the events in a dance structure. She led your eye along the curve in which the musical energy was propelling the dancing, she showed you the distinct episodes happening along that curve—where the middle was, when the finale was coming: and in these dances, with their odd phrase lengths, starts and stops of impulse, and unexpected moves into open expressivity, Verdy's pointed articulation was more than welcome, it was revelatory. Without her I doubt whether I could have understood the piece as well as, astonishingly, I felt that I did the first time I saw it, and perhaps that meaning would never have become clear to the general audience for whom, equally astonishingly, it almost at once became a favorite work. The hazard of Verdy's kind of explicitness was that when she danced a role too often, she could seem too earnestly to be teaching you how to understand it, but a season's layoff brought her spontaneity back.

What carried over between *Episodes* and *Symphony in C* was also the unusual sense of motivation that Verdy gave to her movements: without defining any narrative or psychological motive, she made every movement seem purposeful and necessary. This is not to say that before I saw Verdy I had found Balanchine's dance movements purposeless: he gives a greater sense of purpose to movement than any other choreographer. But there is a special drama, an urgency, created when one becomes aware of a sense of motive *in itself,* which has the effect, almost, of *naming* it—when, for instance, to one's awareness of the inventiveness with which Balanchine brings the ballerina on the stage in the first movement of *Symphony in C,* Verdy's inflection added a slight pressure that let one consciously and pleasurably name the event one was watching: "the ballerina's entrance." Or that moment when the dancer's partner was about to appear, and a special alertness on Verdy's part, without any mime effect, made one more aware than ever that this was indeed the moment at which the ballerina was to be joined by her partner and that it was a dramatic moment, even though it had no specific narrative or psychological implication. On a larger scale, I came consciously to name the first movement of *Symphony in C* "the allegro movement" after I had seen the sharp attacks of Verdy's phrasing, with the result that I felt my understanding of Balanchine's conception of allegro dancing in general had deepened.

While Balanchine was investigating, testing, and enjoying the dimensions of his new ballerina, other concerns were on his mind, one of them being the acquisition of Erik Bruhn. It was perhaps chiefly Bruhn's joining the company in 1959 that led Balanchine to revive *Theme and Variations,* but having Verdy on hand was certainly an additional motive. Bruhn could not adjust to the hectic pace of the New York City Ballet, however, and he left before the revival was ready. The premiere was danced by Villella and Verdy in February 1960. The ballet was then quickly withdrawn; I remember only dimly enjoying Verdy and Villella. When the ballet became a permanent part of the repertory in 1970, as the last movement of *Tchaikovsky Suite No. 3,* it became clear that it represented for Balanchine an important test of style and prowess; what we were watching in the 1960 revival may have been Balanchine's attempt either to demonstrate, or to explore, Verdy and Villella's capacity to pass the test. He may have decided that Villella failed, for it seems unlikely that he could have been disappointed in Verdy's performance: he made the *Tchaikovsky Pas de Deux* for her in March and *The Figure in the Carpet* in April. It was with these two roles that I recognized Verdy's high distinction as a classical dancer, and it was with *Liebeslieder Walzer* the next fall that I placed her in the highest category of dancers I had seen.

Verdy nevertheless remained distinct from the other dancers in a way and to a degree that, though beautiful for me, was for some others problematic. Her identifiably European charm and chic, her piquant and witty delight in the audience's pleasure, was so far from the norm at New York City Ballet that it displeased many loyal followers of Balanchine's typical style, although I have a hunch that these fans would not have been troubled by the same qualities in, say, Alexandra Danilova, a notably audience-charming dancer who seemed in the forties to my American eyes consciously and marvelously foreign, both Russian and Parisian. But the nature of Verdy's musicality and her virtual incapacity to dance without creating a sense of drama, if not necessarily a sense of character—these were, in fact, complex and deep issues, about which there was ample room for debate. I myself occasionally felt a bit surprised by my enthusiasm for Verdy's musicality, since its pointedness seemed a bit old-fashioned when compared with the subtle inflections within a single tempo I had come to love in Toscanini and in most of Balanchine's dancers. But the distance between Verdy's style and that of her surroundings created for me a beautiful and enjoyable tension of variation, which was of interest in itself, as well as something I was pleased with myself for appreciating. I remember an enjoyable argument at the 57th Street automat (that splendid large space was one of the places we went to for coffee and postmortems) with Haggin and Marvin Mudrick, a friend of ours from the *Hudson Review,* after a performance: Haggin was supporting Verdy's style strongly against that of Kent, Mudrick was supporting Kent against Verdy, whom he identified as a "soubrette." Verdy was my special interest, and I couldn't accept Mudrick's limiting category for her, but I really did love Kent, too; so, with a sense of having admirably wide sympathies, I took the position that both were great dancers.

The difference between Verdy's style and the style of the rest of the company was exciting for me to discover and to try to describe to myself, but it led to wide disagreements about the new dancer, which came about very quickly and split down lines that seemed to me to represent different ways of feeling about the Balanchine Enterprise. I had, for instance, met the author and illustrator Edward Gorey a few times in Cambridge and had been an early fan of his witty Gothicism, and I had talked to him occasionally at the ballet. But I didn't share his taste in many instances, for it didn't seem something to be taken entirely seriously. I gathered that he disliked Verdy and was a Hayden fan, perhaps a Wilde fan, certainly later an enthusiastic McBride admirer. I always respected McBride (coming to deeper interest in her only much later, when she danced "Rubies"), and Gorey's taste had as good a claim to respect as my own, but to me his preferences represented cliquish loyalty and jealousy rather than disinterested judgment. Later on, however, I encountered Arlene Croce's criticism, and it was clear she too was not very interested in Verdy—not nearly as interested as she was in McBride, about whom she wrote an important piece, naming McBride *the* American ballerina—and that gave me something more serious to think about, for I much admired Croce's writing. On the other hand, the degree of Haggin's enthusiasm for Verdy also seemed a bit extreme. When he reported that Denby had said about Verdy, "We've never seen anything like this before," I was of course impressed because Denby was still the final arbiter, but I didn't quite go along with this judgment. I now think Denby may not have meant the absolute praise Haggin heard, but in the Sino-Byzantine intricacy and diplomacy with which Denby conducted his professional relationships, he may have said something that would please Haggin by its apparently absolute agreement with him and would please Denby himself by its ambiguity.

It seemed to me that Balanchine showed in *Liebeslieder Walzer,* the greatest role he made for Verdy, that he agreed with me, that he too enjoyed Verdy's distinctness. I was slow to respond to *Liebeslieder Walzer,* a long ballet with a small cast (only four couples), set to music which was not high on my list in 1960. Balanchine uses both sets of the Brahms waltzes, Op. 52 and Op. 65—practically an hour of music with basically the same texture and tone, often a sugary one, suitable to the often-maudlin words. I liked part one of *Liebeslieder Walzer* enormously the first time I saw it, and I certainly noticed the difference between the first and second parts, but my attention wandered during the second, and I lost track of the piece. When I finally discovered its endless riches, it took over my imagination as no ballet had since *Apollo*.

I first became interested in the way the ballet was built in relation to the way it was cast. Above, in writing about *La Valse*, I pointed to one of Balanchine's basic structural habits— the way he makes a formal coda out of the final ball scene by bringing onstage the couples from the first half of the ballet in the order in which they originally appeared. That order is the ascending order in which they rank in the company's roster. A development of this principle governs *Liebeslieder Walzer*. In 1960 Hayden, Wilde, and Adams were the senior ballerinas of the company, with Hayden having slight seniority. Balanchine tended to use Adams for particularly idiomatic work, like the pas de deux in *Agon*, and he set *Movements for Piano and Orchestra* on her in 1963, although, in a famous bit of ballet history, her pregnancy kept her from dancing the premiere, which went to the eighteen-year-old Suzanne Farrell. Hayden danced the Tallchief roles: *Allegro Brillante, Pas de Dix*, and *Swan Lake*. Wilde was always slightly further down the roster, and, in any case, she would not have been chosen for the glamorous new project, I suspect, because she was even less a conventional stage beauty than Hayden. In casting his new ballet, Balanchine, in accordance with his standard practice, gave the leading role to Hayden, in the sense that it was she who danced the final pas de deux and variations; but the structure of the music (in conjunction with his genius in figuring out how to use that music) allowed him to give Adams the penultimate pas de deux, which he made as important and as fully fleshed out as the final one—and thus to give both ballerinas equal roles, although the "honorary" higher status went to Hayden. This is a practice that continues, enjoyably, at the New York City Ballet today, in this ballet as in most others: the calls are taken not in order of priority in the company at the time of the performance but in the order of priority of the dancers for whom the roles were made.

The way Balanchine matched the other two prima ballerinas, Jillana and Verdy, with Hayden and Adams was something I enjoyed thinking about, and in turn it was the avenue through which I entered real understanding of the piece. Jillana had been a principal since 1953, but she had never been given major premieres before 1960 and had rarely been given lead ballerina roles. She made a big impression on me as the Coquette in the 1960 revival of *La Sonnambula*, the Tallchief role in the original Ballet Russe version, which Tallchief had danced with bold sensuality, whereas Jillana danced it with subtle, soft, and sexy malice. She had a powerful presence as one of the company's "beauties" and was definitely a major player, ready for a big juicily feminine role, so it seemed natural to find her in as big an assignment as *Liebeslieder Walzer*. But to me, Verdy's role in the new piece proclaimed itself the last step in the sequence of roles covering a wide variety of styles by which Balanchine established her as a central dancer in the company. In the now-lost *Figure in the Carpet*, the ballet immediately preceding *Liebeslieder Walzer*, Verdy had opened with two rich group dances called "The Sands of the Desert" and "The Weaving of the Carpet," in which she often held the stage alone in long passages that were on the largest scale of dance eloquence. These powerful dances showed that working with Balanchine had not dimmed her impulse to create drama, but it was now a musical drama she was creating. Without telling a story or representing a character, she made watching the dance itself an exciting dramatic discovery of its structure. As I thought about *Liebeslieder Walzer*, I realized that it was "about" something in a way and to a degree new in Balanchine: about its own structure, its own double nature; and I saw that Verdy was at the center of this structure and meaning.

The first part, set to the Op. 52 waltzes, consists of social dances by four couples, the women wearing ballroom dresses and heeled shoes; the second, to the Op. 65 waltzes, is a formal suite of dances in the classical mode, with the women in ballet skirts and pointe shoes. The first part moves among several modes of illusion. The singers face us and sing directly to us, keeping us aware that we are in a theater watching professional performers. But Brahms's music—a bit hard to sing and play but within the compass of good amateurs—puts us in the social world implied by that music, in which the singers and dancers appear to be guests at a musical party in late nineteenth-century Europe, perform-ing with and for each other. And another kind of performance is taking place as well: the dancing couples are playing at being lovers, and because that kind of performance happens in any ballroom, there is a nice blend of artifice and verisimilitude at this level of illusion. The play-acting at love often generates the illusion that the couples are actually in love— which often happens in a ballroom, too. Finally, in the deepest illusion, one of the couples seems involved, almost "implicated," in a complex love affair that has a history, is related to character, and passes through different phases of intimacy and through distinct, if ambig-uous, dramatic events. But even for this couple, the deeper feelings and meanings arise naturally and easily out of, and in the end fall back into, the social behavior of young people entertaining themselves and each other by flirting, joking, teasing, competing, becoming estranged, coming together again. At the end of part one, when the curtain comes down, all illusions fall away into the reality of being at the New York State Theater.

Part two lifts the dancers out of this social behavior, this social group, and this physical space. The musicians remain onstage in their social costumes, but the dancing women are now unmistakably ballerinas, the men their cavaliers, and the opening group dance establishes the changed mode immediately with large soaring lifts that transcend the physical and social behavior of the ballroom and register human acts and relationships in the grander vocabulary of formal art. In the first part the dances were brief, almost gamelike encounters, with everyone taking turns, pas de deux casually interspersed with pas de quatre and impetuously improvised pas de trois (giving everyone a chance to dance with everyone else); group dances had marked the beginning, the middle, and the end of the party. In the second part the opening section is the only full group dance: during the last song, which is set to a serious Goethe poem, the dancers, who have all disappeared, drift back onstage in their social costumes once more, to listen to the singers, whom they applaud. The pas de deux in this part are intricately interlocked and more fully and formally developed than those in the first part, representing a version of the classical adagio-variations-coda structure. The meaning of *Liebeslieder Walzer* comes from watching the same four couples dance successively in these two modes.

In the first performances Balanchine embodied this meaning most pointedly by casting Verdy as the woman involved in the complex love affair in the first part—although, conversely, he may have conceived the role, and the meaning of the whole ballet, by meditating on how to use Verdy. The other three ballerinas had strong dance identities in the waltzes but they did not create characters and their dances did not imply a story, whereas Verdy's role in the first section was unmistakably a characterization and her dances made up a drama of distinct events occurring in a significant order. When you watched the ballet, you paid absorbed attention to all four ballerinas, but Verdy you really *followed*. Then, in the second part, Balanchine shifted her dance mode by giving her two exceptionally pure classical adagios and a showstopping prestissimo coda. It was as if he were pointedly exhibiting her place in his company: she was its dramatic actress but also a brilliant mistress of his dance style, and thus in one person she embodied the dialogue of styles that made up his subject.

In the opening symmetrical group dance, which sets the ballroom space and the social tone of the first section, Verdy was indistinguishable from the others, but in the third dance, "Die Frauen," a public display of sentimental masculine homage to Woman, her characterization and her drama began. The dance is a pas de quatre with echoing sequences—one lift echoed by another and so on—and since Verdy's echoes were smaller and softer than Hayden's original movements, she seemed more submissive; there was the further implication that she and her partner, Nicholas Magallanes, appeared to have a private understanding of the public ceremony they were participating in. The sense of a private understanding continued in Verdy's next pas de deux, the fast, happy "Wie des Abends schöne Rote," as she smiled down with an almost wifely privilege on the man she loved. Then the two joined the other couples as equals in "Ein kleiner, hübscher Vogel nahm," with its fast drive, enchanting maneuvering of ballroom chairs, lovely ladies waving their arms with conscious grace—an entirely public event of self-entertaining party behavior.

At such a moment it could seem possible in retrospect that the special Verdy character and drama had been simply an illusion, perhaps even an inappropriate one, created by her own style and not by the piece itself. But in Verdy's next dance Balanchine authorized her dramatic performance with dance imagery that was odder and unhappier than that in the first pas de deux. In this slow duet, "Wie schon bewandt war es vorehe," Magallanes disturbingly hid his eyes from Verdy with his white-gloved hand—something seemed to have gone wrong, they appeared to be almost estranged, and the lack of explanation for these feelings deepened your uneasiness. Then followed a fast pas de trois in which she flirted joyously with both her lover and another man: had the trouble been resolved? or were the lovers merely obeying the social occasion?—by now you could not help asking such questions. The vague unease gathering beneath the social surface came into the open in Verdy and Magallanes's second slow pas de deux, "Nicht wandle, mein Licht": as Magallanes carried what seemed to be the inert, doomed body of the woman he loved across the stage, you felt that you were watching something you perhaps ought not to be. That the other couples were still present did not diminish but, surprisingly, increased your sense that the couple shared a private, isolated emotion, perhaps an unhappy one. In Verdy's final gesture here, she seemed to be forgiving Magallanes for some liberty taken or some hurt experienced, or perhaps to be accepting some unexpectedly powerfully charged sexual invitation he had extended. The two remained for a moment rapt in their private drama while the others began the final group dance of whispered arrangements for future meetings—perhaps at the next dance, or perhaps in a private rendezvous. Finally, Verdy and Magallanes joined in as lightly as the rest, giving no sign of the private encounter we had just witnessed, and the social tone was restored.

Part two of *Liebeslieder Walzer* takes a different departure from social behavior and tone, not toward intimate dramatic relationships but toward the impersonal intensity of high formal art. Like the slow movements of *Concerto Barocco, Symphony in C,* or *Divertimento No. 15,* the many pas de deux in part two of *Liebeslieder Walzer* have nothing to do with character, and they are neither happy nor sad. But like the pas de deux from *Agon,* they do

Violette Verdy, Conrad Ludlow (left), and Nicholas Magallanes (right) in *Liebeslieder Walzer,* 1961 (photo ©1994 Martha Swope; choreography by George Balanchine ©The George Balanchine Trust)

seem to represent human relationships, for they are unmistakably love duets. They are composed in an exceptionally pure and basic, an almost ascetic dance vocabulary, a choice Balanchine may have made to counter the lushness of the music. Brahms's third and sixth waltzes in Op. 65, for instance, are slow soprano solos that contain similar melodic lines over luscious harmonic progressions; Balanchine accepts the repetition by setting both pieces as classical adagios, but he pierces the oversweetness by the purity of his figures. He sets a repeated, sumptuously modulating sequence in the first pas de deux (at the words "Und einen nach dem andern gab ich dem schönen, aber unwürdigen Jüngling hin") with an exquisitely temperate circle of traveling lifts, timed and spaced with a discretion that clarifies and ennobles the sentiment. You noticed the purity of the figure the more keenly when Verdy was its vehicle: by remembering her personal drama in part one, you realize how completely part two had transcended personality and drama for all the couples. Part

Violette Verdy and Nicholas Magallanes in *Liebeslieder Walzer,* 1960 (photo by Fred Fehl; courtesy the Dance Collection, New York Public Library for the Performing Arts, Astor, Lenox, and Tilden Foundations; choreography by George Balanchine ©The George Balanchine Trust)

one of *Liebeslieder Walzer* concerns young people in love, social dancing, and private drama; part two is about the power of art.

There were sublime simplicities throughout this second section—Adams's dreamily slow beats as she was lifted, for instance, or her turns in attitude in her solo. Hayden's powerful formal pas de deux with Jonathan Watts in part two made you think back to their dances in the first part, which had been rich in resonant, though not quite, in the Verdyan sense, dramatic, gestures—Watts pushing Hayden tenderly away from him or toward someone or something else, the repeated wide circular sweep of her foot just skimming the floor, Watts darting around her in witty courtship play, touching her waist fleetingly every time he circled her; their second pas de deux seemed to end with a quarrel.

In contrast, Balanchine began their grand pas de deux in the second part, the climax of the ballet, with a simple chain of supported turns in attitude, and again his timing and phrasing of an elementary figure of classical adagio reached sublimity. Yet the two parts of *Liebeslieder Walzer* were subtly intertwined, with the almost pointedly original figures in the formal second part keeping us in touch with the imagery of the first part. Verdy's prestissimo coda was appropriately pure allegro dancing, but it ended in drama, as she whirled brilliantly, then stopped breathtakingly, with her head hidden against her lover's chest, movements that harked back ambiguously to the love affair of the first section. In the second half of the Adams-Carter pas de deux, following Adams's slow beats, she ran over to stage left rear, facing away from us; Carter followed, lifted her high up on to his chest (tilting her toward us in an intensely eloquent inflection), and carries her backward on a diagonal to stage front right, then turned her around as she flowed up into a high arabesque which completed itself as she rose on pointe—and then the whole immense event repeated. Far stranger, though not more moving, was the journey Hayden and Watts took at the end of their adagio: with secretive, almost religious devotion she brought her leg forward slowly under her long ballet skirt three times, then rose up on its pointe to continue the strange pilgrimage. The windmill exit referred back to the playfulness of the first part, though more formally.

When Farrell succeeded to Adams's role, she followed the standard New York City Ballet style of making a powerful impact without explicit drama. She danced with the fast fresh lyricism of Adams's beautiful original performance, and if she was for me more thrilling, it was not because she made dramatic points but because she danced on her own immense scale, giving the steps their fullest dimension. Verdy, on the other hand, made her dramatic points explicit and overt as part of her method: both she and Balanchine wanted you to notice them. While you believed in the character and the dramatic events Verdy represented and the emotion she projected, you also recognized that her performance represented a certain style—you could almost name it. With Farrell and the other two ballerinas, you received the powerful impact of the nondramatic dance eloquence Balanchine and his dancers are famous for, yet the contrast with Verdy made you more conscious than usual that Balanchine's style was also a "style." This tension between styles was echoed and amplified in the contrast between the sections; this is what *Liebeslieder* was about in the sixties; and it is why I can say that at least part of the ballet's original subject was Verdy's place in the New York City Ballet.

Verdy gave herself gamely in March 1961 to *Electronics,* a leading contender for the "worst Balanchine ballet" booby prize, in which she was paired with Villella, in costumes that resembled plastic underwear, against noisy electronic music and a cellophane-ice-

Balanchine and Violette Verdy with Mimi Paul (left) and Gloria Govrin (right) making *Electronics*, 1961 (photo ©1994 Martha Swope)

palace-world-of-the-future decor. It was a moment for comfortable jokes about a favorite artist's blooper. There was a delectably corny modernism in the unbearable music, the decor, and the steps—dancers rolled around the stage in emphatic revolution against ballet norms. Perhaps Balanchine himself was joking—Verdy thought he might be. I remember the piece well because of my interest in Verdy, and I had no trouble separating the dancer from the dance; what stays in my mind most vividly is her proud, courageous bearing, to which Balanchine had entrusted the superb long *Serenade*-like opening sections of *The Figure in the Carpet* and by which I had been so moved in *Liebeslieder Walzer*. In *Electronics* that bearing wittily accented the impersonation she made of giving her all to a flop, and Villella seemed just as gallantly devoted. The indulgent pleasure with which I luxuriated in the foolishness of this flop, so boldly sponsored and faithfully delivered by artists with whom I was on the most gratifying terms of admiration, concern, and curiosity—this is a different kind of reward for following artists' careers closely. And the genius of Balanchine,

Verdy, and Villella let me laugh at this product of their joint endeavor without compunction, as I so often cannot with artists whose less secure talents command our indulgent dishonesty about their failures.

And then came *A Midsummer Night's Dream*, Balanchine's first original full-evening narrative ballet, which premiered in January 1962, a month after my college gave me tenure. Only a fellow academic will comprehend the anxiety unique to this process, which I now see as even more complex and mysterious than it seemed at the time, when my attention was focused on simply getting through. But while maneuvering my way along this hazardous path—or hoping that was what I was doing, since so much of the process was and remains hidden from me—I won new friends and supporters and confirmed the loyalty of old ones. I was sustained most, perhaps, by the energy and confidence derived from having finished the book on Dickens, which pleased me and continues to please me by the sound of conviction with which it is written and by its openness of expression, which I continue to aim for in my writing. Coming right after all this, seeing *A Midsummer Night's Dream* felt like receiving personal congratulations from Balanchine. Later I realized that giving a sense of bonanza to everybody in the audience must have been his intention. And soon my thinking about the whole issue of Balanchine's motives and meanings in composing *A Midsummer Night's Dream* led me to the development of a new way of following Balanchine, as a maker of an entire repertory.

Verdy and Villella shared the center of *A Midsummer Night's Dream*. Villella was the focus of the narrative first act, as Oberon, and Verdy was at the center of the ceremonial and abstract second act, dancing the classical pas de deux that marks the moment of most intensely private emotion in the ballet. It was in part the full-evening format of the ballet that led to the sense that the Balanchine Enterprise was putting on a special display of its new riches. As a capstone to her development as a Balanchine dancer, Verdy was given the apex of classical dancing in the piece, with d'Amboise as her cavalier; he was a popular favorite who was then in the prime of his open American style, not yet ingratiating himself too insistently with the audience. Other senior artists danced strongly at the premiere: Hayden as Titania, Jillana as Helena, Magallanes as Lysander, Moncion as Theseus; but Hayden was soon replaced by Adams and Farrell, and Jillana by Mimi Paul. Most of the important dancing in the dramatic first act had been given to new performers: Villella, McBride as Hermia, Schorer as the Blue Butterfly, Arthur Mitchell as Puck, Gloria Govrin as Hippolyta. The emphasis on young dancers in this ballet seemed to be a manifesto. Balanchine and Kirstein had founded the School of American Ballet in 1934 to effect a major change in American dancing—someone once told me that Balanchine had said "nobody here could dance when we came"—and in the early 1960s this investment of time, energy, and genius began to pay a huge dividend in highly gifted dancers, who were trained from childhood in Balanchine's increasingly bold style and technique and yet were remarkably different from one another in temperament, physique, and dance identity—one could imagine Balanchine being dazzled by this profusion were he not unlikely to have ever been dazzled by anything.

*A Midsummer Night's Dream* renewed the sense I had formed from *The Nutcracker* that Balanchine took pleasure in the large format as a chance to surprise his public with his narrative powers, abilities that his abstract ballets might not seem to promise. The most obvious exhibit was the skill with which he condensed the action of Shakespeare's play into a broadly legible sequence of formal dances, interspersed with fast, crowded transitional narrative passages. The up-and-down fortunes of the lovers had the super-legibility of farce, yet Balanchine kept their cartoon gestures of ardor or pain light and fresh, until he deepened them with sudden strokes of dramatic power or pathos—the wild animal grandeur of Helena's despair, for instance (which Paul made immense when she took over the role), or the pathos of the long solo for Hermia, in which Balanchine gave us our first full look at a dancer who was to become a favorite instrument, Patricia McBride. Her supernormal, well-behaved American prettiness made a strikingly original and tactfully up-to-date image of Hermia's happy complacency in love, which allowed Balanchine to surprise you with the depth of the character's predicament and with McBride's fascinatingly *normal* dance identity, in Hermia's spacious solo of bewildered abandonment, danced to the intermezzo, Mendelssohn's supreme blend of passion and fantasy.

The mime gestures in which Oberon and Titania quarrel over possession of the little Indian boy adroitly solved a problem about the training of American ballet dancers. Mime was not taught at the School of American Ballet, and Balanchine was in any case taking a gamble in using so old-fashioned a theatrical vocabulary in 1962. His solution—like much of his artistic strategy—was to give these large mime gestures an edge of parody, making you see the style clearly in and for itself, and to count on the straightforward force of his dancers to charge this artifice with serious narrative motive.

Years later I learned from Villella of the tension between him and Balanchine at this time and the effect it may have had on his handling of the mime. Balanchine resented Villella's not taking his all-important company class at the beginning of every work day, and Villella resented Balanchine's refusal to understand why—that, largely because of the physical training he had submitted to at Maritime College, he had become unable to take Balanchine's uniquely exhausting class and continue dancing through the rest of the day.

Edward Villella with members of the New York City Ballet in *A Midsummer Night's Dream,* 1962 (photo courtesy the Dance Collection, New York Public Library for the Performing Arts, Astor, Lenox, and Tilden Foundations; choreography by George Balanchine ©The George Balanchine Trust)

The effect of the estrangement had been that Balanchine did not teach Villella even the basic steps of the role of Oberon until shortly before the premiere, and he never coached him in either the dancing or—more important—the mime, which Villella worked out for himself with Stanley Williams, his teacher at the School of American Ballet. When I heard the story, I saw both sides of the dilemma with equal sympathy and I still do, and I felt lucky not to have known about it when I first enjoyed the beautiful results that were achieved despite it. Later I was told that Balanchine had intended a stronger accent of parody in the mime sections than Villella actually delivered, a possibility that fits his other stylistic habits and choices and gives credibility to the rumor of the seventies that he had wanted to cast the tiny Gen Horiuchi and the tall Nina Fedorova as Oberon and Titania. But a charming, if mild, parodic effect is what Villella achieved at the premiere, as the film record bears out.

A structural choice in *A Midsummer Night's Dream* that gave me another illusion of almost being in collaboration with Balanchine was his decision to tell the entire story in a long first act, giving the shorter second act over to formal dancing. This disappointed some critics, but I was luxuriating deeply enough in the Balanchine Enterprise to understand how and why it worked, and to feel that I would have done it the same way myself. The second act begins with the ceremonial wedding of the three couples in Theseus's grand palace; this is followed by a formal entertainment for the company danced by professional court dancers—a ballerina, her cavalier, a corps of six couples; the act closes with a transformation scene in which the people from the court world leave in a grand procession, the palace merges with the fairy world of Oberon and Titania, and the curtain comes down on the fairy king and queen blessing their subjects and retiring into separate realms of sleep, as Puck sweeps the stage in epilogue. All the human characters, who in the first act had danced in a large, open, rather relaxed ballet vocabulary, come onstage for the second act moving in the more stylized, emphatically turned-out, self-presentational parade walk of formal ballet procession or in stately arabesque turns—slow, almost hieratic movements in which the passions of the first act have come to rest in permanent, stable images of custom and order.

When the court dancers arrive, they entertain first with a formal allegro dance—elegant and expensive. Then the lead couple perform a classical adagio which is an abstract embodiment and celebration of love, intensely quiet and private, yet at the same time completely public, as pas de deux intimacy mysteriously is able to be in Balanchine. Here we are watching an ideal image of the lovemaking to which the marriages will lead: entirely without religious reference, this pas de deux is nonetheless a spiritual contemplation of and a blessing on our ordinary, life-sized feelings. Most exciting and moving is the fact that the divertissement dancers are indeed "dancers," professionals from a realm that is different from that of the lovers in the drama. That professional dancers should generate the deepest emotion in the ballet was a kind of confession or profession of Balanchine's conception of the nature and function of art, and that it should be Verdy to whom he entrusted this meaning was the capstone of my experience of following her development in the Balanchine Enterprise.

The ending offers a related effect and meaning. When the King and Queen of Fairy bless the butterflies, moths, and fairies who are their worshipful subjects, we see in their gestures of parental concern a nice play between realms of being, for Titania and Oberon represent us in congratulating the students at the School of American Ballet who are playing some of these roles—and are being used by Balanchine with commercial shrewdness to guarantee the paying attendance of their parents, relatives, and friends.

The absence of fast, intricate dancing in much of this last act lets the audience concentrate on the Mendelssohn music in a communal salute to a cultural heirloom—the couples on the stage serve as our surrogates in paying their respects to the Wedding March. Likewise, the last glimpse of the fairy world is set to a reprise of the overture, the music with which at seventeen Mendelssohn invented western Europe's musical language of romantic fantasy. *A Midsummer Night's Dream* seems to me in its entirety a community-creating work, celebrating familiar arts, customs, and sentiments and the traditions from which they derive. And it brings into harmony the different ways we have of being interested in art: we are ordinary people, going to the public theater, but we are also becoming with ease connoisseurs of an art of high artifice; at the same time, Balanchine's personally motivated and publicly presented use of Shakespeare and Mendelssohn makes of our being members of a common culture a living experience.

# NINE / *Making the Repertory*

Tenure gave me a security that freed me to go to New York more often, so that I was able to see more performances of *A Midsummer Night's Dream* when it was new than I had of any other Balanchine work: four immediately after the opening and as many the next season. I saw *Liebeslieder Walzer* several times during this period, too, and became absorbed in working out its meaning and its role in Violette Verdy's career. And I was bewitched by two smaller works that had premiered while I was coming to New York less frequently: *Donizetti Variations* in 1960 and *Valse et Variations* (later *Raymonda Variations*) in 1961. I had seen them a couple of times when they were new, but now I really came to know them and to develop an almost embarrassing love for them. I also became more familiar with *Agon*, *Square Dance*, and *Episodes*. These new ballets brought Balanchine before me in a role I had not been fully aware of earlier, as a maker of repertory.

In the first years of the New York City Ballet I saw easily enough that Balanchine was adding popular and accessible pieces like *Firebird*, *Swan Lake*, and *The Nutcracker* to the repertory in order to bring general audiences into the theater, where they could then learn to like *real* Balanchine ballets: *The Four Temperaments* or *Concerto Barocco*. But I saw no further. I realized gradually that a less obvious kind of repertory formation was going on when I began to wonder why Balanchine had decided to compose another full-length ballet, *A Midsummer Night's Dream*. This work carried on the marketing function of *The Nutcracker*, but there was obviously more to it, and as I began asking what Balanchine might be up to, I made a connection between *A Midsummer Night's Dream* and *Donizetti Varia-*

*tions* and *Raymonda Variations,* a connection that gradually developed my sense that Balanchine was consciously engaged in building repertory in a way I had not previously understood.

Part of his motive was to solicit both an elite and a general audience without losing touch with his own special interests and inspirations, and I took special pleasure in his success at doing this. I had always loved the command Mozart and Shakespeare held over elite and popular audiences alike, and Balanchine's performance in this respect became perhaps the supreme measure of his dimension as an artist. *A Midsummer Night's Dream* trains a general audience in the concentration needed for *Agon* or *Divertimento No. 15* or *Liebeslieder Walzer. Dream* welcomes you in its narrative first act with its large, easy, and fluently shifting variety. Untrained audiences can enter easily and with no severe test of their attention; by the time of the transfiguration of the behavior of love evoked in the sublime adagio pas de deux in the second act, even the most inexperienced audience can measure the depth and meaning of the experience they are having as beautiful and moving, if hard to name.

I had the sense of belonging to both the elite and the general audiences and of watching myself in this double identity; this benign double consciousness became a distinctly pleasurable part of my involvement with the Balanchine Enterprise. There was something pertinent to my personal and professional life in my double identity and my pleased awareness of it. Getting tenure meant that my college accepted the intellectual value of concentrating on the experience of art, and the growing size and prestige of the Balanchine Enterprise meant that the general culture accepted and valued that enterprise. I felt in tune with the company and as intellectually and artistically prosperous as the Balanchine Enterprise must have felt.

Although I saw myself as merely playing the role of member of the general audience for these ballets, I was at the same time genuinely in need of the education offered by even such an easy assignment as the first act of *A Midsummer Night's Dream.* A more important education came through the intensity of my interest in *Donizetti Variations* and *Raymonda Variations.* As I became familiar with them, I felt a half-ashamed eagerness to see them, as if I were waiting for a dessert I liked too much; I had a crush on *Donizetti* and *Raymonda.* And when I asked myself why I should be ashamed, I understood the function they were serving in the Balanchine Enterprise.

*Donizetti Variations* (originally, *Variations from "Don Sebastian"*) was from the first unassuming—easily (and correctly) categorizable as a "utility" work, but composed with high professional expertise and made special by a kind of joking that probably brought to other minds than John Martin's the "cornfield" Martin indulgently referred to in his exact praise of the ballet:

> If the musical excerpts from Donizetti's opera do it justice, it is easy to understand why it is little known. Certainly, Balanchine understands. Not that he makes fun of it, but rather that he is meticulously fair to it, which can be more deadly in a nicer way. Stylistically, he has hit the nail on the head, as he so frequently does in such cases; and, again according to his custom, he has turned the situation into an excellent opportunity for composing fresh and brilliant bits, from whatever cornfield, for his dancers to get their teeth into.

Martins was writing such sophisticated and acute criticism as this from the early 1950s until the end of his career, but I came to appreciate it only well after his career had ended, by reading the many excerpts that Nancy Reynolds reprints in her indispensable *Repertory in Review*. I had not read his reviews in the *New York Times* during the fifties, because I had been angered by his condescension to Balanchine throughout the thirties and forties.

My view of *Donizetti Variations* does not, however, coincide with his in every respect. It is true that there is a lugubrious town-band cornet solo in the score, but otherwise the music does not strike me as particularly corny, and even the cornet solo might have been as knowing a strategy on Donizetti's part as were the parody steps Balanchine set to it—I cannot find an authority to help me on the question, although there is a similar cornet solo in Hershey Kay's brilliant adaptation of John Philip Sousa in *Stars and Stripes*. But Martin's cue that Balanchine had a certain "stylistic" allusion or intention in *Donizetti* might have helped me to understand Balanchine's purposes back then had I encountered it. I'm not sure; Martin is as vague in naming the stylistic nail that Balanchine hits as I would have been, and I can't find a precise term even now, when I think I have a firm grasp of the style aimed at and achieved. And, in fact, not having a term for this style is the best way to experience it.

*Donizetti Variations* is set for a principal couple and an attendant crowd of six women and three men, an unusual combination, and the structure of the variations Balanchine worked out for the group is also special. Variation structure in classical ballet normally begins with a group variation from the secondary dancers—the "demis" (often women only)—followed by the entrance of the ballerina and her cavalier, who dance their pas de deux; which is followed by solo variations for all the dancers in a succession that often works up the scale of the dancers' ranking, as well as the ranking of the levels or genres of dance represented by each variation, ending with particularly brilliant virtuoso variations for both

Violette Verdy in *Donizetti Variations,* ca. 1962 (photo ©1994 Martha Swope; choreography by George Balanchine ©The George Balanchine Trust)

principals and a final group dance. In *Donizetti Variations* Balanchine does not give the attendants any solo variations. There are three group dances for the entire cast; two pas de deux for the principals; a variation for the ballerina, who flirts with three of her men friends; a variation for the cavalier, who flirts with six of his women friends; a dance of motiveless group mourning (this is the dirge of the cornet solo); and a fleet and rambunctious finale. In 1960 I might have defined the mode of this ballet as a fond American translation of the basic Italian opera-ballet style called for by the music; not because I knew much about Italian opera ballet but because I assumed Balanchine did since he had twice been the choreographer for opera companies. What I saw most clearly as reference to American behavior was the cavalier's solo with the six women, a dance that asks the audience to laugh affectionately at his male complacency as he basks in the adoration of his little court. The role was made on the excellent Jonathan Watts but, as I remember, was quickly taken over by Edward Villella, who made this potentially corny *Oklahoma!* show-biz routine into a fine-grained,

Violette Verdy and Peter Schaufuss with members of the New York City Ballet in *Raymonda Variations,* ca. 1975 (photo courtesy David Lindner; choreography by George Balanchine ©The George Balanchine Trust)

idiomatic portrait of an Italian-American postadolescent dreamboat (vintage World War II, in my opinion) ruling his roost in an idealization of the neighborhood borough life from which Villella actually came.

I found other echoes in *Donizetti Variations:* the peasant pas de deux in *Giselle* and other classics are in the background somewhere, and for me there was a memory of the bridal couple's suite of dances from Balanchine's own *Le Baiser de la Fée,* which I had loved so much in the forties and missed so badly in the City Ballet repertory—but since none of the actual steps refers exactly to this possible model, perhaps I was only enjoying the memory of Danilova and Frederic Franklin from my earliest days as a member of Balanchine's audience. I am now aware of another echo, which did not suggest itself to me until my first experience of the Danish ballet tradition, when the Royal Danish Ballet came to America in the mid-sixties, and it occurred to me that there might be a connection between Bournonville's *Napoli* and the mode of *Donizetti Variations.* Even now I have not worked this out with certainty or satisfaction. I enjoy thinking that not only in *Donizetti Variations* but in the earlier *Scotch Symphony*, Balanchine was silently recalling his brief stint as balletmaster in Copenhagen, but neither ballet is Bournonvillian in technique or tone to any significant extent. So I have no name for the genre *Donizetti Variations* represents.

Melissa Hayden was given the premiere of *Donizetti Variations*, but by the time I began seeing it repeatedly Verdy was dancing, and it is she whom I remember. (It was in a minor comic role in this ballet that I first noticed the very young Suzanne Farrell.) And although Patricia Wilde danced the premiere of *Raymonda Variations* when it was called *Valse et Variations* in 1961 (a generous parting gift to this dependable dancer), it is again Verdy whom I remember best, and with the most pleasure, even now that the role has become a much-used vehicle for the display of virtuosity and style.

*Raymonda Variations* falls into the genre of the Petipa tradition in which Balanchine grew up, of course, but there's more to it than that—Balanchine means his title very seriously. Because both use music from Glazunov's *Raymonda*, *Raymonda Variations* reminded me of *Pas de Dix* the first time I saw it, although Balanchine uses different music (he returned to the *Pas de Dix* music only in *Cortège Hongrois* in 1973, his somewhat perfunctory farewell ballet for Hayden), and *Raymonda* does resemble *Pas de Dix* in having variations for demi-soloists as well as for principals. At first it seemed less remarkable than *Pas de Dix* because it lacked Tallchief and her superbly sensuous solo à la Orientale, but after a while the variations for the soloists began to make a greater impression on me than had those in *Pas de Dix*. Eventually I realized I was watching dances designed to exhibit dancers of much greater individuality and power: tiny, delectable Suki Schorer and splendidly grand Gloria Govrin and Patricia Neary. A passage that has stayed with me as a locus classicus is the reentry of the two Amazons in the finale, zinging in on the high wire in a transfiguration of synchronized prowess that rhymes with the ballerina's electric entrance in the opening dance, spinning down the diagonal line of soloists and corps. The energy and freedom of moments like these kept me returning hungrily to this ballet, as Villella and Verdy's charm kept me wanting to see *Donizetti Variations* continually. And I gradually realized how deeply and fully imagined these "variations" were and thereby came to see where the ballet fit in the Balanchine repertory.

The stage sets for both *Donizetti* and *Raymonda*, without visual distinction, solidly confirm the identity of each ballet and its place in the repertory. The current set for *Donizetti* is standard village-square theatrical vernacular. The set and costumes for *Raymonda* feature sugary pink and blue candy colors, which combine with Glazunov's almost scandalously syrupy echo of the Rhinemaiden music from the *Ring*, which Balanchine uses as a prelude, as well as with the exactly calibrated choreography, to create the ballet's distinct tone, which again I can't name exactly—"serious parody of Petipa," perhaps. But their unnameability did not hinder my eventually secure grasp of the modes of these works as I came to understand them. Both *Raymonda* and *Donizetti* were engineered to teach me and make me experience the range of tone and genre possible within the limited category of a "variations" ballet. All Balanchine's ballets have depth and substantiality because they are made up of serious, fully worked dancing, and they are exhilarating because of the energy of Balanchine's invention and the intellectual power of his structural—in particular his rhythmic—decisions (what you would call the rhythm of his editing if these were films); and all his ballets are calculated to come to three-dimensional life in the identity, the special bravura, flair, and elegance of particular dancers. But works like *Donizetti* and *Raymonda* serve another function: they help us experience distinctions between the modes, styles, and genres of ballet—to develop the eye for difference on which discriminating pleasure in all the arts depends and then rewards with what James Joyce, in *Stephen Hero*, identifies as an *epiphany:*

> By an epiphany he meant a sudden spiritual manifestation, whether in the vulgarity of speech or of gesture or in a memorable phase of the mind itself . . . He told Cranly that the clock of the Ballast Office was capable of an epiphany. Cranly questioned the inscrutable dial of the Ballast Office with his no less inscrutable countenance.
> —Yes, said Stephen. I will pass it time after time, allude to it, refer to it, catch a glimpse of it. It is only an item in the catalogue of Dublin's street furniture. Then all at once I see it and I know at once what it is: epiphany.
> —What?
> —Imagine my glimpses at that clock as the gropings of a spiritual eye which seeks to adjust its vision to its exact focus. The moment the focus is reached the object is epiphanized. It is just in this epiphany that I find the third, the supreme quality of beauty. . . . First we recognize that the object is *one* integral thing, then we recognize that it is an organized, composite structure, a *thing* in fact; finally, when the relation of the parts is exquisite, when the parts are adjusted to the special point, we recognize that it is *that* thing which it is. Its soul, its whatness, leaps to us from the vestment of its appearance. The soul of the commonest object, the structure of which is so adjusted, seems to us radiant. The object achieves its epiphany.

It is the metaphor of adjusting one's vision to focus that I find so valuable here, tricky as it may be to disentangle from the other reverberations of Stephen's language, which Joyce himself calls "applied Aquinas." Our capacity to perceive works of art—or to perceive anything exactly—depends on the fineness of our focus, our ability to distinguish one thing from another; this leads to an expertise, which is pleasurable to us both as aesthetes and as human beings, in seeing the range and number of things there are in the world and the fineness of the distinctions between them. Exactitude in distinguishing one thing from another leads to a capacity for and a pleasure in the consciousness of such discrimination, which reaches the point of revelation when one has the experience of seeing the work of art as *that* work of art it in fact is, the dancer as *that* dancer she in fact is. There is perfect harmony between such expertise and works of art that are especially designed to reward it. In spite of the disparity between the scholastic abstruseness of Stephen's language and the mondaine worlds of *Donizetti* and *Raymonda,* I think that in composing these two easy and appealing works, Balanchine aimed at increasing his audience's sense of the range of tone, style, genre, and emotional density of which ballet is capable, teaching us how to experience that range expertly and how to prepare for the epiphany of recognizing what we are experiencing for exactly what it is—despite our inability to name it. And those moments of recognition give great pleasure and are of great value in our everyday lives.

Classical ballet is often said to be, and actually is—even in Balanchine's immense extension of its language—a limited mode of art that works with a limited vocabulary. The single "word" *arabesque,* for instance, is repeated in ballet far more often (though in an infinite variety of variations) than any single word or group of words in a poem in English. Although the same is true of the tones in music, there is an absolute lack of denotation in musical tones that does not apply to the bodily movements of ballet, which always carry a faint reference to everyday human movement. For this reason it makes sense to say that ballet retains the sense of being made up of a limited number of images when compared with music. But what Balanchine accomplished in his career was not only an immensely inventive range of variation of this narrow vocabulary but a sharp focus on the distinction between these modes and genres and types and styles, so that although he may not cover the huge range of emotion, theme, and tonality Shakespeare does, he gives an almost equal sense of variety and multiplicity by the exactitude of the distinctions between his various works.

Balanchine's sense for exact distinctions in genre is matched by his use of dancers. Just as I began to see that he was making many different and exactly differentiated ballets, I began to see that the company was filling up with a large group of exactly differentiated dancers. All Balanchine's ballets help dancers to form dance identities and then to enlarge, reveal, and project them, yielding an epiphany of their whatness as dancers—their souls. Most choreographers try to do this; they point to the differences between dancers by contrasting a lyrical with an allegro dancer, a short with a tall, a soubrette with a potential prima, by calling attention to a jumper, a turner, powerful legs, delicate arms. Balanchine brings this process to epiphany more often than most, especially when he is working in the variation mode.

He began with his choices as director of the School of American Ballet and of the New York City Ballet, inviting into the school and into the company only dancers with interesting identities—not exactly temperament or physique or correctness or musicality or an immediately obvious expressivity, but perhaps only the capacity to interest the eye, to interest *his* eye, for it goes without saying that he had a genius for spotting the identity of unformed dancers. He studied these dancers in class and in performance and made roles for them that showed us (and the dancers too) who they really were. From the first I paid special attention to Suki Schorer, for anyone could that see she was fine and musical and expressive; but the roles Balanchine made for her, of which the variation in *Raymonda* was one of the first, brought the whatness of her size, charm, and expressivity to epiphany. Likewise, Gloria Govrin and Patricia Neary were exceptionally, even dangerously, tall dancers, but *Raymonda Variations* helped you see the radiance, the splendor of their size.

Judith Fugate is the exception that proves the rule; exploring her case is perhaps unfair to a dependable trouper, but I cannot resist so instructive an example. I first noticed her when as a child she danced Don Quixote's first ideal image of femininity—a tiny blonde girl in danger. Kneeling on one of his huge books of romance, imploring his aid, she was absolutely entrancing. In due course she turned up in the corps and soon began dancing solos. She was pretty and assured, and she had the gift of making her movements clear to the eye. But she remained at the rank of soloist throughout Balanchine's life, and I agreed with this decision, although I could sympathize with Fugate's frustration at never having been promoted. Even as a soloist, she danced only a limited range: she was a fine second violin in *Concerto Barocco*, but she was never to my knowledge given the second lead in *Tchaikovsky Piano Concerto No. 2*, never tested in the third theme of *The Four Temperaments*, and I can understand why. When Peter Martins changed the casting practice at the New York City Ballet to one that relies on seniority, a more common and democratic method that gives more dancers a chance at more roles, Fugate was promoted to principal and began to dance the prima ballerina roles, to my regretful but never-failing boredom. And when I saw my only performance of Martins's *Sleeping Beauty* a couple of years ago, the fact that

Aurora was danced by Fugate (and the Lilac Fairy by Valentina Koslova) meant that I didn't really see the ballet, because neither of these well-trained dancers had a distinct enough identity to show me the soul of her role.

Mimi Paul was tall and powerful, like Govrin and Neary, but she was elegant, too, and she had a depth of fantasy that made her ideal as a heroine. When she replaced Jillana in *Liebeslieder Walzer* and *A Midsummer Night's Dream* in about 1963, her own achieved powers, in addition to my training in the Balanchine school, enabled me to see her whatness at once, and with the greatest excitement. She was very different from Jillana, but I enjoyed making the comparisons; comparing various dancers in the same role had become a substantive part of my pleasure in following the Balanchine Enterprise during the sixties and seventies. My comparison of Paul with Jillana worked to the disadvantage of neither, for I continued to regard Jillana's performance in these roles as being as fine as Paul's; when Jillana retired, Paul was a marvelously satisfactory replacement. (Jillana proved irreplaceable as the coquette in *La Sonnambula,* although for some reason Balanchine never tried Paul out in this role, for which she seems to me suited. Apart from some marvelous performances by Farrell as the sleepwalker, however, this ballet fell into disrepair soon after its revival in 1960 and never had the benefit of Balanchine's rekindled interest.) After coming to know Paul well in *A Midsummer Night's Dream* and *Liebeslieder Walzer,* I began following her career as one of my special interests. Until she left the company I never quite realized how seldom Balanchine choreographed for her, but the three big roles he created for her, in *Don Quixote* in 1965 and in *Jewels* and the "Valse Fantaisie" section of *Glinkiana* in 1967, were thrilling revelations of her identity, although perhaps they came too late to make her feel close to the center of Balanchine's attention: this is one of the saddest aspects of Balanchine's obsession with Farrell.

An instructive comparison emerged in the second season of *A Midsummer Night's Dream,* when Allegra Kent began dancing the second-act pas de deux in alternation with Violette Verdy. At first I found her much less interesting than Verdy. In fact I had temporarily lost my eye for Kent's special quality, probably because she had been on leave so often during 1959–1961, but when she began to appear regularly in the repertory she reinstated herself as a major dancer in my eyes. Her pas de deux in the second act of *A Midsummer Night's Dream* lacked the emphases I had loved in Verdy's performances, but it soon came to have an equal value for me, with Kent's own quality showing itself in her unique and beautiful *lack* of emphasis as that word is often understood.

By 1963 I was following so many strands of the Balanchine Enterprise, keeping track of so many dancers, and turning Balanchine's repertory over in my mind so often and with the greatest pleasure that it was in a state of near-euphoria that I came down to see the premiere of *Bugaku* on March 20, 1963. And I felt confirmed in my pleasure, and in the certainty of my judgment, by what seemed to me the communal euphoria surrounding me. The curtain calls after the first performance of *Bugaku* were not as long or as obsessed as the calls being taken at that time night after night wherever they appeared by the superstars Margot Fonteyn and Rudolf Nureyev, but in the applause for *Bugaku* I believed I was hearing the effect of the education Balanchine had been giving his audience for so many years.

This time he was giving us a surprise: the odd flavor of *Bugaku* enlarged the sense of special occasion. He was working out a new mixture of modes: he had been impressed by the Imperial Japanese Gagaku, musicians and dancers who had appeared in New York two years earlier, and in *Bugaku* he grafted images and movements of that exotic theatrical tradition into the ritual and technique of his own art. If doing so brought him closer to the brink of kitsch or camp than he usually worked, it only made the power and tact of the achievement the more thrilling. In David Hays's brilliantly lit minimal arena—an elegant sort of bullring—Balanchine had, for once, a handsome set to work with, and Hays's clear decor gave an invaluable edge to the effect of the piece. Toshiro Mayazumi had been commissioned to write special music with an Eastern/Western flavor, and what he produced, though certainly not a major score, effectively got on your nerves just excruciatingly long enough to let you recognize the solid theatrical and erotic power it achieved. In correspondence with the music Balanchine aimed at a more explicit eroticism than he ever had attempted before, not even in the pas de deux from *The Prodigal Son*—for the first time his dancers took off their clothes to make love—and he had never before invented anything as perilously close to the unacceptable as turning Kent's extended leg into a phallus. But this erotic adventure was produced with his familiar tact and taste, and he had the matchless services of Kent and Villella in peak condition: they had the beauty, the athletic power, the command of technique to bring Balanchine's conception to full embodiment. And, to cap it all, their dance identity gave a wittily American normalcy to this work of extreme artifice.

And then Suzanne Farrell came on the scene.

TEN / *Farrell*

Suzanne Farrell's emergence and ascent at the New York City Ballet, which was to change the Balanchine Enterprise in dangerous ways, changed my relation to it so much that her appearance became the most important single event in my involvement with Balanchine's career. She changed everything, in a complex process. I had felt myself absolutely in tune with the Balanchine Enterprise before she came on the scene, and if her arrival was still able to deepen my involvement immensely, the reason is that she emerged in 1963 not only for me but for Balanchine himself, and he thereafter focused his energy and imagination on her in the most explicit and finally the most dramatic way.

Farrell had joined the corps in 1962, but I didn't notice her at first because I had not yet gotten very far with my project of making myself familiar with the new members of the corps as soon as they appeared. It may, in fact, have been Farrell herself who initiated the project; I didn't want to miss the next such dancer, although no one remotely comparable turned up until Gelsey Kirkland came along in 1968. I do remember one of Farrell's first little solos, a comic turn in *Donizetti Variations,* in which she comes onstage late to join the other five girls of her group, finds them inexplicably posed in melodramatic grief, stares at them for a moment, and then with a little shrug decides that she must be supposed to grieve too. Farrell got the point across well, as have many young dancers in their time, and she must have made this little piece of business particularly legible, since it made me notice her. But either I missed her other early, minor solos or I didn't notice anything special in them. For me, as for the general public, Farrell emerged as an important dancer only on April 9,

1963, in *Movements for Piano and Orchestra,* a major work of the Balanchine-Stravinsky repertory.

It was an unexpected and dramatic debut, quite apart from the quality of Farrell's dancing. Balanchine had set the lead on Diana Adams, but her unexpected pregnancy made her unable to dance the premiere, so that, officially, Farrell was a last-minute substitute. But neither then nor later did anyone think of the premiere of *Movements* as anything other than Farrell's debut as a star—and as Balanchine's particular star.

When I first saw *Movements* it seemed clear that Balanchine was moving further along in the style he had begun in the pas de deux from *Agon* and in much of *Episodes,* but there was a big difference, as well. Although the lead couple again moved carefully through a sequence of difficult balances, the sense of crisis in *Agon* was gone, as was the irony and wit of *Episodes.* Farrell and d'Amboise's style in *Movements* called to mind the careful concentration of a pair of athletes who were demonstrating five of their workouts. There was no dramatic illusion, no theatricality; there were not even any entrances or exits—at the end of each section the dancers repositioned themselves, using the businesslike walk of gymnasts. Stravinsky's punning title warns us not to expect familiar musical genres or even a familiar way of making music—this is not a suite or a sonata or ordinary musical development but simply "movements"—and Balanchine likewise avoided familiar dance images and even familiar principles of dance motion. The steps followed one another in the rhythm and pace of steady, even walking, with neither conventional dance flow nor a clear dance beat, and the divisions of the overall structure followed each other without familiar devices of contrast, climax, or cadence. *Movements* is called a ballet for lack of an alternative term, but it never looked to me much like dancing: it is an absorbing event that has no theatrical or even rhetorical effect that happens to take place in a theater.

The new ballerina matched all this. She made no dramatic points, she gave no personal inflection to her steps; she held attention entirely by what seemed the virtually unsponsored continuity of the changing configurations of her body; the strong impact she made was not quite stage presence. I noticed too that she did not sweat as ordinary dancers did, a characteristic that acquired different meanings as my understanding of Farrell and her self-presentation changed over the years. Suzanne Farrell in *Movements* seemed a further and perhaps the final extension of Balanchine's "Don't act." It appeared that his new ideal dancer was not even going to be an instrument of dance as I ordinarily understood it. Maybe the new imperative would be "Don't dance."

I was tremendously impressed but not exactly delighted by the new ballet and the new dancer, and this has remained my reaction to *Movements.* Stravinsky loved the ballet, as he

Balanchine and Suzanne Farrell in class, ca. 1962 (photo ©1994 Martha Swope)

wrote in *Themes and Episodes*, because it gave him "a tour of a building for which I had drawn the plans but never explored the result." His is a wonderfully generous tribute, which I cannot resist misapplying to the music itself: perhaps not until he saw Balanchine's choreography for *Movements* did Stravinsky come not so much to *understand* the piece he had just composed as at last to *like* it. But Balanchine's choreography never had that effect for me. I have never come to love *Movements;* both the music and the dancing took a path that I couldn't really like or quite follow, and in my judgment it was a path that did not offer much for Balanchine either. *Movements* is a genuine and distinguished work, with an achieved identity, but for me it marked a dead end, into which Balanchine's loyalty to Stravinsky temporarily led him, a path away from his genius and almost away from his inclination.

I recognized my lack of sympathy with this ballet when I found that I could never listen to the music while I was looking at the dancing. I had not liked the music for *Agon* or the

Webern music for *Episodes* at first either, but now I appreciate both scores. I don't often listen to either by itself, but while I'm looking at the ballets, I consciously follow and enjoy the music in relation to the dance. With *Movements* this has never happened, and this failure has been for me the final answer to all the plausible arguments in favor of serial music in principle. Again and again I *plan* to listen to the music, only to realize after a few minutes that I've forgotten or failed to, which is to say that the music has not made itself available to my ears, whatever it might offer my eyes were I were to study the score.

I recognize that the music and I have both failed when I realize that I have lost my place in the dance. I have no dance training, and I cannot name most of the steps or sequences of steps to myself as I see them, but I do have musical training, I sing sol-fa silently to myself whenever I listen to music, and I usually know where I am in a ballet by knowing where I am in its music. Because I never know where I am in the music of *Movements,* I've never gotten to know the ballet either—sometimes I even forget how many movements there are in the piece. What I do, therefore, is wait for memorable configurations, the moment when Farrell is held upside down, for instance—I realize a few seconds in advance that one of these is about to occur, but I haven't really been following. In *Movements* I miss what I think of as continuity in dance, and for me that is to miss the sine qua non, not only of the art of ballet but of all art. *Agon* lacked a familiar dance *flow,* but I felt a powerful continuity despite that absence, so I had no trouble following the ballet and finding it important. What I'm saying about *Movements,* of course, is that for me it isn't important art. It now seems a move toward the minimalism that came to the fore in modern dance soon afterward, and the entire development proved to be for me a move away from interesting dancing. In a certain sense *Movements* did say "Don't dance."

Perhaps Balanchine himself realized this. I come by this fantasy by working backward from *Meditation* (1963), the first ballet he made explicitly for Farrell, and the one in which she came to the forefront of my attention. Balanchine made *Meditation* with what now seems to me the mischievous intention of astonishing and teasing the audience—together with the less characteristic intention of making a confession. After the withholdings and absences of *Movements,* he gave us in *Meditation* a moody love duet set to a sugary trifle for violin and orchestra by Tchaikovsky. The stage is darkly lit, and a man sits dejectedly on a chair; then a woman enters in sensuous chiffon under a brilliant deep orange-red spotlight, moves in bourrée toward the man and is supported and lifted thrillingly as he begins to respond to her presence. I court banality in this description, and for a portion of its first audience *Meditation* was banal. But my friends and I admired it immensely from the start, and we believed we understood its meaning and especially its *purpose* as clearly as Balanchine himself had—that purpose being to show that Suzanne Farrell was not just the company's latest interesting dancer but a dance genius of a wholly new kind, and to show too that Balanchine was in some sense of the word in love with her.

In *Movements* Farrell had maintained the same dynamic level as she stepped from one balance to another; in *Meditation* she danced with a powerful momentum of dance flow which surged through an immense dynamic range, from very "loud" to very "soft," covering a great deal of space, with the highest, swiftest arabesque I had seen until then. But the differing effects of *Movements* and *Meditation* were both manifestations of the unique energy from which all her movement flowed. I felt that Balanchine was inviting me to study this extraordinary phenomenon, and I set to work immediately. As I brought my response to consciousness, I realized that in both *Movements* and *Meditation* Farrell's energy surged out in a continuous jet of movement to which my own body answered with an exhilarating kinesthetic sympathy, while my eye and mind answered with an aesthetic and spiritual delight in the clarity of the complex organic images the energy formed. Under the theatrical conditions of *Movements*—the plain leotards for costumes, the bare stage with a simple blue drop and brilliant lighting, the even dynamic level of the steps—Farrell's instinctively sustained energy gave almost palpable three-dimensional embodiment to Balanchine's cool analytic exploration of Stravinsky's score. In *Meditation*, on the other hand, with its moody lighting and costumes, its hint of narrative, and its half-dramatic dance vocabulary, her energy generated a direct expressivity that brought familiar, even banal, emotive gestures back to life. I guessed at once that this protean potentiality was what Balanchine valued in Farrell and that in making *Meditation* immediately after *Movements* he was calling atten-tion to the dimension and range of this potentiality. And when I saw this, as I immediately did with great excitement, I knew that my following of Balanchine's career had taken a major step, for I now had the sense not only of *agreeing* with him about this new dancer but of *collaborating* almost at first hand with his taste and judgment and with the project he was so clearly embarked on. If Balanchine from that point on made the exploration of Farrell's dance genius his chief project, so did I. And when her dancing lit up role after role in the standard repertory, I felt a glow of personal gratification as my judgment was confirmed— sometimes I was so excited that I very nearly took the credit for her dancing.

I felt secure about another appealing but conceivably more problematic aspect of Farrell's dancing in *Meditation:* the direct erotic power that Balanchine had brought out of her. Never had I seen a movement so bewitching as the way she held her elbows back and away from her body when she moved impetuously forward in bourrée or chassée; never had chiffon clung more ravishingly to the curve of a dancer's hip. I was enchanted and I saw that enchantment was, in fact, the meaning and motive of the piece: *Meditation* was Balanchine's love poem to Farrell. And it did not matter to me that this meaning was almost unmediated. Eight years earlier, I had realized that the choreography for Allegra Kent in "The Unanswered Question" section of *Ivesiana* expressed Balanchine's sensual pleasure in her extraordinarily fluid body, but "The Unanswered Question" is a fully worked structure of art that objectifies the erotic pleasure that must have been its source, and the same is true of the far more explicitly erotic choreography for Kent in *Bugaku*. There is some feeling of private erotic fantasy in *La Sonnambula* (in which a poet learns to control the movements of the sleepwalking wife of his host, and is murdered by the man in consequence); but the stylized romantic atmosphere keeps the private, personal emotion under control.

In contrast, *Meditation* comes close to seeming an erotic daydream of Balanchine's. The choreographer was not only allowing but obviously encouraging Farrell's Farrellisms—those impetuous arms—so that the girl in *Meditation* was unmistakably a flesh-and-blood dancer named Suzanne Farrell, whereas the ravishingly beautiful Kent in *La Sonnambula* had been a character in a theatrical illusion. Since Balanchine's infatuation with Farrell was to subject the company and the audience to such a troubling drama later in the sixties, and since the elements of that drama were visible in *Meditation,* I perhaps ought to have felt a twinge of apprehension at the change in Balanchine's habits as an artist, and perhaps others did. But the ballet did not make me in the least uneasy; it was an entirely positive experience.

But if I began now to think about Balanchine as a man, that never meant seeing him apart from his work but always pondering how and with what motives he went about *making images* on the stage, new images, of all his dancers, including the one with whom he was in love. I knew I was a far from disinterested observer, since I felt an unmistakably personal excitement about Farrell, but I also knew from the first that my lack of disinterestedness did not represent a mistake of judgment. If, in loving *Meditation,* I felt a new collaboration with the artist whose work I had been following for so many years, that feeling came to me as a gain in intensity rather than as complicity or loss of perspective.

*Meditation* marks the point at which my friends and I diverged in judgment from B. H. Haggin and Edwin Denby, a disagreement that might have given us pause but did not: their faint reserve about Farrell simply seemed oddly obtuse. This may have been the moment at which I left my teachers behind, but that did not worry me, so great was the power of Farrell's genius and so exciting an act of life was the creative energy and imagination with which Balanchine was opening himself to it.

The people with whom I discussed ballet accepted Balanchine's intense interest in

Farrell and approved of it, since we all got the point of *Meditation*, but it was not clear how widespread this awareness was. *Meditation* was perceived as an embarrassing misstep to so perceptive and sound a critic and judge as P. W. Manchester, who wrote in the *Christian Science Monitor* on December 16, 1963: "Balanchine goes along with both romanticism and sentimentality. In fact he dives in head first. He might well have subtitled the piece 'Homage to Soviet Ballet (Highlights Division),' because that is exactly what it looks like. He keeps his dancers mooning around in a yearning sort of way. They both spend a lot of time kneeling on the floor clutching each other's ankles. There is no development, and we know it is going to end only because we hear the climax in the music." Of Farrell she wrote, "No one looks lovelier when she is yearning than Suzanne Farrell with her long fair hair streaming to her waist over the snowy draperies of her simple dress." If Manchester missed the difference between the Balanchinian and the Soviet brand of ardent yearning, the fault is as much Balanchine as anyone's, since Manchester's taste was at least partly educated by the Balanchine style, and she was in effect scolding the master for backsliding.

But the words *his dancers* and the rather neutral account of Farrell's "loveliness" may represent not failure to notice the infatuation being expressed in front of her but rather the sad reticence about what were presumed to be private issues that was characteristic of Balanchine's critics. On the other hand, Manchester had written about the erotic pas de deux in *Bugaku* in a tone, unusual in this finely disinterested critic, of shocked prudery— maybe she thought things were going to pieces generally in the Balanchine Enterprise. Allen Hughes, of the *New York Times* (no very impressive authority, to be sure), had not thought well of *Bugaku,* either, so I wouldn't have been surprised if he had disapproved of *Meditation,* but in fact he rather liked it (December 11, 1963). He praised Farrell warmly and like me found it astonishing that this was the same dancer who had danced with such cool athleticism in *Movements* just a few months previously. But warm praise did not match the level of my own and Balanchine's excitement.

What eventually came to be the serious Farrell problem began about this time because of the rapidity with which Balanchine let the dancer work her power on many central roles in the repertory. For me this development was, of course, no problem at all. And at first, it was exactly *power* that I was aware of: the scale of her dancing, her body, and her energy; this quantitative aspect of Farrell's genius still strikes me as central. As I wrote of Farrell in a piece for *Partisan Review* in 1968 about a role she began to dance in 1963:

In *Liebeslieder Walzer,* as in *La Valse,* she happens to be completely correct in style, but this is the least of the virtues of these incandescent performances. When Diana

Adams danced *Liebeslieder* the characterization was basically the same; she too was the most exuberant, joyous, young and free of the four women, as Verdy was the most mature and experienced. And Adams was as lovely, and danced as beautifully as one could ever want. Then Farrell's very first appearance in the role made you believe you had never really seen it before. Some people explained it by speaking of her actual youth; others murmured reprovingly about "untamed" wildness. Denby, in what was almost the first critical statement I couldn't share, thought some of her movements brash—to him she seemed to be showing distaste for her partner when she pushed him away from her. But this youth, sweep, speed and impetuosity need no taming: her fantastic energy releases itself in fantastic grace. Of course you have to believe your eyes to see this, just as you have to believe your ears to hear that Toscanini's performance of the Haffner Symphony isn't too fast to be graceful. Some things don't seem humanly possible, but when they happen in front of you it doesn't make good sense to get annoyed. Think of the configurations of Farrell's body in the most eloquent moment in the slow duet of the first part of *Liebeslieder,* for instance, when Stowell folds her over in his arms before he raises her up: Farrell unifies this sequence by instinctively fluid modulating movements that no head-intelligence could contrive: it is like a happening in nature.

The transformation Farrell worked for me in the slow movement of *Symphony in C* was a more complex affair: she, along with Mimi Paul, carried on the revelation of this ballet that had begun when I saw Violette Verdy dance the first movement soon after she joined the company in 1958. Once Verdy had revealed the allegro essence of this movement, I located a dim print of Maria Tallchief's performance in my memory—or, what is more likely, I had so strong a sense of Tallchief's identity through *Pas de Dix* and other roles that I was able to construct a memory of what her performance in the Bizet must have been. But there wasn't enough in my memory to build on to resurrect Tanaquil Le Clercq's performance in the slow movement, and I still draw a blank about it, despite efforts to extrapolate some hint of an image from what I now know of her marvelous *Concerto Barocco*. And I don't have any memory of Kent's performance in the slow movement in the late fifties and early sixties, although I saw it repeatedly. Before I saw the public broadcasting documentary about Balanchine I might have claimed an admiration for her performance as, say, "beautiful and delicate on a small-scale" (I am invoking Haggin's style, since it was his taste I would have been following). But the excerpts in the Balanchine documentary and especially those in another public broadcasting documentary, "Balanchine's Ballerinas" (1989), are more

Mimi Paul and Conrad Ludlow with members of the New York City Ballet in *Symphony in C,* 1964 (photo ©1994 Martha Swope; the ownership and the rights for *Symphony in C* belong to John Taras)

idiosyncratic than I realized at the time—Kent seems proud and isolated, courageous and vulnerable in her oddly, nobly inflected reading of the role. My failure to remember so special a performance is the more puzzling since I was seeing it just when I was beginning to understand the first movement through Verdy's instruction. In truth, I did not get the point of the second movement in itself until it became the arena of competition between Farrell and Mimi Paul: at once it became one of the things I most wanted to see. Their performances overlaid and obscured all memories of Kent and Le Clercq. Now I feel not only stupid but remorseful at having let something as beautiful as Kent's performance slip so easily from my mind—this is the oblivion she and other supplanted dancers felt they were entering as role after role was taken from them and given to usurping youth. For youth did take over.

The competition between Farrell and Paul in *Symphony in C* began in 1963 when Kent was away from the company on a pregnancy leave and had to be replaced. The decision to

Suzanne Farrell and Conrad Ludlow with members of the New York City Ballet in *Symphony in C*, 1964 (photo ©1994 Martha Swope; the ownership and the rights for *Symphony in C* belong to John Taras)

replace her in a popular work like *Symphony in C* was a routine practical one, and the fact that the slow movement came both to Paul and Farrell did not seem at the time to represent a takeover by the young ballerinas. As I remember, the formidable, even fanatical Paul got the assignment before Farrell, but the two alternated regularly from 1963 until 1968, when Paul left the company to dance the classics at the American Ballet Theatre. The competition between the two dancers soon became an intense rivalry and may have appeared to Farrell and Paul to be anything but benign, but to me it seemed entirely positive: I was swept along in the energy of Balanchine's enthusiasm about his new dancers. I remember the impact of the sheer size of Farrell's and Paul's bodies, a largeness which seemed in itself to offer a reading of the role, a revelation of it, although I had often seen the movement danced by Le Clercq, who was about the same height as Farrell and Paul. When Balanchine said, "The tallest is better because you see more," I understood exactly what he meant in relation to Farrell and Paul in the slow movement of *Symphony in C,* and I agreed with him:

they seemed exactly "so much to look at." And Balanchine's pleasure in the size of many of his new dancers also taught me a lot. I learned to look at dancing better because Farrell's and Paul's size made the configurations of their bodies clearer for me; following Plato's advice in *The Republic* about reading the large letters first and then checking the smaller ones to see whether they said the same thing, I learned to see more clearly the details of less grandly articulated bodies, like Verdy's, McBride's, Schorer's, and, in the seventies, Gelsey Kirkland's.

At the time I considered Paul's performance the equal of Farrell's, and I wonder how I would compare them were I to see them again. In this role, as in so many others, Paul gave the impression of both fanatical concentration and fantasy-laden inspiration, as if she were enacting a personal scenario while she was performing the steps—in the big traveling lifts she was dreaming if ever dancer was dreaming. With Farrell, I was struck from the beginning with a special physical phenomenon in her performance. In the traveling lifts she gave the illusion that she was already beginning the return flight before she had completed the first, yet the first flight was fully realized before your eyes—it was a magical effect, and I remember enjoying wondering how she did it. It did not come across as a trick, as did Maya Plisetskaya's rubber arms in *Swan Lake*, nor did it seem even consciously intended: it certainly had something to do with the speed and the precision with which her brain sent messages to her limbs, but then those talents were the locus of her genius in any case, and what they created came to reality in the realm of poetry, although it may have begun in superior neurological integration and athletic prowess.

It took the dimension of Paul's and Farrell's dancing to make me really *see* those extraordinary, and now famous, traveling lifts that are a kind of refrain in this movement. Years later, when John Clifford reported in an interview printed in *I Remember Balanchine* that Balanchine had called these lifts "the moon going across the sky," I was unsurprised at how deeply they mattered to Balanchine himself—and yet it had taken Paul and Farrell to bring them clearly to my attention.

Mimi Paul seemed to be such a great dancer to me that I wasn't aware of anything invidious in the comparisons I continually made between her and Farrell. It is true that Farrell's position in Balanchine's regard led to his giving her key roles in his repertory: *Apollo, Concerto Barocco, Agon,* Titania in *A Midsummer Night's Dream.* Those roles had a richness and a meaningfulness that imparted itself to her—it made her a key dancer in the viewer's memory and imagination. Well before the absolute proof offered by *Don Quixote* I knew that Farrell was for me by far the greater dancer. But Paul was not forgotten in the repertory: she was a great presence, particularly in the Jillana roles in *A Midsummer Night's Dream* and *Liebeslieder Walzer,* and there were some talismanic blessings, signs of being chosen, from Balanchine when he gave her the third-theme pas de deux in *The Four Temperaments* and Adams's role in *La Valse*. She replaced Kent in *Bugaku* early on and was interestingly different from Kent, more powerfully intense in her artifice though without Kent's limpid naturalness. Paul danced *Swan Lake* long before Farrell, and I enjoyed trying to figure out why: I concluded that Balanchine thought that Paul was already fully what she was going to be and therefore ready for *Swan Lake*, but there was no need to hurry Farrell's *Swan Lake*, since she had not yet become all her immense potentiality promised.

Part of Balanchine's motivation for making *Don Quixote* came from the fact that the company had moved to Lincoln Center and needed new works to show off their big new stage. There had been a passionate debate about the validity of creating a center for all the performing arts, and I had taken both sides in comfortable ambivalence—I was a bit cynical about the idea of marketing all of New York's performing arts together in one mall, and I liked both Carnegie Hall and the old Metropolitan Opera House, but I was resigned to the fact that "high concept" packaging was how the arts were bound to be sold in mid-century America. I had no strong loyalty to City Center; indeed, I was skeptical of the loyalty claimed by many fans toward this awkward space and stage: there were few good seats there, and while it turned out that those seats—at the front of the mezzanine—gave a better view than any of the seats in the new theater, this was the way things often happened, and one had to keep matters in perspective.

I found nothing notably grandiose in the new format for the New York City Ballet at the New York State Theater. Balanchine's preoccupation with size when the company moved to Lincoln Center did not worry me. True, I liked the overblown new sets for the snow scene in *The Nutcracker* no more than anyone else, nor yet the vulgar decorator swags in *Brahms-Schoenberg* or the pompously swelling columns of St. Petersburg in the new sets for *Tchaikovsky Piano Concerto No. 2*, but I saw no overall tendency toward the overblown in style or dancing. I had an almost complete trust in the New York City Ballet, which derived from my trust in Balanchine, who enjoyed working for an institution and did not seem impeded by it. I saw no reason why this state of affairs should not continue under the pressures of the larger theater and the inclusion into such an enterprise as Lincoln Center, nor did fear prove to be justified.

Both *Don Quixote* and *A Midsummer Night's Dream* recall Balanchine's youth: he claims his authority in Shakespeare's play on the circumstance of having played a bug when he was a boy in a St. Petersburg production that was accompanied by the Mendelssohn music (Nancy Reynolds quotes Balanchine as saying, "I still know the play better in Russian than a lot of people know it in English"); *Don Quixote* was a Petipa subject before it became a

Balanchine one. There is something both endearing and arrogant in Balanchine's loyalty to his middlebrow upbringing in art and literature, although his musical understanding was of course from the beginning thoroughly professional and highly sophisticated. *Don Quixote* is less successful as a whole than *A Midsummer Night's Dream,* but it carries a more urgent weight of personal presence and motive, and it is far more ambitious, more assertive, more demanding of the audience. It was also—and seems to continue to be—entirely dependent on the dancer who inspired it, as *A Midsummer Night's Dream* is not, although there has been some difficulty replacing Edward Villella as Oberon.

A less endearing, more arrogant loyalty to his own past appears regrettably in the fact that Balanchine commissioned the score from Nicholas Nabokov, an old Russian expatriate friend and colleague from his Parisian days. Everybody agrees that Nabokov's weak music proved a serious handicap, although no one seems to have tried to find out what Balanchine himself thought about it. Nabokov had enjoyed a little success in the thirties and forties—a couple of ballet commissions, including an orchestration(!) of the *Goldberg Variations* for William Dollar and Ballet Caravan in 1938 and a commission from the Boston Symphony Orchestra in the early fifties—but he had entered cultural politics at UNESCO long before he composed *Don Quixote,* and there was no apparent justification for Balanchine to think that he could produce anything better than the score turned out to be. When I heard of the plan to hire Nabokov, I myself guessed, and hoped, that Balanchine himself was going to take a hand in the composition, using Nabokov as a stalking horse, but there is no evidence that he did so, and the choice of Nabokov may be accounted simply misplaced loyalty to an old White Russian friend—although perhaps one catches a glimpse of a need on Balanchine's part to keep the center of attention on himself by choosing a weak composer. On the other hand, no one has ever come up with a better suggestion than Nabokov: Stravinsky was out of the question on every count, too old to contemplate such an exhausting commission and too engaged in his own experiments with new technique to be ready to adapt to another's needs, even Balanchine's—I wonder whether he was ever even considered.

Another big difference between *Don Quixote* and *A Midsummer Night's Dream* is that in the later, more personal, more troubled, more problematic piece Balanchine found himself incapable of original or even interesting decisions about format or style. Unlike the brilliant solution given to the narrative problems of *A Midsummer Night's Dream,* the mode of *Don Quixote* is conventional and perfunctory, and the overall workmanship more uneven than that of any other work in the Balanchine repertory. The second act is masterly throughout, but both the first and third are insecure in tone, although each has rich and brilliant sections. On the other hand, Balanchine's way of reading Shakespeare had been rather

Suzanne Farrell as Marcela in *Don Quixote*, 1965 (photo ©1994 Martha Swope)

conventional and impersonal, an enterprise of "general culture" rather than of personal motivation and interpretation, whereas his reading of Cervantes was full of the pressure of personal involvement and yielded a lively sense of an artist feeling and thinking his way through to his own conception.

His choices in *Don Quixote* may seem odd at first. The ballet begins slowly, sketchily, and without much dancing. Don Quixote himself is not strongly characterized in the first two acts, and his relationship with Sancho Panza—the famous duality of spirit and flesh, appearance and reality—is barely sketched in. What interests Balanchine is Don Quixote's dreams of beautiful women and the progressively more humiliating consequences of these dreams. This reading, though not irrelevant to Cervantes, is, of course, central to Balanchine's imagination throughout his career, while it directly represents the predicament in his personal life at the time of composition.

Don Quixote's first dream establishes key aspects of feeling and tone, for the first "lady in distress" the Don dreams about while reading his great books of romance appears to us as a tiny girl kneeling on one of the books and imploring aid with touchingly comic gestures of her fragile little arms. This image defines the innocence of the Don's chivalric belief in the purity and vulnerability of women and evokes an amused but moved and respectful response to that ideal. There follows a somewhat incoherent progression of encounters. The next woman is a variation of the child, but she comes from the real world—a young serving-girl so devoted to her master as to dry his feet with her hair: this is Farrell's first avatar. She disappears up a staircase into a golden light, then reappears in the Don's fantasy as the ideal Dulcinea; at this point the Don formally initiates his role as knightly adventurer. For a while not much happens. He strides about slowly, nobly, correctly, and comically, waiting for injustices to come along: the point isn't made with much flair. He rescues some prisoners, who turn on him in mild slapstick. Both the Don and Balanchine seem at a loss.

But in the bright village square there suddenly appears the theatrically promising image of a dead poet and his guilty mistress, Marcela, Farrell's next incarnation. The crowd reviles her, at which the Don rescues her, and she expresses her gratitude for the Don's noble act and noble opinion of her in one of Balanchine's greatest dances. Marcela belongs to a sophisticated courtly world, and her dance is a knowing exhibition piece in an artificially pastoral style; she herself seems to be a professional actress or dancer, now stalking elegantly this way and that on pointe, now balancing herself charmingly on her shepherdess's crook, now leaping with bold athletic prowess, and finally drifting away with delicate coquettish backward glances. Yet this exhibition dance has dignity and purity too, as if she had been created into sincerity of feeling by the Don's belief in her, and the way Farrell's straightforward sumptuous energy enlarged pastoral artifice was a master achievement of style that we were not to see the like of until she and Balanchine created the grand amplifications of rococo in *Chaconne* and *Mozartiana* at the end of his career. From this height of emotion Balanchine bangs the action down to farce again as the Don destroys a puppet show in order to save another lady in distress, who turns out to be the little girl from the first dream, her fragile, charmingly stiff little limbs now enacting a tiny parody of classical adagio. This balletic joke diminishes our involvement in the Don's dreams and humiliations, and at the end of the act we feel that we are once more collaborating when a grandduke and duchess discover the Don as an amusing curiosity and lead him back to their court.

The brilliant second act is filled with Balanchinian enlargements of the divertissements characteristic of nineteenth-century narrative ballet. A gorgeously sinister ceremonious entrance of courtiers is trailed by lost-looking Don Quixote; then follows a superb series of assured, exotic, rather sensual dance entertainments. The Don watches courteously but without comprehension. The atmosphere of sophisticated corruption thickens as the courtiers draw the Don into a suave formal dance during which he is made the butt of quiet malice that culminates in open ridicule. After he has been abandoned in disgrace, a vision of Dulcinea enters to comfort him: their pas de deux transforms conventional ballet adagio into the poignant trompe l'oeil of a strong young woman supporting a tired old man.

The third act begins with the Don's long dream about Dulcinea and her court of pure and beautiful women, a rich set piece that appears at first to be a completely happy idealization, all curving softness and effortless grace, in contrast to the assertive sensuality of the second-act dances; with rueful understanding we see Dulcinea now fresh and free, lifted gloriously by a handsome young man instead of supporting the aged and humiliated knight. But the Don's happy dream does not last. Dulcinea's variation becomes agitated and fearful; it is interrupted by a man and woman in black—the evil magician and his erotic accomplice so beloved of romantic ballet. When these figures threaten Dulcinea, the Don wakes up in alarm and charges into the most deluded of his battles to save an ideal. At last Balanchine introduces the windmills and the imaginary giants, to spectacular effect. But the spectacle is charged with deep painful feeling by now; we feel admiration for the Don, but shame too, and an intense protectiveness toward him. When his furious impotence reduces him to crawling about on all fours like a mad dog, he is captured by impersonal but not unkind officials, who bring him home in a cage to die. On his deathbed he is admonished by a (much too long) procession of religious figures; in the background the burning of his books of heroic romance becomes a hellfire. In spite of these warnings his final vision is again of Dulcinea, but after his death the serving-girl lays a homemade crucifix on his breast.

*Don Quixote* gave me my most vivid first-night memory. I had followed every step of the publicity and was absolutely primed, my friends the Harriers equally, and we talked our responses through during intermissions and afterward until we found the right words. At the end of the first act we were in consternation: *"not enough dancing"*—just what we thought we would never say about a Balanchine ballet. And our response has remained constant, despite Marcela's great solo. After the second act, we were very impressed; the divertissements at the duke's court had seemed marvelously choreographed, cast, and performed, especially the "Pas de Deux Mauresque" for Suki Schorer and John Prinz; and we had given ourselves over fully to the passage when Dulcinea seems to support the Don, while he is of course supporting her, in the magical pas de deux which was the more moving—and perhaps not even entirely an illusion—at this performance because Farrell was so incomparably strong and Balanchine himself, almost fainting with exhaustion, was dancing the Don. But it was the opening of the third act that did me in, with the stage softly full of the beautiful women Don Quixote is dreaming about; at Farrell's entrance, as she bourréed downstage through the group, her arms in a ravishingly Farrellesque port de bras, I still remember saying to myself, "There it is," and I've never stopped feeling that.

The *Don Quixote* premiere changed my habits briefly: after the ballet and the long talk about it afterward I had trouble falling asleep, and when I came wide awake, feeling fine, at about six in the morning, I was the one that time who went out to buy the croissants at Sutter's.

About the dances for Farrell, which are inevitably the great things in *Don Quixote*, suffice it to say that they are the dances of Dulcinea—they are the frank embodiment of ideal womanhood as conceived by an expressive genius working at the height of his powers. But almost equally rich and assured are the court dances in the second act, which had the additional interest of presenting so many of Balanchine's other new dancers in exciting new roles. These divertissements form a richly varied gallery of the sensual women who are not Dulcinea, who are powerful in their attraction without her combination of cool virginal inaccessibility and clear athletic prowess. And it was marvelous for me to see that, in the middle of his infatuation with Farrell, Balanchine had given such time and energy to the rest of his dancers. He seemed to view each of them afresh, as Suki Schorer testified to Nancy Reynolds when she described the "Pas de Deux Mauresque" that she and John Prinz made so memorable: "It was a very easy dance, but effective. Slow, undulating, very soft, on and off pointe, sometimes with flexed foot. I always felt it was kind of Slavic, and John had a few jumps where he touched his feet to his head. It was one of the few places in the score where there was any melody. I liked it particularly because I didn't have to move fast, hop around, or 'be cute.' It was as if Balanchine looked at me in a new way."

Suki Schorer and John Prinz in the "Pas de Deux Mauresque" from *Don Quixote*, 1965 (photo ©1994 Martha Swope)

I was enchanted too by the witty animal power of Gloria Govrin and Arthur Mitchell in their "Rigaudon Flamenco" and the exquisite sensuality of Patricia McBride's "Ritornel," a solo dance accompanied by a child bearing a large Middle Eastern fan; the girl was Colleen Neary, the thirteen-year-old sister of Patricia Neary, who had so imperiously danced the first divertissement, the "Danza alla Caccia," with Conrad Ludlow and Kent Stowell.

Mimi Paul and Marnee Morris, Farrell's rivals in long-legged, "tallest" ballerina style and stature, were Farrell's attendants at Dulcinea's court in the third act; they led the sumptuous group dance, which could be called Balanchine's homage to the great white ensemble dances in *Swan Lake* and *Giselle* if *homage* were not too limiting a word to describe dances drenched in a beauty both deep and familiar, and yet so original in tone, so fully developed, and so richly worked. Both Paul and Morris performed rich and difficult variations, and the difference between the variations showed how carefully Balanchine had been watching the dancers in the morning classes that began the day at the New York City Ballet. Farrell inevitably had the most exciting and most demanding variation, which led back into the dramatic action through its shifting moods—from reckless, intrepid independence and athletic prowess through constant changes of speed and direction to vividly agitated awareness of danger, which convincingly awakens the Don from his dream and leads into his final, deluded attack on the windmills.

*Don Quixote* confirmed the confessional implications of *Meditation* and seemed to bring them to resolution. By creating, and at the premiere himself dancing, the role of Don Quixote, and by casting Farrell as Dulcinea, Balanchine identified her as the center of his life and art but defined his interest in her as one of traditional idealization; the ballet's narrative line and tone enacted a melancholy acceptance of her inaccessibility.

In actuality, his infatuation and her resistance intensified and began to generate irrational behavior on both sides until the conflict between their wills led him in effect to fire her in 1969, in an action that threatened every aspect of the Balanchine Enterprise, particularly the interests of the audience. Long before, by the time of *Don Quixote* if not earlier, the situation had come to public knowledge (though with surprisingly little newspaper publicity), and serious concern inevitably arose as to whether Balanchine was neglecting or mistreating—if not actually betraying the trust of—his other dancers by giving so much attention and so many roles to Farrell. But despite my interest in the whole company, I was so swept along by Farrell herself and by Balanchine's ardor that I was only intermittently aware that the enterprise itself might be threatened by this excitement. Occasionally it occurred to me that Farrell's prominence might be hurting the morale if not the careers of other dancers in the company, yet for the most part I accepted that possibility as regrettable but essentially beyond Balanchine's control, since it seemed both natural and desirable that he should follow the direction of his inspiration. I did not feel that a great injustice was being done, nor did it occur to me that I myself might be guilty of injustice, or at least insensitivity, to other dancers in my commitment to Balanchine. I felt no obligation to bring the situation into focus as a moral or even a practical or political issue; even now, I don't feel that I was obtuse or insensitive in having failed to do so.

I was loyal chiefly to Balanchine's interests in this matter, because it was his genius and the products of it that engaged me. Had his infatuation led to such company discontent that it threatened the embodiment of his conceptions in performance, I suppose I would have believed him to be hurting himself and his art; but to my eyes he was not doing that, and it wasn't in the nature of my involvement with Balanchine's career to have a disinterested, sensitive concern for the feelings of those dancers who were unhappy about their lack of claim to his attention during these years. It had always been for the value of his ballets as works of art that my attention was centered on his career, and because what he and Farrell were making together offered a rich and beautiful new episode in that career, I wasn't deeply concerned with what their partnership might be displacing.

The only instance in which I thought Balanchine to be unjust in a casting decision during these years was entirely a mistake on my own part, a rather interesting and symptomatic one. I still ruefully remember feeling troubled at Balanchine's decision to cast Allegra Kent instead of Violette Verdy in the 1966 film of *A Midsummer Night's Dream*, although Verdy could not, in fact, have danced in the film: she was on leave, involved with her new marriage, and performing as guest artist with England's Royal Ballet and with other European companies for two years before the film was made, and she underwent major surgery during the time the film was made. I'm not sure why I did not remember these facts when I saw the film: perhaps the lapse was a sign of my nervousness about Verdy's place in the company, my worry over what was going to happen to her, perhaps, or my worry that my high estimate of her dancing might not be justified: this might explain the sense I had when I saw Kent dance "her" role that she was being mistreated. I was actually deeply moved by Kent's dancing, naturally enough, since she was one of my favorite dancers and the role fits her marvelously, but I must have been nervous about the comparison I had to have been making between her performance and Verdy's. I was also worried and discouraged by the fact that Kent's was the only dancing applauded by the audience with whom I saw the film. The preview I went to was attended for the most part by people who were professionally involved with dance, and in my fantasy I took their applause to imply a preference for Kent over Verdy—"Now *this* is the way it should be danced." But what the applause is more likely to have meant on this occasion, I now realize, is "*This* is what I call really great dancing, not that Farrell girl's brash over-athletic exaggeration that is all we get to see these days." Farrell's Titania, a marvelous outpouring of grace and power, had not been applauded. But neither had Villella's splendid Oberon—the truth of the matter may be that the timing in the film left a moment for applause after Kent's performance but not after the solos of any of the other dancers. In any case, my mixed-up response now seems to show that I was experiencing some tensions, but no more so than others inside and outside the world of the Balanchine Enterprise.

The film was not a successful venture, and it did not really deserve to be, for it was made too quickly on too small a budget, by mediocre and somewhat incompetent filmmakers, apparently with little supervision by Balanchine. The makeup is so peculiarly atrocious, particularly that of Farrell and Villella, as to suggest that nobody checked the results of the day's shooting. Villella told me much later that not only had he never seen the entire film in the theater but that he hadn't even seen the daily rushes. It fits in with Balanchine's uneasiness about filming his ballets that, having decided to have this film made, he paid little attention to the process; the films made by the Canadian Broadcasting Company in the early sixties and in 1969 and 1971 seem to owe their excellence to the high standards of the CBC rather than to careful supervision on Balanchine's part, and he did not become interested in filming until he began working for public broadcasting in Nashville in the mid-seventies.

But for me the film is more than satisfactory: it is superbly danced by Farrell, Kent, Villella, Mitchell, Schorer, McBride, Paul, and Govrin and beautifully performed by the orchestra under Robert Irving, but the crucial thing about it is that it confirms my sense that the morale of the company in 1966 was high in everything that presented itself to the spectator, whatever backstage tension, hurt feelings, or ill will were being caused by the Balanchine-Farrell relationship. This is recognizably the company I was watching night after night with the greatest pleasure, and the film still gives me pleasure, both in itself and as a record of a great enterprise. Balanchine's infatuation with Farrell was a real problem; she did dance too often; many of the other dancers were right to have felt mistreated and ignored; Farrellitis was a real disease and a serious one. And yet what I felt nightly in the audience was that everyone onstage wanted to be there because the New York State Theater was where the life of their profession was taking place. The film of *A Midsummer Night's Dream* bears this out.

In the early 1960s I began to write for *Partisan Review* after my friend Richard Poirier became one of the editors. In 1964 he asked me to contribute regular articles about ballet, and I can offer another sort of record about the state of the Balanchine Enterprise during the mid-sixties and about the nature and dimension of my concern about the Farrell-Balanchine drama by quoting and commenting on the accounts I wrote for *Partisan Review* from 1965 to 1968.

There were three review articles in which I covered the New York and Boston seasons of the New York City Ballet, the Bolshoi Ballet, England's Royal Ballet, the Danish Royal Ballet, and the Boston Ballet. The results were what might have been expected: admiration for Balanchine was the steady theme, and my pleasure in expressing judgments was in full play—I made wisecracks like "Plisetskaya is the Joan Crawford of ballet" and offered rather earnestly phrased praise of Margot Fonteyn and Rudolf Nureyev. My judgments took the form of the comparisons that had been my critical method since high school. I judged Frederick Ashton's *The Dream* and Kenneth Macmillan's *Romeo and Juliet* unfavorably by pitting them against *A Midsummer Night's Dream* and *Don Quixote;* I registered skepticism about what had received a good deal of publicity as "dance acting" at the Danish Ballet and the Bolshoi by comparing it with Jillana's performance as the Coquette in *La Sonnambula* at the New York City Ballet, which had gotten little publicity but was for me just as dramatic and more interesting, since it took place in a better ballet. It would be nice if my judgments had not always been so invidious, but were I to rewrite the pieces today, in a more generous spirit toward Ashton, for instance, my comparisons would still produce the same basic judgments, perhaps more gently phrased; were I to rewrite my comparison between Macmillan's art and Balanchine's, the result would be even harsher.

I argued the validity of comparison explicitly in the first of these articles. There, describing the dancing of the Boston Ballet, I discussed the Ford Foundation grants awarded to the School of American Ballet and the New York City Ballet in 1963, as well as to other schools and companies that had adopted Balanchine's style and technique. I acknowledged, and expressed sympathy with, the disappointment these grants had occasioned for other companies and schools, and for the critics who supported them, but inevitably I asserted that it was the job of the Ford Foundation to make the grants on the basis of comparisons and that they had made the right judgment in awarding those grants to Balanchine and his followers. That these awards installed Balanchine as the lord of ballet in America was something about which I had no regret, nor have I ever felt that Balanchine was spoiled by institutional success.

When I described *Don Quixote* in 1966 I praised Farrell highly but in almost generic terms: "By far the most beautiful thing of all is what Suzanne Farrell dances and the way she dances it. She is the latest of Balanchine's 'creations' and now, at nineteen, she gives the illusion of being the most wonderful dancer one has ever seen. Balanchine has created such illusions before. By calling her a creation of Balanchine, I do not mean for a moment that she is anything less than a dancer of the highest class in her own right, but merely to stress the fact that she is working in the best possible climate." By 1968 I had decided to introduce my article about the recent season with an account of Balanchine's dancers rather than of his choreography, and my description had a "long overdue" rhetoric to it that probably did not disguise the fact that it was I myself who had reached a new phase in my engagement with Balanchine's art.

I argued that in the ballet world of the 1950s and 1960s, where ballet dancers, especially expatriate Russians like Rudolf Nureyev, had become superstars, the Balanchine method had begun to yield a kind of dancing that was not only as good technically as that of the superstars but in performance better because of how these artists were being used by their teacher and choreographer. I argued that the great dancers at the New York City Ballet, "who are guided by [Balanchine's] taste and style, are not his puppets or slaves, yet they haven't, probably because of the magnetism of the Balanchine name, been given quite the attention and admiration they deserve." The proper attention and admiration I proceeded to give took the form of an extended contrast of the styles of Verdy and Farrell, followed by briefer descriptions of Villella, Paul, Kent, and McBride, with a few remarks about Mitchell, Moncion, and Morris. My emphasis on dancers rather than choreography expressed genuine admiration for performers who really did seem to me great artists, yet my choosing to build the piece in this way was perhaps an attempt at damage control in relation to the Balanchine-Farrell drama. I was implicitly claiming that Balanchine was not neglecting his other dancers in favor of Farrell but was keeping them steadily in mind and richly fostering their careers and their growth. And I went on to produce evidence for this in a review of the new *Jewels*, which I presented as a ballet that had been lovingly fashioned to exhibit the special qualities of the dancers I had described.

"Emeralds," the first section of *Jewels*, is set to Fauré's *Pelléas et Mélisande*, and when I first learned of this my vague memory of the music made me wonder how Balanchine, who loves music that has a strong beat and solid theatrical power, was going to handle this luxuriously silky score, which contains almost no beat. And "Emeralds" is unlike anything he ever did. To suit the slow, even flow of the "Prelude" he created a shadowless green paradise of motionless motion, mondaine and elegant. And for me it was very moving that Verdy should be the presiding spirit of this civilization. The curtain rises on the traditional

Violette Verdy in "Emeralds," 1967 (photo ©1994 Martha Swope; choreography by George Balanchine ©The George Balanchine Trust)

static pose, but this time of an unusually elaborate grouping of dancers, an intricate bouquet, and I had never before been so moved by Verdy's pride and courage as I was in watching the authority with which she brought this great silent configuration into motion. Both she and Paul subsequently had brilliant and unusually full variations; Verdy's, to a finely embroidered spinning song, was a rhapsody of innocent self-enchantment—the concentration with which she examined her curving arms and hands was connoisseurship rather than narcissism; Paul's variation, set to a ballad with long, arching phrases, sent her in large circles of exploration about the stage. Paul had the great choreography of "Emeralds," a pas de deux with Moncion that represented the private life of this artificial paradise. Balanchine derived the whole dance from the quiet andante beat of the music, which yielded an even, hypnotically measured walk, interrupted at unpredictable intervals by extensions and lifts. The lovers were obeying a difficult exotic convention of courtship, different from the love relationship in classical adagio. Paul's fastidious temperament and Moncion's remote gallantry made this love-walk, in which even the mechanics of

Mimi Paul and Francisco Moncion in "Emeralds," 1967 (photo ©1994 Martha Swope; choreography by George Balanchine ©The George Balanchine Trust)

partnering are artificially codified, appear to be the demanding correctness of another culture.

"Rubies," to Stravinsky's *Capriccio*, darkens the charm of the music's motor rhythms by heavier accents. Patricia Neary's provocative poses in the opening section called to mind the sexy show dancing of the twenties and thirties, but they were more static and weighty. Near the end of the first movement, when her limbs were manipulated by four men, the effect was funnier than similar things in *Agon*, yet the quiet music kept it from being openly comic. McBride's and Villella's thorny, difficult, deliberately graceless pas de deux lacked all suggestion of conventional courtship or lovemaking, yet this couple showed an almost uncanny rapport in their difficult twisting maneuvers. Villella's solo had explosive animal force and McBride's solo an insistent nervous drive—they were alarming creatures. The finale would have been as lighthearted as *Card Game* but for the irregular phrase lengths. The high point, at which Villella circled the stage with his gang, crystallized the period-

Edward Villella with (from left) Deni Lamont and Paul Mejia in "Rubies," 1967 (photo ©1994 Martha Swope; choreography by George Balanchine ©The George Balanchine Trust)

piece nostalgia and parody you sensed throughout the ballet—it looked like a trick-cyclists' act. But its loose carefree charm was fiercely charged by Villella's brilliant speed, and the spins as he left the stage were just this side of violence.

"Diamonds" opened with the only miscalculation in the piece: the first movement is too thinly choreographed. Balanchine had wisely decided not to use the first, sonata-form movement of Tchaikovsky's Third (*Polish*) Symphony (as fifteen years earlier he had decided not to set the first movement of Mendelssohn's *Scotch Symphony*), but when he came to set the beautifully original "alla Tedesca" second movement as the opening of "Diamonds," he chose to set it without the principals and in an unusually undecorated tribute to Petipa group dancing, and the result isn't interesting enough: he claimed, inadequately, that he wanted the audience to listen to the music. But he more than made up for the lapse in the immense slow movement that followed. The dimension of this pas de deux is what bowled me over at first. Farrell danced through fifteen minutes of extreme balances and shifts of balance with no breathing spells, and often seemingly with no support. The mode is of abstraction and amplification of adagio, combined with a distillation of the dramatic imagery of nineteenth-century ballet—fleeting references to Odette's fears and alarms in act 2 of *Swan Lake,* repeated Diana-the-archer poses, and other half-narrative motifs that hint at generic dramatic action. Balanchine presented Farrell in "Diamonds" as the ballerina of the future; the range of her technique, the nuances of her style, her special accent in the familiar imagery of ballet (her almost pouter-pigeon profile, for instance) all amounted to a revision of Petipa for our time. There was a note of public manifesto to be heard, quite unlike the personal revelations of *Meditation* and *Don Quixote.* "Prima ballerina assoluta" seemed the intended effect. But these effects were not merely public grandeur. Some gestures and interactions in the pas de deux suggested a grave deep intimacy between the dancers—and this original tonality was perhaps the dance's most beautiful characteristic.

*Jewels* showed a Balanchine eager to present the Balanchine Enterprise as a large, many-faceted endeavor that included dancers of widely differing talent and temperament. The whole structure led to Farrell's appearance as its climax, to be sure, and "Diamonds" celebrated the dimension of her genius, style, and stamina as clearly as *Don Quixote* had done. But *Jewels* as a whole presented a less extreme hierarchical ranking of the dancers in the company than Balanchine's concentration on her might have been expected to have yielded at this juncture. If Farrell was *the* ballerina, Verdy, Paul, and McBride were firmly identified as principal ballerinas as well, and the differences between the four were accentuated and made exciting. Villella's unique status was acknowledged; strong cavaliers like Ludlow, Moncion, and d'Amboise were used freshly. The depth of the company's technique was displayed in stylistically subtle and technically demanding roles for Suki Schorer, Sara Leland, and John Prinz in the "Emeralds" pas de trois and for Neary in "Rubies"; and, in a canny move, Balanchine handled a public-relations issue about ballet in America by calling attention to his increasingly strong male contingent through varied use of the four demi-soloists in "Rubies," who served first as Neary's four cavaliers in a wittily ominous pas de cinq variation of the pas de deux from *Agon* and then as Villella's gang from Queens in the last movement. And all these points were made with Balanchine's characteristic depth and finesse.

In giving special attention in my article to the dancers in the New York City Ballet, I was offering a conscious defense of Balanchine against the complaint, expressed aggressively by Clive Barnes of the *New York Times,* that Balanchine was making a serious aesthetic and moral mistake by replacing "mature" dancers with "unseasoned" youth. Now it is certainly possible that mature dancers have greater depth, refinement, or finesse than twenty-two-year-olds, but Balanchine had continually proven throughout his career that this simply is not the case. His roles in Paris for the so-called baby ballerinas of the early thirties—Toumanova, Riabouchinska, and Baronova—aroused no fretting about immaturity, nor did his roles for Le Clercq in the late forties—she was seventeen when she danced in *The Four Temperaments*. Fairness to Barnes requires that I give him credit for bringing Balanchine's obsession with Farrell to public discussion, however unperceptively he did so; I wasn't nearly as candid in my own writing, and there was a general rule that one did not discuss such matters in public. But Barnes was less admirable when he hinted that he could speak of the tyranny of youth because he had the confidence of important insiders in the ballet world. I don't know whom he might have been echoing; it was certainly not the language of Melissa Hayden, one of the senior dancers who might have felt most threatened by the influx of youth in the 1960s. Her smart, forthright, detailed, and cheerful account of the new state of affairs in the Balanchine Enterprise, which Reynolds quotes in *Repertory in Review,* contains no boilerplate about *maturity* or *ripeness:*

> It was hard to hold your own. No one else danced. There was no transition—it was as though [Balanchine] had closed a book of his life and picked up another book, turned to the first page, and there was Suzanne. He loved the new crop of dancers, they had beauty, they had "bigness"—we were going into a new theater, and he wanted "bigness." We were not small fry any more. His classes changed, technically: he wanted large, flowing steps, covering space, where formerly, for instance, he had talked for hours about the articulation of the foot.

I read that last sentence ruefully, so incontrovertibly detailed is its account of how the Farrell phenomenon changed the Balanchine Enterprise and how hard that change must have been for older dancers to handle.

I now think *Jewels* as a whole may have suffered from the fact that Balanchine was presenting the company as a large unified enterprise when it was perhaps not one. My estimation of the value of the ballet's three parts has shifted greatly as the casting of leading roles has changed; "Emeralds" was my favorite at first but without Verdy and Paul it is hardly worth seeing; without the depth and richness of Farrell's bodily presence, "Diamonds" will always seem a little heartless in its mastery: "Rubies" has emerged as the one that travels best, although no one yet has recaptured Villella's combination of wit, casual charm, power, and grace. I wonder whether all three ballets were not overtailored to the dancers for whom they were made, not only for Farrell but for Verdy, Paul, and Villella. In his eagerness to do justice to those dancers he may have suspected himself of ignoring, Balanchine may have written their special identities too deeply into the heart of the roles themselves and thus made those roles difficult to pass on to dancers with different kinds of individuality.

Almost a year after the public manifesto of Farrell's stature and status in "Diamonds," Balanchine returned to the mode of *Meditation* and *Don Quixote* with another confessional ballet, *Metastaseis & Pithoprakta.* The difficult score by Iannis Xenakis belongs to the major strand of twentieth-century music that stems from Schoenberg's *Erwartung* and perhaps also from Stravinsky's *Le Sacre du Printemps,* in which a connection is both suggested and denied between two ways of transgressing conventional limits: the musical transgression of conventional listenability (whether by extreme volume, lack of continuity, or various kinds of insistence or monotony) and the violent social or sexual transgression of conventional human behavior. Balanchine's ballet transgresses conventional ballet movements. I was unmoved by the first part, *Metastaseis,* a throbbing group convulsion for twenty-two women and six men reminiscent of the "experimental" parts of *Ivesiana* that I found genre-locked and overly intentional; but I reported myself much struck by *Pithoprakta* when I wrote about it immediately following my account of *Jewels* in *Partisan Review,* although I did not come to the obvious conclusions about its meaning. *Pithoprakta* was a pas de deux for Farrell and Arthur Mitchell in which she was costumed as a B-girl in a cheap bar, while Mitchell wore even less; as he reported, Balanchine "never liked me to have a lot of clothes on in that ballet." Here is my strong and I think accurate account of its impact and my evasive analysis of its meaning:

> It begins as a *pas de deux manqué;* and the disturbing image of Mitchell going through the motions of support without daring, or being able, to touch Farrell was turned into something close to horror in the nightmarish twitches, the unmotivated stresses and displacements that took place when the two finally did touch each other, and which continued in their almost dehumanized convulsions when they separated again. The fantastic contrast between this quintessence of disorder and the three utterly different orders of *Jewels*—this is just the latest demonstration of that continuing creative excitement that makes going to see the New York City Ballet a necessity.

I could have gone on to say that the whole need for partnering was negated in the opening section, since Farrell moved without support through balances and shifts that one

Suzanne Farrell and Arthur Mitchell in *Pithoprakta,* 1968 (photo ©1994 Martha Swope; choreography by George Balanchine ©The George Balanchine Trust)

would have thought required a partner. And I could also have pointed out the unsettling ambiguities about the role of the Farrell figure, who might or might not be consciously arousing and refusing to satisfy the would-be partner's desire. And although Farrell's costume marked her behavior as virtually professional sexual teasing, her phenomenal control and assurance as an unsupported dancer made a thrillingly positive image of feminine independence and authority. Mitchell's desperate longing came across as poignant and dignified, but the character was clearly not in the same class as the woman, and the horrifying nature of their coupling when it finally happened seemed to justify what had kept them apart before.

But of course the main point I could have made was that the relationship dramatized in the ballet stood for the relationship between Balanchine and Farrell and that the disturbing aspect of this particular dramatization lay in the fact that Mitchell was black. When he hovered near Farrell, reaching out to touch her and not being able to, he was trying in the most clear-cut and unsettling way to break a sexual and social taboo, and failing. I discussed with my friends the idea that the piece represented Balanchine's sexual insistence and Farrell's refusal to give in to it. And I discussed at length the tact and taste of Balanchine's use of Mitchell's blackness as a shocking metaphor for Balanchine's own unacceptability as Farrell's lover. But if Balanchine had taken taboo-breaking as his subject, I myself was not about to in my review.

In a 1982 article about Baryshnikov's career with the New York City Ballet I took issue with the "tasteful" refusal of the press to point out that Balanchine was ill for most of the time Baryshnikov danced with the company and that therefore he could not work with him as Baryshnikov must have expected when he chose to join the company, and I connected this evasiveness with the earlier refusal to discuss the personal implications of the ballets Balanchine made for Farrell in the 1960s and afterward. But I forgot that I, too, in writing about *Don Quixote* and other Farrell ballets, had never spelled out the implications of that relationship. And I forgot too how fearful I had been of openly discussing *Pithoprakta*. Perhaps I was right to be afraid of the clarity and overtness of Balanchine's expressive act: if you describe what is going on in this ballet to an outsider, it might sound as if Balanchine was out of aesthetic control, and I was perhaps leery of attempting to explain why I disagreed with that assessment. I was not alone in my uneasiness: Reynolds reports a consensus that *Metastaseis* was "the more compelling of the two sections," but that wasn't my sense of things then. *Pithoprakta* made a big impression, although it may have been little spoken of out of nervousness over the ballet's implications and what they promised about the future of the company. None of the reviews Reynolds summarizes refers either to Mitchell's blackness or to the known relation between Balanchine and Farrell: in many of the reviews Farrell herself was barely mentioned, as if the charged casting of the piece was accidental or coincidental.

I discovered later that it may, in fact, have been chance that created the essence of the piece. In her 1990 autobiography, *Holding on to the Air*, Farrell reports: "The motif of the dance was that we barely ever actually touched; but, as was often the case, this had come about by accident. Before the premiere we had filmed our dance as a record of the choreography, but because Arthur was unable to be there I danced the pas de deux alone. Mr. B thought it looked interesting, and when Arthur returned he told him only to pretend to partner me; thus our interactions took on an alienated tone." Had I been a City Ballet insider, I might have known this before I saw the ballet, although whether it would have changed my view or my feelings about the final product I can't be sure; I am sure that I'm glad I did not know it. But it makes little difference, for Balanchine's use of chance was like

Shakespeare's, not Merce Cunningham's; he was perfectly willing to see that what had happened by chance was in fact "what he really wanted to say." Incidentally, Farrell's failure to note the connection between the situation of *Pithoprakta* and what was going on between her and Balanchine is one of the many ways in which her book is disappointing, although it also represents the standard way of handling these issues.

Balanchine's next assignment for Farrell, *Slaughter on Tenth Avenue* in May 1968, was generally not well received, and I suppose it did not deserve to be. But Clive Barnes's heavy pondering of the value of the work and of Balanchine's reason for staging it struck me as disingenuous: "Balanchine's choreography is musical but here very dated. It is a pastiche sanctioned by nostalgia and sanctioned by history, but it remains a perfunctory, feeble work. If the magic name of Balanchine were not attached to it, it would be very properly mocked off the stage." Readers were meant to spot the infatuation with Farrell that caused Balanchine to seek out this particular nostalgia, and Barnes's failure to take notice of Farrell's presence in the ballet was his sly way of honestly failing to see what all the shouting was about as far as Farrell was concerned.

I myself enjoyed both the ballet and the sense it gave me of being again in a semi-conspiratorial relationship with Balanchine in his decision to stage it. Reworking *Slaughter* for Farrell recertified her centrality to Balanchine's career by forging another strong link between her and his past, in this instance his success on Broadway in the 1930s. It was the two narrative dances, "La Princesse Zenobia Ballet" and "Slaughter on Tenth Avenue Ballet," in the 1936 Rodgers and Hart musical *On Your Toes* that made Balanchine a major presence in show business. The occasion reunited him professionally with his first wife, Tamara Geva, who had become a Broadway personage a couple of years earlier: she danced both the ballerina in the parody-Oriental Zenobia number and the stripper in "Slaughter." Vera Zorina, soon to become an object of infatuation and his second wife, entered Balanchine's life when she was chosen to dance the same roles in the ensuing London production and in the Hollywood film that was released in 1939. In asking the audience at the New York State Theater in 1968 to contemplate this corny relic now reincarnated in the phenomenal Farrell, Balanchine was not only being nostalgic but for the first time producing a genuine version of that pastoral America he had jokingly dreamed about in Europe, the country where the girls would all look like Ginger Rogers.

I had not seen *On Your Toes* on the stage but had seen the film some time in the 1940s; by 1968 I remembered very little about the dancing, so the restaging for Farrell satisfied my curiosity about the famous number, as well as enchanted me by the accurate wit of Farrell's striptease style and tone. But her accuracy came into sharp focus for me only many years later, when in the 1984 public broadcasting documentary on Balanchine I saw a clip of Zorina's dancing from the film. A great deal instantly fell into place: Zorina's opulent and openly inviting sexuality told me some of the secret of Balanchine's infatuation with her in the thirties and also offered a fascinating contrast with Farrell's coolly accessible but not in the least inviting sexuality, which invoked not Zorina but the tone and style of the originator of this image in Balanchine's imagination—Ginger Rogers, whose physical, social, and sexual manner James Harvey has caught exactly:

> There's a fleeting but memorable image of her in *Stage Door*, when Adolphe Menjou first spots her in a chorus line at the rehearsal studio. She is in the middle of a line of girls, all in rehearsal clothes, arms linked behind their backs, heads turned to the left, eyes lowered, as they kick their legs out to the tinny piano sound. It's the basic chorus-girl stance, legs out and heads turned away; but for Rogers it's almost epiphanic, capturing something so essential about her that it brings a shock of recognition when you see it: it's that mixture of displayed flesh and averted eye, both presenting and withholding herself at the same time. Just as when Menjou goes backstage at the nightclub to ask her for a date, she seems both agreeable and hostile at the same time.

Regardless of whether Farrell's balletic transfiguration of Ginger Rogers was a conscious decision on either her or Balanchine's part, the result was a revelation about style, both for itself and for the sake of history.

After *Slaughter on Tenth Avenue* an amusing but disquieting rumor went around that Balanchine was planning a *Salome* for Farrell, using excerpts from Berg's *Lulu*. I doubted whether it was to be taken seriously, but I was nervous anyway. Oscar Wilde, Frank Wedekind, and Alban Berg were attractive collaborators—Berg seemed particularly appropriate for the choreographer of the Webern *Episodes*—and there was something appealing about accepting the subject but not the terrible music of Richard Strauss's opera. But Farrell as Salome seemed too angry and hostile an idea to be workable, and as far as I know nothing ever came of it. I took the rumor itself as a sign of general uneasiness.

If, in the last analysis, I was not worried about what was going on in the Balanchine Enterprise, the simple reason was that I shared Balanchine's estimate of Suzanne Farrell. I knew that he was in great personal disorder about his relationship with her, and I saw him revealing this in his ballets, but the ballets seemed to be truly separate from his personal problems; they had been released into the world of art. And everything that I saw about the workings of the company suggested that Balanchine was attending satisfactorily to his job of composing for the public theater and running a large theatrical institution. If I suffered from "Farrellitis" it took the form of a certain oblivion to the other dancers. I hardly noticed that Balanchine gave Villella no good new roles after "Rubies." When in 1967 Balanchine used music of a favorite composer, Glinka, for a four-part work called *Glinkiana,* he included a bland classical suite for Villella and McBride, two cheesy national dances for Hayden and Verdy (Spanish and French, respectively, which both dancers put over well although neither could have derived much pleasure from the experience), and—in the one good section—a fleeting, leaping evanescence for Paul and John Clifford, *Valse Fantaisie,* which was Paul's last role before she left the company. (This section was set to music Balanchine had used in 1953 for a ballet for Diana Adams, Patricia Wilde, and Tanaquil Le Clercq, and it is likely that this is the only music he really liked—the other pieces merely showed his loyalty to Glinka.) *Glinkiana* had no unity or identity apart from its music, and soon only *Valse Fantaisie* remained in the repertory. But although Balanchine's concentration on Farrell may have been responsible for the thinness of *Glinkiana,* I didn't make that connection in 1967—he had made pieces as weak before. And I did not regard the fact that he gave Villella and McBride no other new roles between 1967 and 1970 as a serious lapse—I thought of Balanchine as otherwise occupied.

In 1968, for instance, Balanchine put a lot of energy into the making of *La Source,* to music he really did like, by Delibes; this was a project he was interested in for the music and also for the broader purpose of training a new dancer. He enlisted Verdy's aid in teaching the young, talented, and attractive John Prinz how to be a danseur noble. Bernard Haggin attended the rehearsals, and what he told me about them showed Balanchine giving himself fully to the project. Prinz performed well enough at the ballet's premiere, but he did not have the stamina or the self-confidence to achieve the goal he and Balanchine had set for him. But in itself, the project shows that Balanchine was giving at least some thought and energy to the artistic welfare of his company during this period. He wanted to see Farrell dance very often, true, but this did not bother me, for I wanted to see her dance as often as he did. The repertory was already huge and richly varied; I felt no sense of sterility as I eagerly returned to the ballets of the past. These were not lean years for me nor—I take the chance of saying—for many in the audience.

I thought of Balanchine's relationship with Farrell as being in the service of his own inspiration—he gave as much imagination, concern, and attention to the needs of all his

Violette Verdy and John Prinz in *La Source,* 1968 (photo ©1994 Martha Swope; choreography by George Balanchine ©The George Balanchine Trust)

dancers as he could, while reserving the time and energy he needed for the task to which his vocation was calling him most intensely. And this still seems to me the right attitude to take.

So far was I from believing that things were amiss in the Balanchine Enterprise that my chief concern during this period was not worry about the company but the defense of Balanchine against Clive Barnes's attacks. For Barnes, Farrell's style, technique, and manner, far from representing the dancing of a genius and the fulfillment of the Balanchine tradition, presented instead the arrogant preening of an incorrectly trained dancer who was indulged by her master out of sexual infatuation rather than artistic insight. And Barnes expressed elaborate regret at Balanchine's practices because they denied audiences the rich performances of mature and seasoned dancers and denied those dancers the chance to bring their careers to fulfillment in important roles. In this view, Balanchine either had never had, or had lost, an eye for the depth of workmanship, discipline, and feeling that comes only from years of dancing and living. The old charge of overathleticism surfaced again, and Balanchine was accused of showing a lack of regard for spiritual, dramatic, or imaginative qualities in dancing, of preferring the muscular power of youth because of its embodiment of some cruel conception of the ideal body and also, so the implication went, because young dancers lacked the experience and the will to resist his tyranny.

The charge of injustice toward other dancers still worries me. Maybe Balanchine's concentration on Farrell did hurt the chances of her coevals, Mimi Paul, Marnee Morris, Suki Schorer, Gloria Govrin, and Patricia Neary; maybe it prevented them from ascending to prima ballerina status; but there is no actual evidence of this. It is true that Paul announced publicly that she was leaving the company for American Ballet Theatre because she felt neglected, but her interest in dancing the nineteenth-century classics was surely also a factor in that decision. She, however, was securely ensconced in the rank of principal dancer at the New York City Ballet and she was receiving a share of rich roles; she may not have been in the favored position of Farrell, but whether that means she was neglected is another story. She danced Giselle for the American Ballet Theatre without much success, and she did not have time to grow into the role—nor did she have a Balanchine to learn from; she soon retired into teaching, and I should imagine that most people think she should have stayed with Balanchine.

Govrin, Neary, and Schorer were each in their different ways out of scale for prima ballerina status, although Balanchine himself may have encouraged Govrin and Neary to believe otherwise. Since my fondest memory of the two of them is of their dancing the finale of *Raymonda Variations* in 1961, they must have become brilliant dancers early in their careers. Although they may have felt they were underused over the next several years, the record does not bear this out. Govrin made a hit on the company's 1962 tour of the Soviet Union and had great success in 1964 as the Good Fairy in *Harlequinade* and as the second lead in the first movement of the *Brahms-Schoenberg Quartet* in 1966, but she was in and out of the company because of overweight and finally disappeared.

Neary was given a brilliant major role in "Rubies" in 1967 but at the second rank. She is supposed to have taken Balanchine's denial of her off-the-wall request to dance *Swan Lake* as her reason for seeking her fortune elsewhere. Balanchine's refusal to grant her demand did not show insensitivity to her interests, given her lack of conventional stage beauty, but of course she did not see it that way. On the other hand, although she may have left in anger she remained within Balanchine's orbit later as the head of the Geneva Ballet, to which she brought a large part of the Balanchine repertory.

Schorer's repertory gradually expanded beyond the soubrette roles she danced with perfection in *A Midsummer Night's Dream* and *Harlequinade,* and Balanchine found new qualities in her in the "Pas de Deux Mauresque" in *Don Quixote* in 1965 and the pas de trois in *Jewels* in 1967; but she returned to the soubrette category in *La Source* and eventually decided on early retirement in 1971, having with Balanchine's encouragement discovered early her gift for teaching by trying her hand at the School of American Ballet. As I have mentioned, she did, in fact, achieve ballerina status in my eyes in the first movement of *Symphony in C* at the end of the sixties. Certainly her pleasure at not having to be "cute" in *Don Quixote* carries an undertone of discontent with her repertory, and I am sure that from time to time she did feel stuck in soubrette roles. But it is hard to determine whether Balanchine should or could have been more sensitive to her feelings earlier than he was. There isn't time for everything, and Balanchine needed Schorer's theatrical identity in his repertory—despite his preference for tall dancers, his conception of a complete repertory for a complete company involved roles for small dancers, ballet tradition being full of such roles. Schorer was already getting the chance to dance in a different mode by being cast in the floating "Unanswered Question" dance in *Ivesiana* and other more lyrical roles; later in her career she danced principal roles like the Paul role in "Emeralds," with its sweeping solo and its mysterious pas de deux; she had early been given the Le Clercq variation in *Divertimento No. 15,* and so on. And Balanchine did, eventually, "look at her in a new way" in *Don Quixote.* What this adds up to for me is that in a large company, even with several coaches and different casting practices, not every dancer will be satisfied with the direction and the speed of her career; perhaps it was one of Balanchine's gifts to remain slightly impervious to this kind of chronic but irremediable dissatisfaction.

Morris presents a more troubling case. I singled out her perfectionism for praise when I wrote about the company in 1967, and from the beginning I was moved by her dedication, but I don't remember finding her dancing thrilling until I saw the tape of *Who Cares?* in which she danced the wonderful "My One and Only" solo with what Arlene Croce calls her "vanilla-wafer charm." It was never clear how interesting Balanchine found her. She re-mained a soloist for a long time, longer perhaps than she might have done had Farrell not absorbed Balanchine's attention. It seemed her destiny to dance the second lead in *Concerto Barocco* while Farrell danced the lead, and although she did the angel of death role in *Serenade* early on, she never danced the heroine. Balanchine did not make roles for her worthy of her gifts until *Who Cares?* and *Tchaikovsky Suite No. 3* in 1970, after Farrell had left. It did not occur to me at the time that Morris was being unfairly kept at a lower level, although her unhappy departure from the profession shows that her sense of self-worth may have been badly damaged by the way she was treated in the Balanchine Enterprise. Her fine performances in *Concerto Barocco* and as Polyhymnia in *Apollo* and her fragrant

Marnee Morris in *Who Cares?* 1970 (photo ©1994 Martha Swope; choreography by George Balanchine
©The George Balanchine Trust)

presence and dancing in *Who Cares?* are on record in the Canadian Broadcasting Company
videos from 1969 and 1971.

I was annoyed that Barnes focused on Farrell's immaturity, but in the long run I was
educated by having to answer his charges—it started me thinking about what maturity
looks like. An older dancer might have a more richly inflected, more ripely nuanced reading
of a role than a nineteen-year-old girl—experience ought to mean something, and this has
actually been true of some great dancers. But it is not the way great things necessarily
happen, as Glenn Gould was making clear in the music world at the same time that Farrell
was dancing. In the familiar sense of the word Gould was more mature at twenty-five than
he was at forty—less eccentric, less mannered, less interested in showing you the inner
voices of music that does not have interesting inner voices, and so on. There is a natural
musical good sense in the debut recording of the *Goldberg Variations* in 1955 which, as
embodied in that extraordinarily sensitive pianistic athleticism, makes it some of the
greatest piano playing ever done, technically, imaginatively, and emotionally, whereas the

1980 recording of the *Goldberg Variations* is a bit overemphatic and discontinuous in its pedagogy.

Dance is a physical art in which maturity brings inevitable and painful problems, not to speak of actual disabilities. I became aware of the cost of a certain kind of maturity when Maria Tallchief returned from her maternity leave after 1962: she *looked* the same, the configuration of her body in outline was what it had been before, and her phrasing, attack, and continuity were all recognizably Tallchief, but when you go to the ballet you also participate in the dancing with your body, and my body told me that her distinctive power was gone. Gradually she recovered a bit, but not enough, of the old force; although she rightly continued until 1965 to command the status of senior ballerina in the company, she was no longer for me a dancer who created major experiences.

Farrell's thrillingly swift or gorgeously slow extensions into arabesque, taken by themselves, might seem analogous to a new record set by an Olympic athlete—a testimony to advances in athletic education and nutrition. It was not the swiftness alone of those extensions that made them extraordinary, however, but the combination of swiftness with a delicacy of articulation, which yielded an alive, spontaneous flame of energy that you actually saw and felt as it created those arabesques and united all of her gestures into one continuous unfolding and outpouring.

This great gift was apparently not a matter of head work, of taste or conscious planning on Farrell's part, as far as one could see, and it was perhaps in part because her face remained so uninvolved, so unthoughtful, throughout the performances of the sixties that people accounted for Balanchine's predilection for Farrell only in terms of personal infatuation. I discussed this characteristic of Farrell's in my *Partisan Review* piece about the dancers at the New York City Ballet:

> She is not, and probably never will be, a notably warm or dramatic dancer in herself. And she seems almost entirely to lack Verdy's artistic intelligence and dedication: she doesn't seem to shape her roles by conscious decision. Farrell's grace, taste, warmth—her personality itself—all these seem the unconscious external manifestations of quintessential physical gifts. Denby, in one of his wonderful simplicities, wrote that the basic secret of ballet dancing, as of all kinds of dancing, is how to keep your balance when you are moving very fast and changing direction suddenly. Farrell has this gift to a degree you never thought possible. . . . When the radical simplicity of Farrell's dance inspiration isn't doing its job, nothing more complex or

intelligent or civilized is there to take over. I have never been lucky enough to see Verdy's *Sonnambula,* but I have it on the best authority that she enters with an electrifying intensity that hasn't been seen since Danilova's unforgettable performances, and I can easily believe it: her musical and dramatic sense would make her want to carry through the implications of the agitated music. . . . But it's clear Farrell doesn't really understand the music. She stalks in on pointe most beautifully, but never projects the meaning that the sleepwalker is desperately, inexplicably, suffering. Yet later in the *pas de deux* you almost stop breathing during that slow, high arabesque at the right front of the stage, an effect that didn't come from understanding the meaning—which nobody would miss anyway—but simply from making the movement on the largest scale possible.

A couple of chance encounters with Farrell confirmed my sense of her basic manner of proceeding. One Saturday or Sunday afternoon, after a performance of *Don Quixote* in which she had seemed even more magnificent than ever, if that was conceivable, I was discussing her dancing with friends in the Lincoln Center plaza when she appeared under the arcade of the New York State Theater, accompanied by Edward Bigelow, the company stage manager (I learned later that Balanchine detailed him to escort her everywhere, for various kinds of protection—against fans maybe, rapists perhaps, suitors certainly). My excitement about the performance led me to go up and say something like, "You were really wonderful this afternoon," to which she had literally nothing to say, nor did she show the least hint of "manner" or style or even courtesy in acknowledging my compliment: she looked at me blankly, even a bit hostilely, as if I had said something a little offensive, then turned away. Her brushing me off matched my account of her identity gratifyingly, but it did not make her inability to receive praise any more gratifying. And I had another unencouraging experience at the Empire Coffee Shop on Broadway at 63rd Street, a dreary place to which members of the company often went after the evening performance: my friends and I would go there to see them.

One evening we watched for what I remember as being close to an hour while at a nearby table Balanchine tried to mesmerize Farrell—talking nonstop to her about subjects we were just too far away to catch, although his gestures suggested he was describing ballets or dancing he had seen. She was barely managing to stay awake while he was talking, but he seemed not to notice. This public drama was enthrallingly interesting and exciting at the time; it did not seem as poignant and slightly queasy-making as it does now. I can't quite bring back why we took it so lightly then, since we certainly understood that Balanchine was trying to win Farrell and that she didn't want to be won. But it was the imperviousness of her ordinariness that really struck me; she seemed unreachable. That unreachability is why I did not think of including her in the group of dancers to whom I considered sending my article about the dancers at the New York City Ballet.

I sent it instead to Verdy. I thought of her as having intellectual—and in particular musical—interests that Farrell did not have. This judgment came partly from what I had heard about Verdy from Haggin, who had not met her socially but had observed her in rehearsals, had interviewed Villella about her, and had appealing anecdotes about her that made it clear she was someone with good things to say—her articulate wit, in fact, was becoming quite famous. Her dancing confirmed this identity; indeed, I had focused on her cultivated stylistic habits in my article: her musicality, the sense she gave of having points to make, of thinking her roles through deeply. And my decision to send her the article had the most satisfactory results in the form of a warmly and elegantly phrased answer that led me to take the step of getting to know her. The *Hudson Review* was celebrating its twentieth anniversary in 1968 and Fred Morgan, its founder and editor, gave a party on a boat circling Manhattan, to which I was invited and to which I decided to take Verdy, both to get to know her myself and to show her that I had smart friends—and also, I think, to avoid the anxiety of having to do the entire job of entertaining her, since Haggin and other friends of mine who wrote for the review would be on hand. The evening worked out exactly as planned.

Verdy turned out to be brilliantly intelligent, articulate, and self-aware as an artist and woman, and as charming, chic, open, and warm as her stage persona had promised. Soon after this party I arranged to meet her during the company's summer season in Saratoga Springs, New York, where my friends Jane Mayhall and Leslie Katz (who were connected with Yaddo, where I had met them) gave a party in which they introduced her to Yaddo people, after which she became a regular dinner guest at that artists' colony during the City Ballet's annual July Saratoga season. I felt privileged and proud to have made an arrangement which gave pleasure all around, and I was able to introduce Verdy to people who became important friends, advisers, and even gurus of hers.

It was through getting to know Verdy that I first became aware in detail of what many dancers of the New York City Ballet were having to endure because of Balanchine's preoccupation with Farrell. And I heard the story with a highly ambivalent attention. I remember vividly a conversation at dinner with Verdy and Madame Guillerm, her mother, a powerful woman whom I immediately liked and respected. (I was to discover later how famously, almost infamously, powerful a ballet mother she was, and I was to think about her relationship with Verdy a lot during her last years, when she had become completely estranged from her daughter.) The subject of our conversation was not just "Farrellitis" but Balanchine's general way of treating his dancers. Mme Guillerm claimed credit for having had the wisdom to keep Verdy from quitting many times when she had been upset by the way Balanchine was neglecting her, and her argument was just what mine would have been: that Balanchine's company was the only place to be in the ballet world and that no manner or amount of ill-treatment would justify depriving oneself of the education and prestige of being there. I do not think that Mimi Paul had yet left the company, but she was frankly discussed as an example of how not to behave on this matter, although Mme Guillerm's expression of disapproval—"Mimi is selfish"—seemed old-fashioned and not quite to the point. I knew what she meant, however. During this evening I learned that Verdy had once gotten together the two most important people of her artistic life, Balanchine and Pierre Boulez, at a dinner party, with disappointing results: Boulez did a lot of talking, Balanchine did none, and no sense of rapport was achieved. I felt warmly sympathetic with her for attempting this enterprise; it was the kind of thing that I myself might have attempted and been equally disappointed in.

I had come to know Villella when Haggin brought him and McBride to MIT and Wellesley to help illustrate his lecture on the relation between *Apollo* and traditional pre-Balanchine ballet. And when Verdy and Villella both came to Boston to dance *Giselle* with the Boston Ballet in 1968, I gave a party for them. My best memory of enjoying and being excited by knowing dancers is of sessions between *Giselle* rehearsals in Boston when I talked with Villella and Verdy about many things, including what it was like to rehearse *Dances at a Gathering* at the New York City Ballet. They had both always been candid about having found the Balanchine Enterprise physically difficult to be a part of, but their main point now about Jerome Robbins concerned the way he kept dancers standing around while he was waiting for his inspiration to happen, instead of following Balanchine's practice of calling them for rehearsal only when he was ready to choreograph for them. (Since everybody seems to agree that Balanchine did not work out his choreography before he was actually working with dancers, the suggestion is that he regulated his own habits by his respect for dancers; he would at least decide in advance which dancers he was going to use for what music, and then even if that did not work out ideally, he would remain committed to his basic first idea.) Verdy and Villella reported that Robbins would also insist that different dancers learn the dance he was making at the same time, so that he could ask them, "Now show me how it looks on you, Kay [Mazzo]," and so on. He would make different versions of a single dance and make the dancer learn them all: "Now show me version 4,

Allegra." I enjoyed the implicit compliment Villella and Verdy paid to Balanchine for not having Robbins's bad habits.

I thought Verdy's and Villella's *Giselle* in Boston wonderful, but I don't remember consciously thinking that one of the reasons why it was taking place was that neither dancer was getting much attention from Balanchine after *Jewels* in 1967. I was aware that Balanchine had made no difficulty about their appearing in these ventures, but I asked neither them nor myself about the implications of this fact. Much later it occurred to me that in the days before Farrell, Balanchine must have wanted all his dancers on hand all the time, just as he wanted to see them all in company class every morning. He let some dancers appear on television because that did not take them away from New York, but his dancers almost never made guest appearances with other companies except as part of the New York City Ballet outreach program. But I discussed none of this with Verdy and Villella in Boston. I remember simply feeling glad that they were expanding their dancing by appearing in Boston and Washington, not only in *Giselle* but in *La Sylphide,* which I saw only on film. The two did talk about Balanchine's relationship with Farrell but not pointedly or explicitly enough for me to be alerted to watching the company for signs of disintegrating morale. And now I am unclear about why they did not say more: partly out of good manners and courteous reticence, and partly, perhaps, because they could easily gather how enthusiastic I was about Farrell, and they did not want to go into the subject.

I have continued to see Verdy often and with great pleasure, but I'm ashamed to say I haven't really learned much about ballet or about Balanchine from her. Some of this derives from my reluctance to learn anything about ballet technique—time after time I have planned to attend ballet classes regularly in order to learn the terminology and to train my eye to recognize correctness, but good intentions have never gotten me there. On the other hand, I'm not sure what I would have learned even if I were equipped to understand Verdy's professional perspective. I think the cold truth is that I never wanted my own judgment of Balanchine and of his style and technique to be affected by any outside influence, even one so authoritative as that of one of his leading dancers.

I realize now how seldom I actually discussed the ballet with Verdy, in general or with regard to particular works. I praised her dancing often and enthusiastically, though no more than I wanted to or than it deserved, yet I didn't really bring up ballet subjects. We talked a great deal about Balanchine, but it comes back to me that there was a distinct limit on the questions I asked, the issues I raised. I certainly was nervous about expressing my admiration for Farrell when I was with Verdy, and this nervousness may have had an inhibiting effect on any talk about ballet; and there was one painful episode in which I did offend

Verdy by my enthusiasm about Farrell. But I also remember something much pleasanter: after Farrell had returned to the company I mentioned to Verdy how strange, though thrilling, Farrell had looked when she first danced the *Tchaikovsky Pas de Deux,* and this appealed to Verdy's authoritative knowledge about the body in ballet, as well as to her generosity, for she enjoyed explaining to me in detail exactly how a ballet originally made for a short body—her own, in fact—would necessarily force a tall dancer like Farrell to adjust the choreography to her own body, a process which could take a long time.

It occurs to me now that a less anxious and more imaginative—and nicer—person than I would have found a way to ask Verdy more questions and would thus have learned more than I did. Even so, an embarrassingly large percentage of those questions would have been about Farrell. When Farrell came to do Verdy's last Balanchine role, *Sonatine,* Verdy had left the company, and I never talked to her about Farrell's marvelous performance, which I liked as much as I had Verdy's; I do not know whether Verdy ever saw Farrell's performance—probably not, but I should have tried to discuss it in technical detail with her. When I praised Farrell's performance in an article for *Raritan,* I drew on what I had learned from Verdy by bringing up her analysis of Farrell's *Tchaikovsky Pas de Deux,* and I would have learned more had I questioned her more searchingly about all sorts of matters. One source of inhibition was my continuing nervousness at the thought of becoming an insider in the Balanchine Enterprise. That is one thing that kept me from asking Verdy for the full details of the Balanchine-Farrell drama. And the result was that in these years I was thoroughly preoccupied by this drama while remaining in ignorance of most of the facts about it, and I was in consequence unprepared for the denouement.

The end of the Balanchine-Farrell affair took place on May 8, 1969. While Balanchine was continuing to pursue Farrell unsuccessfully, she had begun to go around with a young company dancer, Paul Mejia. When Balanchine discovered this, he stopped casting Mejia in the few solo roles he had been beginning to get, but then intercession by friends and colleagues persuaded Balanchine to restore Mejia's roles. By 1968 Farrell and Mejia were in love and had decided to marry; the marriage took place in February 1969, whereupon Balanchine ordered Mejia not to come to the theater any more, although he did not officially fire him; again Balanchine was persuaded to restore a few of Mejia's roles. But Farrell decided to put her belief that she could convince Balanchine to accept her marriage to the test on the occasion of the Spring Gala Benefit Program on May 8. Two new works were to be previewed, John Clifford's *Prelude, Gigue and Riffs* and Robbins's *Dances at a Gathering,* with the program to be filled out by *Symphony in C.* As a special treat for the benefit audience, Villella was initially down to perform one of his early parts, the third movement of *Symphony in C,* which he had outgrown years earlier, as well as the leading role in *Dances at a Gathering.* At the last moment he decided not to do the Bizet, whereupon Farrell and Mejia suggested that Mejia, who had often danced the role, take Villella's place. When Balanchine refused, Farrell gave him an ultimatum: unless Mejia danced the third movement, she would not dance the second movement as planned. Balanchine again refused, Farrell offered her resignation, and Balanchine accepted it; he replaced *Symphony in C* with *Stars and Stripes.* Mejia never returned to the company, and Farrell did not come back until almost six years later, making her reappearance again in the slow movement of *Symphony in C* early in 1975.

This is the version of the story I heard almost immediately after the event, I forget from whom, and although I have heard variants of the details, this seems to be what happened. My response was the one I was to have when Villella told me about his difficulties with Balanchine: I saw everyone's side. I felt shame for everyone—for Balanchine's jealousy and lack of self-control, for Farrell's overestimation of her power, for Mejia's insignificance as the bone of contention—but I also felt the justice of everyone's grievance. Farrell's departure from the company for six years was human energy wasted. Everyone suffered, no one profited, not even in amour propre—neither Farrell nor Balanchine nor, of course, the audience.

The dancers who inherited Farrell's repertory—Karin von Aroldingen, Kay Mazzo, and Sara Leland—did gain a prominence they probably would not have had if Farrell had not left, but the circumstances under which they advanced cannot have given them much pleasure or satisfaction, and the general judgment is that they did not bloom in the Farrell roles. Mazzo replaced Paul acceptably in *Liebeslieder Walzer* and became a major dancer in her own right in two roles Balanchine created for her in 1972, *Stravinsky Violin Concerto* and *Duo Concertant;* her face and bearing were distinctive and her dancing elegant and clear, but it was dry, too, and her range and energy were limited. Leland and von Aroldingen danced a great deal, and they danced well in a couple of good new roles, but in my judgment they rarely rose above the rank of utility dancer. Indeed, Balanchine used von Aroldingen to replace Farrell so often that she became something of a pariah among us Farrell fans—so much so that I was surprised to be so touched by the beauty of his tribute in the roles he made for her in *Vienna Waltzes* and *Robert Schumann's "Davidsbündlertänze"* after Farrell returned. *Meditation* and *Pithoprakta* were dropped, but Balanchine kept all the other Farrell ballets in the repertory. With *Don Quixote* this was a problematic decision: Mazzo's and Leland's failure to carry the Dulcinea role ought perhaps to have led Balanchine to drop a ballet that depended so centrally on Farrell, but he may not have been ready to acknowledge that fact, and the brilliant roles for other young dancers in the second and third acts made it an important repertory piece.

I missed Farrell when she was away, but her absence was not an entirely negative experience, for I was fascinated to watch her roles in other hands. I felt I was seeing her and enjoying her dancing behind her replacements, and I discovered in that way why I found her dancing so exciting. I would never have been particularly bothered by Mazzo's inadequate performance in *Movements for Piano and Orchestra*, since I was not a great admirer of the ballet, but in fact Mazzo's performance had the effect of positively *showing* me the marvelous body power and energy under Farrell's imperturbability. I would have said that *Don Quixote* was not worth seeing without Farrell, but I watched both Leland and Mazzo in it several times, and learned more about Farrell from each experience. I would have continued to go to *Jewels* because of Verdy, Villella, and McBride, but I don't remember ever leaving early so as to miss Mazzo's "Diamonds": I was checking why it seemed so weak and juiceless. I saw Mazzo's performance so often, in fact, that it seemed a long time before a better substitute for Farrell was found, although my program shows that it was actually in the fall of 1970 that I first saw Allegra Kent in the role.

Kent's strangely strong and soft *Agon* had alternated with Farrell's dancing of it before Farrell left, and Kent continued to dance it in Farrell's absence. But "Diamonds" was harder and took longer, since it asked for a stamina that only Farrell had in those days and that Kent did not quite have, though hers was in other respects a magnificent performance. The dress rehearsal for her first "Diamonds" and the performance itself form one of my great ballet memories. It was September 2, 1970, in the days when the company still had an early fall season, and I had returned that very day from Venice. Kent's performance was excitingly unlike Farrell's—the only mode for acceptable replacement, of course—New York was brilliant and glamorous in the early fall weather, and my friend Richard Harrier and I felt ourselves perfect Gautier *flaneurs* as we took our drinks between rehearsal and performance at the sunken café outside the General Motors building across Fifth Avenue from the Plaza Hotel. This was a building you were not supposed to like, since it had replaced the more elegant Savoy Plaza, but on that day its café went right along with Kent and "Diamonds," the sunlight and the street life, to make New York the only city in the world worth coming home to from Venice. Only New York had Balanchine.

I thought of Balanchine during this period as missing Farrell in the simplest way. I saw proof of it in *Tchaikovsky Suite No. 3*, a new ballet that he had created by reviving *Theme and Variations* (which he had set for Ballet Theatre in 1947 to the fourth movement of the

Tchaikovsky suite) and adding new choreography for the first three movements. When I saw the premiere on December 3, 1970, Farrell's absence, and presence, seemed to me to be the subject of all the new sections, and the experience registered as far from negative. The new material is not first-class Balanchine, but I was enthralled to see von Aroldingen, Mazzo and Morris being asked to impersonate the missing Farrell. Every gesture of this composite ballerina, particularly in the opening elegy, reminded me of Farrell: it was an elegy for her as *Meditation* had been a love poem for and to her. *Elegie* does, in fact, rather resemble *Meditation* in tone and mood, though it is more elaborately worked and not as good. The lyricism of *Meditation* goes by quickly, but *Elegie* lingers over its poetry of love and loss; the choreography does not so much suit the music as underline its near-banality. It was entirely characteristic of Balanchine to use the resources of his St. Petersburg tradition, however banal, to express his loss. He remained committed to the scale of Farrell's dancing, again particularly in the *Elegie*. Von Aroldingen, who danced this section, was tall and blonde with regular, handsome features, a muscular broad-shouldered body, and some real presence; she had attracted notice for some time in the corps and had danced a few solos before this, and she went on to inherit many Farrell roles and to play a major role in Balanchine's private life until his death. But since she entirely lacked Farrell's electric flow of energy and infallible sensitivity, the scale of her dancing often gave the effect of coarseness and overemphasis. Mazzo and Morris handled their impersonations with more finesse, though with nothing like Farrell's impact.

The chance to make comparisons such as these was at hand during every performance of the New York City Ballet during Farrell's absence, and I took the opportunities offered. It would have seemed to me folly to "try to be fair," to give credit where credit was due or not to let the best be the enemy of the good or to want to understand the other dancers' points of view. I was of a mind that George Bernard Shaw captures so wittily when explaining his own predilection for exaggerated comparisons: "For my part, I should not like to call Schumann a sentimental trifler and Brahms a pretentious blockhead; but if the average man was a Mozart, that is how they would be generally described."

ELEVEN / *Disconnected*

The loss of Suzanne Farrell interrupted the steady attention and sense of forward movement with which I had been following the Balanchine-Farrell relationship, and while she was away, from May 1969 to January 1975, my relation to the entire Balanchine Enterprise suffered an intermission in focus and collaborative illusion. Changes in my own life further complicated things. My life as a teacher was branching out. I had become more involved in department and college politics during the sixties, serving on important college committees and as chairman of the department. In 1966 I began to spend two and a half weeks every summer teaching film at a Danforth Workshop in Liberal Education held at Colorado College, and this new and enjoyable work led to teaching film at Wellesley and to writing about it; it also led to thinking about the student activism that was on everyone's mind at the workshop. Eventually I spent a year in college administration as acting dean of my college. None of these changes lessened my interest in Balanchine or the time I spent watching his ballets (although I could not go to New York often in 1972–73, when I was dean), but they all worked together to interrupt the current of my interest; following his work during these years stopped being the organizing center to my life that it had been in the Farrell years.

I even deserted Balanchine's art itself to some degree, though only briefly, in an unexpected fallout from the most dramatic experience of these years. In the fall of 1969 Bernard Haggin and I broke off relations. I had often let myself be persuaded to rehash earlier episodes in our relationship in which we had either quarreled or been temporarily estranged—particularly episodes in which he thought I had failed him. These misguided and difficult sessions never satisfied his standards of certainty about what had happened and why, so consenting to take part in them was always a mistake on my part; but he was insistent and I was, to put it mildly, deeply under his sway. In February 1969 he raised one of these issues again in a long letter—it was about a quarrel he had had with our friend Paul Bertram in Paul's room in Leverett House at Harvard in, I think, 1955—and I must have answered evasively, because we were estranged briefly at the beginning of the summer. But I wanted to get along with him, and I tried to interest him in a student strike that had enlivened the session of the workshop in Colorado Springs from which I had just returned. As a rule he was hostile to the radical student activism of the sixties (I heard a lot about the Students for a Democratic Society leader Mark Rudd's activities at Columbia, a culture and a milieu Haggin knew well and loved); but I too was ambivalent about what my students and I had been through in the workshop and still quite high on the experience, so I did succeed in interesting him with my account, and the summer passed by in a friendly enough mood.

In the early fall Haggin turned cold toward me again in the lobby of the New York State Theater—what happened, I think, is that I always disappeared as my actual self from his mind when he was not seeing me in person—and soon after my return to Cambridge I received in the mail a manila envelope containing annotated Xeroxes of our correspondence through the years over the incident with Bertram; on a separate postcard Haggin asked me to study the correspondence and answer the questions he posed about it. He realized that I might not want to read what he had sent me, he said, but asked me, in that case, to "do him the courtesy" (those were the words) of telling him. I returned the envelope unopened, with a letter trying again to explain why I thought it a mistake to rehash an event long past in order to decide who had been "right" or had "behaved" better. He answered in an abusive postcard, without salutation or signature, telling me that he had always been disgusted by my dishonesty and cowardice; we never spoke again.

I wasn't blameless in earlier misunderstandings and conflicts, or in the final break, but he wasn't either, and his pressure to put me in the wrong had become intolerable. His life was already strewn with broken friendships, as I well knew, so I was not really surprised to find it happening to me in my turn, nor was I surprised when he then broke with our friends the Harriers because they would not agree with him that I had been wrong in my relations with him—and then in turn he broke with still other friends who would not agree that the Harriers should have supported him. I had the impression at the time that I had handled this crisis pretty well, and, in fact, I did not do badly, but part of my reaction to it was suppressed and unknowingly led me, in an odd ricochet, to plan a long article about not

Balanchine but Robbins—an act of distinct independence from Haggin, although it had an ambiguous relation to my feelings about Balanchine.

Haggin had little interest in Robbins, to put it mildly, and I agreed with him in that. We loved *The Afternoon of a Faun* and liked *Fancy Free*, but for both of us such early ballets as *The Age of Anxiety* and *The Guests* had only a sophomoric meaningfulness, and *The Cage*, while undeniably a powerful theatrical experience, appalled us by its confessionalism. *Interplay* shrewdly caught a key aspect of American taste and behavior, but it was not an aspect that concerned us much, and we made a similar assessment of the popular new *Dances at a Gathering*, which we had discussed amicably the summer before the break. I didn't loathe it, as Haggin did, but we both thought it shallow in its expertise and distastefully manipulative, and that was enough for us to make good conversation out of it: we never used the word *meretricious*, but it—including its etymological implication—was in the air.

We both found fault particularly with the opening piece of *Dances*, for which Robbins happened to have chosen music with special value and meaning for the two of us, Chopin's Mazurka Op. 63, No. 3, in C Sharp Minor. In his teens and early twenties, Haggin had hoped to become a concert pianist; when he realized that he did not have a major gift he had turned with disappointment to teaching the piano and then, in the late twenties, which were also his late twenties, he had found his true vocation in criticism. His parents had bought him a unique, pre–World War I Mason and Hamlin piano, which he was in the habit of playing for a half hour or so every day when he was in New York; he liked to play when he was in Cambridge in the summer, too, and he would come over once or twice a week to use my piano, which gave me a chance to hear him. It was quite an experience. He always practiced by playing one or two of his three favorite pieces—the slow movement of Bach's *Italian Concerto*, Haydn's Andante and Variations in F Minor, and this marvelous mazurka, which he played with quiet, elegant, plangent verve.

But as we thought about the dance, far from spending even a moment's pleasure on the happy coincidence of our taste with Robbins's, we moved immediately to being "appalled" (one of Haggin's favorite states—mine too, I suppose) by Robbins's mistakes in setting the mazurka. Haggin had a wonderful reading of measures 66–77, the coda, a passage that deepens the ruminative, plaintive texture and tone of the melody with delicate canonical writing, and he had worked out a quietly thrilling phrasing for the climax, in measures 73–75, which I've never heard from any other pianist. At the beginning of this quiet coda the choice Robbins made was to send Edward Villella on a circle of turns about the stage—not exactly brilliant turns but fast and virtuosic enough to seem to us unmusical, aggressively overinventive, arbitrary, willful, and egotistic. These were our inflamed terms, and they still seem fair to me. And this "wrong" choice for the coda only confirmed the hunch we had had about the tone and taste we were in for when Villella later touched the floor reverently in a This-Is-Our-Land gesture. I'm deliberately making us sound like Fanny Price and Edmund Bertram giving Mary Crawford bad marks in Jane Austen's *Mansfield Park* because I want to emphasize the strength of our conviction that the difference between right and wrong in art was capable of its appropriate kind of verification in public discourse—as I think such things both need to be and are.

> "But was there nothing in her conversation that struck you Fanny, as not quite right?"
>
> "Oh! yes, she ought not to have spoken of her uncle as she did . . . "
>
> "I thought you would be struck. It was very wrong—very indecorous."
>
> "And very ungrateful I think."

I remember finding slimy the rejection dance Robbins made for Kent, in which she is turned down by one after the other of several men she comes on to. Overly charm-filled American folk numbers, like the one of the girls walking in the moonlight and the boys horsing around, had a Rodgers and Hammerstein stink for us. Robbins had made Violette Verdy a minimalist sketch of a dance right at the center of the ballet, in which she represented the spirit of the house or some such thing; Haggin thought it a foolish invention that she brought off brilliantly, but I credited Robbins for an expert coup de theatre that gave our favorite so marvelous a moment at a crucial stage of her career. And I enjoyed the bravura acrobatics involving Sara Leland much more than Haggin did and considered the fast numbers for Villella to be as brilliant as they were meant to be—and very useful for Villella's career at a crucial moment. For me the seriously bad dance was the adagio for Villella and Patricia McBride, ersatz in emotion and gravely pretentious to boot, but I don't remember whether Haggin agreed with my judgment. And we both, of course, were "appalled" at the portentous hogwash Robbins cooked up for the finale, to the Nocturne Op. 15, No. 1, in which all ten dancers look up in awe as a cloud or a spaceship passes by. The fact that the ballet was greeted as a major American masterpiece added to our animus and our pleasure in vilifying it.

I have no memory of discussing the Farrell drama with Haggin that summer, although we could hardly have avoided talking about it. It is true that in our high judgment of Farrell, as I have already reported, my friends and I had wandered from our more-or-less complete agreement with Haggin about the dancers at the New York City Ballet—not that he disliked Farrell, for he admired her greatly, but that she did not seem to him as transcendently special and new as she did to us. Both Haggin and I had talked with Verdy about "Farrellitis," and although I don't remember any active disagreement about Balanchine's casting practices, there may well have been some difference in our way of seeing the break with Farrell that made me suppress all memory of discussing it with him. For me, Farrell's departure meant the loss of something immense while for Haggin, it represented a lesser loss, and even perhaps a gain, since he may have expected that Verdy would now regain some of her repertory.

The first premieres held by the New York City Ballet after the Farrell casualty and my break with Haggin were of Robbins's *In the Night* (to Chopin nocturnes) in late January 1970 and of Balanchine's *Who Cares?* (Gershwin, arranged by Hershey Kay) in early February. This is the point at which my following the Balanchine Enterprise began to drift, for I don't remember whether I went to see either of these premieres: even the physical experience of going to the ballet had become difficult since I had to be on guard not to run into Haggin. I must have been avoiding him intellectually and emotionally as well. I remember disliking the Robbins piece, but I paid attention to it because of Verdy's role with the new Danish dancer, Peter Martins. But I cannot remember when I first saw *Who Cares?*—I doubt it was at the premiere but I'm not sure. Haggin's review of it in the *Hudson Review* contrasted it as Balanchine's "unpretentious masterpiece" with *Dances at a Gathering*, which Haggin called a pretentious fraud, but this was more than I felt at the time about either ballet. The fact is that although I admired *Who Cares?* and genuinely liked it in 1970, I hadn't yet caught its whatness—my understanding of it, my epiphany, came in the late 1970s, when it became one of my absolute favorites.

As if to balance my inattention to *Who Cares?* I became thoroughly absorbed in Robbins's *Goldberg Variations* after I saw it in May 1971. I admired the brilliant finale, and, without exactly liking it, found the whole ballet immensely interesting to think about—its mixture of success and failure, of will and imagination, seemed to me a major issue. This would almost certainly not have been my reaction had I been seeing Haggin constantly at intermissions—the violence of his dislike would have given me pause, and my fascination with the new work probably would not have withstood his onslaught. But without his supervision, I became an expert on *The Goldberg Variations*, so that when Ted Solotaroff, the editor of *New American Review*, asked me to write an article, I proposed a long piece on Robbins's career in serious ballet and show business, analyzing the gap between his great gifts and his lapses of sincerity as an artist. Solotaroff accepted with what I took to be real interest, and the subject I proposed still seems to me an important one, which nobody has even now taken up. But I became painfully stuck writing the piece and never finished it.

Writing has always been harder for me than it should be: I wish that once in my life I could have the facility to begin a piece by getting a few clear sentences down in coherent order. I always spend hours and days on false starts, writing and rewriting sentences of awkwardly arranged and wordy prose that do not say what I really mean, until I find a beginning—usually a certain tone—that satisfies me. Even then, there are always further obstacles to overcome. With the Robbins piece, this difficulty hit its peak: what I wrote turned to dust again and again before me, but again and again I wouldn't admit it, staying with implausible opinions that weren't remotely mine: I was on the wrong path, but I wouldn't, and then couldn't, turn back. I never did discover what I really meant to say. And I didn't know what was happening: only long after abandoning the piece did I realize the degree to which my trouble had been caused by the break with Haggin.

I had locked myself in between contradictory impulses. I was trying to dissociate myself from Haggin by writing about an artist he almost despised, because I believed I had some good points of my own to make. But all along Haggin had been the audience I wrote for, and I was still writing for him—but with the subject I had chosen that was not possible. He was my audience because he had secured my first commission for me, to write a review for *The Nation*, before I was twenty, because I had checked my responses to art against his from then on, and because he remained my model for clear thinking and sureness of taste and judgment (despite the general view that he was simply a terrible-tempered and crazy man—which was true). He himself knew he was playing this role for me and for other readers, and he spoke often of the trials of being a "ghostly father" (although he never called us his "sons"), and I too considered myself to be well aware of having cast him in that role. I once showed a section of this book to someone who knew both Haggin and me well, and he claimed that I hadn't found my true subject, which was my difficulty in gaining independence from Haggin. I don't agree that that is my subject, but, as the old lady said, "How can I tell what I think till I see what I say?" Maybe that's what I've been saying all along.

Eventually (I cannot remember exactly when) I saw *The Goldberg Variations* once too often, and I was suddenly filled with distaste for the virulence of Robbins's egotism, for his forcing his invention by choosing to do all the repeats: the piece disintegrated before me. This view has held steady since. I finally abandoned my view that Robbins had a great gift that he often betrayed. *The Afternoon of a Faun* is genuine and beautiful, but the best I can say about Robbins apart from this work is that he is formidably, and often enjoyably, expert at working an audience and at getting what he wants from dancers. I had a painful experience of these gifts at a performance of the New York City Ballet in the late 1980s; I had been wavering back and forth about the performances of the Balanchine ballets I was looking at, thinking them not too bad one moment, lifeless the next, when the very first movements of the dancers in Robbins's *Glass Pieces* reminded me what it is like to see a ballet danced when the maker is watching. Robbins's capacity to bring dancing up to pitch may not be the most sublime gift in the world but he has it, and it is a sine qua non for the survival of dance: Balanchine had it in excelsis, of course, and for several years now we have been seeing his repertory danced without the benefit of this supervision.

The fact that I have little to say about the next important event in Balanchine's career, the Stravinsky festival in June 1972, stems not from failure of attention or interest on my part; I missed the whole thing because by the time it was announced, I had already committed myself to the Liberal Education workshop in June. I envied the friends who were able to go to every performance in that great week, and I felt sad and almost guilty to be missing such a moment in a career I had been following so closely. Balanchine claimed that he wanted to show that Stravinsky was still alive, but he must have meant also that he wished to prove that his own genius was still alive, as was the Balanchine Enterprise. And it was not he alone but the whole company of dancers, musicians, and choreographers that offered twenty-one new ballets in that one week of celebration and mourning: eight by Balanchine, three by Robbins, three by John Taras, two by Todd Bolender and one each by Richard Tanner, John Clifford, and Lorca Massine.

A major creation of the festival was Peter Martins, who came to life as a Balanchine dancer in the two roles Balanchine made for him. Martins had just joined the company as a guest artist when Farrell left, and although impressive for physical beauty and size, he was only an adequate dancer. He and Farrell made a fine couple, and Verdy had reported that he was a splendidly reassuring partner in *In the Night*, but as a serious dancer he didn't really figure for me—nor for other people, I think—until his new Stravinsky roles. In *Far from Denmark,* his autobiography, he describes with impressive honesty and detail the painful process he passed through at the New York City Ballet before realizing that he had to give his will over entirely to Balanchine in order to achieve anything significant in the Balanchine Enterprise. I was not on hand to watch any of this happening, but I knew that some major development of dance identity had been achieved when I saw *Stravinsky Violin Concerto:* the large and handsome body had at last gotten wired and Martins had become an interesting dancer, not just a beauty.

He seemed the natural choice for male leads in the new ballets, but I was at first surprised that Balanchine paired him with Kay Mazzo in both *Stravinsky Violin Concerto* and *Duo Concertant* instead of giving one of the roles to, say, Patricia McBride, which would have seemed more fair and would have given McBride a more important place in the festival. I concluded that he had become "interested" in Mazzo, but now I think that he was trying to make her interesting enough to be interested in. Balanchine may also have been more motivated by the box-office appeal in the contrast between Mazzo's delicate, almost brittle, wistful and vulnerable fragility and Martins's large blonde handsomeness—at a key moment in *Duo Concertant* when Martins is protecting and consoling Mazzo, for instance, his hand covers her face entirely. But it was clear that in choosing Mazzo for both ballets Balanchine was again exempt from any mechanical "justice" in casting—some would say, of course, that he had callously exempted himself from these concerns. Melissa Hayden, Verdy, and McBride were the senior ballerinas in 1972, but none of them was given a large assignment in the Stravinsky festival, since McBride's beautiful role in the great *Divertimento from "Le Baiser de la Fée"* did not have the weight of the roles for Mazzo, Karin von Aroldingen, and Gelsey Kirkland. What was going on, I now think, was not simply that Balanchine's muse was guiding him to Martins and Mazzo but that he was also taking care of company concerns other than the need to give the dancers their fair share of the roles. Mazzo perhaps and Martins definitely were destined to be major presences in the company for the next several years, and Balanchine was interested in exploring their possibilities with them.

The structure of *Stravinsky Violin Concerto* is unique in the Balanchine canon. The fast outer movements may be Balanchine's tightest compositions; the first is a succession of dazzling entrances and exits, made out of thin air, all prelude and promise with no development and no felt need for any—it starts and starts and starts and then it is all over. When Balanchine called *Stravinsky Violin Concerto* his favorite piece I guessed that he was talking about this structure, and I understood his pride in it. And he probably was thinking also of the slow movements, as he well might have been.

The score has two slow movements; the ballet therefore had to have two pas de deux. This self-assignment was made more difficult by the fact that to a casual ear the two movements are in the same style of thin, frozen eloquence, with a melodic line that is embroidered, perhaps tortured, by astringent ornamentation—the rich Bachian rhetoric of the basic musical form is thinned out and given an edge by the acidic texture. Whether he planned it consciously, what Balanchine produced to this music were two strikingly different movements that also, to a casual eye, look pretty much alike, two pas de deux tailored not only to the techniques of the different dancers but also to the meanings in their different bodily configurations. In these pas de deux Balanchine composed his most neurotic, twisted, screwed-up, modern, "difficult" images of love relationships that, again, differed in mood and in mode of communication between the partners and yet were easily recognizable as lying in the same region of language and artistic mode. The astringency of the music, the almost inhuman acrobatics of some of the passages (von Aroldingen's circular walk in back-bend, her hands touching the floor, while Bart Cook studies her noncommitally, for instance—as if his lover had revealed herself to be a powerful insect from another planet), the clarity of the movements, the oddity of the partnering methods and their super-visibility—all these added up to a metaphor for the steady, involved, cool analytic observation of difficult and strained human behavior and relationships that is the meaning of the dance. And this was new in Balanchine's work—nor was it to be repeated afterward. The exhilarating energy of *Who Cares?* had been Balanchine's first response to the Farrell disaster; now the objectivity of *Stravinsky Violin Concerto* seemed to express a new attitude toward difficult relationships. But whatever function these expressions served in Balanchine's personal emotional economy, they were fully self-contained works of art in the theater.

The opening of another new Balanchine-Stravinsky work, *Symphony in Three Movements*, establishes its adventurous mixture of modes—the lines of girls in white are reminiscent of show dancing but are weightier and more intense: Balanchine seems here to be hoping to match the almost cataclysmic force of the score. But to me he does not succeed, and I have always been somewhat disappointed by the loose form and rhythm of the dance. I am fond of it, but that is not a word I want to use about Balanchine's work. It is certainly genuine, but it makes me feel slightly condescending toward the applauding audience.

When I finally saw the new Stravinsky pieces I was very impressed with them, but I didn't feel as close to Balanchine as I had when he was choreographing for Farrell in the 1960s. I felt that I was out of things in general, and missing the Stravinsky festival made me feel left out in a plain and simple way. When I saw *Meditation* in 1963 it seemed to me an invitation to admire and study Balanchine's new dancer, and when I responded it seemed as if I had joined a project, as if I were working along with him, in an illusion of collaboration. And I continued in this illusion throughout the early Farrell years. But the brilliant *Stravinsky Violin Concerto* was a ballet in which I had no personal stake: I hadn't "worked on it" with Balanchine.

I was unable to recapture this illusion of collaboration with Balanchine until the final rehearsals and premiere of *Coppélia* at Saratoga Springs in the summer of 1974, and it came about partly because I was more an insider with the Balanchine Enterprise at that time than I had been previously. This was the first time I had seen rehearsals, and I was attending and discussing them with interesting new acquaintances. Jane Mayhall and Leslie Katz, whom I had met at Yaddo, had invited me to stay at their house in Saratoga, along with Nancy Goldner, the dance critic, who was writing the text for the program book for *Coppélia,* and Richard Benson, the photographer, who was illustrating the book. Talking with these new friends proved again that the Balanchine Enterprise could be a community-making experience.

During the same summer, through the good offices of Verdy, I watched one of Balanchine's classes and saw the way he was handling Gelsey Kirkland; he was entirely focused on her, patient and even-tempered in the face of her loudly acted-out independence—she did only a fraction of each assignment and fiddled endlessly with her leg warmers and her shoes, behavior that puzzled me at the time and became clear in its more painful implications only much later. I had been excited about her dancing all summer, particularly her first *Harlequinade,* so I was discouraged to hear, after Baryshnikov defected, that she was expected to leave the company to dance with him at American Ballet Theatre—just when I was becoming excited about a great new Balanchine dancer, her intense dissatisfaction with the Balanchine Enterprise surfaced.

The New York City Ballet's *Coppélia* is a reworking of Petipa's 1894 St. Petersburg rescension of the 1870 Saint-Leon Parisian original, and I felt personally involved in it because Balanchine made it in collaboration with Alexandra Danilova, with whom he had come to know the work in his young days at the Maryinsky Theater. She set the first two acts, which he tuned up to his own speed and fullness of detail; then he added a new third act. This collaboration might have been made expressly to bring my following of Balanchine's career full circle. I had loved the high spirits and charm of Danilova's Swanilda in *Coppélia* for the Monte Carlo company in the forties, and the tact of her presentation of a young girl was one of my great theatrical memories. I remembered few of the actual steps that followed her ravishing entrance except for her dance with the ear of wheat, which she kept utterly simple for all its mystery and power.

Balanchine and Danilova had also collaborated in 1945 in reviving *Raymonda* for the Monte Carlo company, which I had seen and enjoyed, although none of the dancing stayed with me except the passages Balanchine himself revived and reworked in *Pas de Dix* and later in *Cortège Hongrois.* At the back of my mind there is a rich, blurred memory of Danilova in the heroine's role in *Serenade,* and perfectly clear in the front of my mind are images of her grand authority in *Le Baiser de la Fée* and the first, sunny version of *Mozart-iana*. Her sleepwalker in the 1946 *Night Shadow* is still the best. I had known for a long time that she taught at the School of American Ballet, but it was not until I read her memoir, *Choura*, in 1987 that I learned how she had come, in 1963, to do so. Her account is as spontaneous as her dancing:

> One day I ran into Balanchine—as usual, on the street. "What are you doing?" he asked me.
>
> I said, "Nothing. I really needed something, so I'm teaching."
>
> "Why don't you come and teach the variations you remember?"
>
> "What variations?" I asked, rather stunned.
>
> "You think and tell me," he said, and he turned on his heel and walked off, leaving me standing there with my mouth open.
>
> I went home and cried a little bit, made myself a drink, and then took myself in hand. Sit down, I said to myself, and think what you can do. *Coppélia, Raymonda*, several old ballets came to mind. So I called Balanchine, and soon I was teaching at the School of American Ballet.

At the *Coppélia* rehearsals I saw the two of them talking and demonstrating steps to each other, but I was too far away to hear and I could not entirely follow what they were showing each other, as happens at most rehearsals I attend. But these hours brought my own experience with the Balanchine Enterprise back to its beginning.

Everything about this *Coppélia* seemed to me new, fresh, and clear—the pristine shaping of narrative in the first act, the beautifully detailed interplay between Dr. Cop-pélius and the young lovers in the second, and the enchanting galope at the end of the third, one of Balanchine's most electric finales, when the lovers' bravura fish-dive is trumped by Marnee Morris's surging reentry with the little girls from the Waltz of the Golden Hours. But above all shone McBride's performance. *Coppélia* carried on my education in her dancing, which I had experienced some trouble bringing into focus. I had found her splendidly clear and strong in *A Midsummer Night's Dream* and in Hayden's roles in *Liebeslieder Walzer* and *Allegro Brillante*, but she stayed just outside the circle of my special interest until I felt her nervous power in "Rubies." Her nonrhetorical eloquence in "The Man I Love" from *Who Cares?* was becoming a deeper experience the more I saw it: it defined and explored a whole new area of dancing for me, and I saw beyond her terrific competence to something more individual. But it was, in fact, not her individuality but her lucid and vivid normalcy that made her the right vehicle for what Balanchine was exploring

Alexandra Danilova at the making of *Coppélia,* 1974 (photo ©1994 Martha Swope)

in *Coppélia*—the relation between mechanical movement and natural movement; the discipline of classic ballet; the relation between dancer and choreographer.

These themes are central to any version of *Coppélia,* of course, but they are explored in Balanchine and Danilova's *Coppélia* with a sharpness of inquiry that brought me back into connection with the Balanchine Enterprise. When McBride, as the flesh-and-blood Swanilda pretending to be the doll Coppélia, pretended to come to life to an oboe melody that resembled a Bellini aria, I felt a contact with the spirit behind the Balanchine Enterprise that was as immediate as when I first saw the wandering bed in *The Nutcracker.* McBride gave herself to this moment with simple sufficiency, entirely without irony, so that when irony arose, as it poignantly did, it came from the action itself, as we saw (though Dr. Coppélius did not) that the life he thought he had created came not from his art but from the everyday life of a village girl who was jealous of her lover's infatuation with the doll the doctor had assembled. This moment gave me an epiphany into McBride's dance identity and temperament, and eventually a new insight into the Balanchine-Farrell drama. A minute later I was shaken by the violent Spanish dance into which McBride erupted when Dr. Coppélius tried to distract her energy—she had been winding up all the dolls—with a

Patricia McBride, Shaun O'Brien, and Helgi Tomasson in *Coppélia*, 1974 (photo ©1994 Martha Swope; choreography by George Balanchine ©The George Balanchine Trust)

Spanish shawl, then ravished by the Scottish dance inspired by the plaid scarf he finds for her next: I remember really *seeing* McBride look down at her dancing feet, and thinking "Danilova showed her how to do that"—as I confirmed later when I saw Danilova teaching the dance at the School of American Ballet. I was having one of those moments of really experiencing what I had known about for a long time: the tension ballet holds between discipline and vitality—and the related theme of the balletmaster as artist-scientist-dollmaker, the sinister and pitiful Dr. Coppélius: creator and crank, artist, dreamer, fraud, Pygmalion with a toy Galatea, hacker with his robot, Frankenstein with his monster, Balanchine with Farrell. Of course, some of these ruminations were strictly my own, but Balanchine vindicated my intellectual flights a year later when he composed *The Steadfast Tin Soldier*, to music from Bizet's *Jeux d'Enfants*, and showed there how deeply he too had been thinking about the image of the doll and its relation to dancing—and to living.

On January 22, 1976, the day of the New York premiere of *The Steadfast Tin Soldier*, I entered the final phase of my relationship with the Balanchine Enterprise. In the afternoon I went with Nancy Goldner to see the dress rehearsal of *Chaconne*, a new work for Suzanne Farrell, who had rejoined the company almost exactly a year before; then in the evening I attended its official premiere, which came side by side with the Bizet ballet. It seemed to me that Balanchine was showing the two new ballets on the same program as a public acknowledgment and exploration of what Farrell's return meant to the Balanchine Enterprise. *Chaconne* is a meditation on a subject and a score to which he had turned repeatedly in his career, Gluck's *Orpheus and Eurydice*, and now his return seemed deeply appropriate, for Farrell had indeed come back, and she was bringing her roles to life again. Balanchine had created a brilliant tour de force for her in *Tzigane*, which premiered at the Ravel festival in May 1975, but now it was time to make her the gift of a grand, serious ballet of appreciation. And like a canny man of the theater, he served up *Chaconne* garnished and glossed by the new toy ballet, both to set it off and to comment on it as an artist and as a man, to reflect it and reflect on it, to put its identity in a deep and multiple perspective of art and artifice.

Between the premieres of *Coppélia* and *Chaconne* I happened myself to be in a passage of confused transition that made me long for resolution. I moved back from administration to teaching, went on sabbatical, abandoned my Robbins project but searched for another; in addition, I was nearing the end of a long personal relationship that had proved fruitless. In October 1974 I left for a six-week European trip that ended the day after it began, when I was hit by a car on the Corso in Rome on the way to dinner at Ranieri's. I spent the rest of the fall in Wellesley recovering from a broken leg, then moved to New York for the spring. Farrell had made her first appearance after her return, in *Symphony in C,* just days before I got to New York, so I missed it, but I saw the New York City Ballet and Farrell repeatedly in the remaining weeks of the winter season and in the spring.

In May the company mounted a Ravel festival to recapture some of the publicity the Stravinsky festival had generated, and I wrote it up for *Dance Life,* a new magazine founded by Connie Harrier's nephew, David Lindner; the note of pent-up opinionatedness I struck is part of the record of my responses to my chosen artist. I seemed anxious to show I was no puppet or running dog of Balanchinism; on the other hand, hardly a paragraph goes by without some strenuous sarcasm directed at Clive Barnes. I unloaded a few opinions that I was already abandoning or qualifying—scorn for Ravel's *La Valse* as "degenerating from camp to trash" and for Balanchine's *La Valse* as "enjoyable and expert claptrap," for Bournonville's *La Sylphide* as "boring," for Adam's *Giselle* score as "poor" and so on. John Taras was given a thrashing for his *Daphnis and Chloe* choreography, which was certainly bad enough. It was characteristic of me to have returned to my writing about ballet in a judgmental and competitive spirit, and I actually felt completely in tune with the Balanchine Enterprise at the Ravel festival—it was with a decidedly proprietary air that I laid about me. And I did get the biggest things right, including *Sonatine,* the new ballet for Violette Verdy that opened the festival: "The piece is small but its masterly simple stylishness is very good. . . . The great thing about *Sonatine* was in fact the lovely new role Balanchine had made for Verdy, a role that recreated her freshness and refocused her clear spirit, her pride in the midst of elegance and charm. It might almost seem as if Balanchine had deliberately also made it a slight piece, knowing that Verdy's mastery would make something important out of it."

The most exciting new piece in the festival was *Tzigane,* for Farrell, and I greeted it warmly:

> In this exhilarating étude for foot positions in the gypsy genre, there are more intricacies and subtleties of choice than you'd believe possible. This was doubly impressive because these thousand tiny choices were taking place inside a bold and assured large dance structure; and it was all triply impressive because it was being danced full out by Farrell, who in roles like this one and in *Diamonds* and *Don Quixote* and *Movements* (among others) is now doing the greatest dancing I have seen since I started going to ballet in 1944. . . . *Tzigane* was exciting not only for the

rapidity and range of its choices of position and direction and balance but for its rapid and sensitive changes of tone and level of intensity, from the directly impassioned and rhapsodic to the wittily self-mocking and then on to open joking. And there was a wonderfully full array of ways of using Farrell's looks, personality and style, beginning with the All-American-High-School-Girl gypsy impersonation of the entrance, reminiscent (probably deliberately) of the *Brahms-Schoenberg,* and then proceeding with extraordinary modifications and amplifications of that body and personality until Farrell's particular dance genius was palpably *there,* in front of you.

Soon after I wrote this, someone reported that Balanchine had told Farrell to do just what she wanted when they were making *Tzigane,* and the two of them seemed so clearly to be living in each other's imaginations in that ballet that I accepted the story without wondering whether it was literally true. In *Holding on to the Air* Farrell explains how *Tzigane* came about: "Finally, he suggested an actual ballet step: 'Now, maybe you can do a big arabesque,' and, always wanting to give him as much as possible, I did a huge, diving arabesque penché. 'We know you can do that,' he countered, 'what else can you do?' and I flipped out of the penché into a deep backbend, head facing upward. His eyebrows rose as I looked to him for comment, and I knew then the fun had begun—we were experimenting again." I did not know that this was the way *Tzigane* had been created when I first saw it, but I sensed something of the process, and from that point on I began to think more and more about the new creative interrelationship between Balanchine and Farrell, in both literal and figurative terms. In *Chaconne* the inextricability of dance and dancer suggested that Balanchine might again have told Farrell to do just what she wanted.

*The Steadfast Tin Soldier* is a candy-box ballet in which dancers imitate dolls imitating people; *Chaconne* is sublime, noble, and heroic—its dancers move like gods. When Balanchine put them next to each other at the premiere, he probably wanted to say only, with his characteristic sniff, that he liked and was interested in both kinds of ballet. But for me, after my summer of thinking about Balanchine as Dr. Coppélius and about dancers as dolls, the ballets commented on each other—if only to say that Farrell was not under any limiting control but instead in free collaboration with her master. No dancers could seem less like dolls than the full-bodied Farrell and Peter Martins as they made their way freely through the perfectly expressive patterns of *Chaconne. The Steadfast Tin Soldier,* by having us watch human beings imitating dolls, refreshed our sense of the beauty and warmth, the grandeur, of the human movement of these superb creatures.

There is a spontaneous equality of man and woman in *Chaconne*. But the toys in *The Steadfast Tin Soldier* mimic the artifice of human gender roles: the soldier's proud bearing, discipline, and gallantry, the ballerina's self-delighting, self-applauding charm and flirtatiousness. Yet there is something moving and genuine about this behavior: when the soldier drops to his knee with a bang to kiss the paper doll's hand, he shows mechanical inflexibility but also marvelously total commitment, both artificial code and fervent belief. When the ballerina suffers—there is something wrong with her lungs, and her wits too, for she unwisely opens a big window and is blown into the fire by the draft—she is the descendent of the heroines of romantic drama and ballet. The stiff courtship pas de deux has unexpectedly touching images of devotion and rapport. But in *Chaconne* ballerina and cavalier are both heroic, their partnership an equal collaboration.

The structure of *Chaconne* worried Nancy Goldner, Arlene Croce, and others at the premiere, for they thought the relation between the parts unfocused. I later decided they were right, but at first I noticed only a slight abruptness, which I thought due to the fact that Balanchine had set various pieces from Gluck's opera at different times over a period of years. For the Hamburg State Opera in 1963, he had composed brilliant rococo dances for the final celebration in the Temple of Love in Gluck's *Orpheus and Eurydice*—a gracious pas de trois, a hard, sharp little pas de deux (the only dance he has kept unchanged despite the fact that nobody can dance it because the turn is too hard), a sweet pas de cinq, a grand exhibition pas de deux with variations, and a final group dance, set to the chaconne of the title. It was Brigitte Thom, the ballet mistress at the Paris Opera Ballet, who restaged the 1973 Paris version of these dances for the New York City Ballet in 1976, but Balanchine must have modified the choreography for Farrell and Martins. He could hardly have asked the Hamburg or Paris dancers for the extraordinary things he demanded of Farrell and Martins, and Croce wrote as if she knew or took for granted that Balanchine had changed parts of it; but Reynolds says nothing about revision, nor does Farrell in the autobiography. At the last moment before the New York premiere, Balanchine scheduled an extra hour's rehearsal for Farrell and Martins and made an andante pas de deux for them that took place on a darkened stage to the "Dance of the Blessed Spirits" with the flute solo: this served as a prelude to the brilliant dances from Hamburg and Paris in the version I saw that afternoon and evening. When costumes came later in the spring, still another opening dance was added, a walk for tall women that is akin in atmosphere to the pas de deux and set to the framing section of the "Dance of the Blessed Spirits." In its final structure the ballet does not move forward in a dramatic progression, like a sonata, but changes rhythm and tone like

Suzanne Farrell and Peter Martins in *Chaconne*, 1976 (photo ©1994 Martha Swope; choreography by George Balanchine ©The George Balanchine Trust)

a suite as it passes through different dance forms. It falls into two distinct halves, one soft and dark, the other hard-edged and brilliant. But it has a unity that can easily be seen as a meditation on Gluck's *Orpheus*—first the sad story, then the happy finale.

The new pas de deux shows the meeting of a man and a woman in a darkly glowing place. Perhaps they are Orpheus and Eurydice meeting in Hades: the dance imagery does not name a motive, but the meeting of man and woman is so dense with possibility that it shows more clearly than anything in *Orpheus* why the story had such power over Balanchine's imagination. In one balance, often reproduced in photographs, Farrell and Martins support each other with interlocked elbows while he turns her on a ravishing tilt; it is ingenious and as solidly engineered as the Brooklyn Bridge, yet onstage Farrell and Martins seem to be catching it on the wing. At another point, in Goldner's inspired words from the March 1976 *Dance News*, "one of Farrell's legs is always lapping the ground and swimming forward, and who's to know whether it's her leg (so alive it could be the encasement for her brain) or Martins's arms that are doing the most propelling?" The brilliantly lit court dances that follow are danced to the music of the happy ending in the Temple of Love that Gluck was forced into by eighteenth-century opera convention, and their sharply inflected style makes a bold contrast with the liquid flow of the Elysian Fields imagery. But just as this dark-light contrast is easy to read as meaning, so there is a consonance, a visual assonance, between the Elysian images and the appoggiaturas and acciaccaturas of stance and placement—the roulades and gruppettos of arms and legs— that ornament the heroic bravura of the exhibition pas de deux and variations in the Temple of Love. And there is a unity rising from the body and spirit of Farrell herself. Gluck's musical language of rococo ornament unites the slow and fast, dark and light, elegiac and celebratory sections of the suite, and the unfailing coherence of Farrell's dancing unites the hard and soft sections of the ballet.

The threat to coherence comes in the final chaconne. Here is Croce's statement of the issue from *Afterimages:*

> What happens in the middle of *Chaconne* is that a whole new ballet crystallizes, a
> new style in rococo dancing appears, which in 1963 was unknown. Balanchine turns
> the clock ahead so suddenly that if it weren't for Farrell's and Martins's steadiness
> we'd lose our bearings. Their first pas de deux gave no hint of what was to come.
> Now, in a minuet, they present a solemn facade or gateway to the variations for
> them both that follow in a gavotte. These are like sinuous corridors leading one on
> and on. It is excess, but it is controlled excess—never more than one's senses can en-

compass yet never less. Farrell's steps are full of surprising new twists; her aplomb is sublime. And Martins achieves a rhythmic plangency that is independently thrilling. . . . Together, from the gavotte onward into the concluding chaconne these two dancers are a force that all but obliterates what remains of the divertissement. Balanchine's ensemble choreography here is musically focused, but visually unrhymed. His yokes and garlands and summary groupings don't quite manage to gather and contain the new material for Farrell and Martins within the shell that remains from Hamburg-Paris.

I now recognize this fault line, but the way I would put it would be to say that the chaconne does not focus my attention and hold my interest. Croce's word *rhyme* asks the finale to make specific reference to the "new style in rococo dancing" of the variations, but we cannot tell what the structure would have been unless Balanchine had achieved it, and he did not. Reynolds's matter-of-fact account in *Repertory in Review* is probably right:

> Perhaps it was two ballets, imperfectly integrated; some identified the elements, rather too superficially, as the Martins-Farrell sections on one side, and all the other parts on the other. In form the ballet was a series of more or less unrelated divertissements, interspersed with dances for the two principals, followed by what promised to be a grand finale but was in fact a large movement in which some new demi-soloists were introduced and previous soloists never appeared. As if to reflect this unexpected choice of dancers, this final movement was diffuse; for once, Balanchine did not clearly tell the eye where to look.

I agree, yet I do not mind the diffuseness, for in practice I do not maintain high structural standards about art that I love: once I decide a work is mine, I expect and even want it to be exactly what it is, so that I hardly notice details that interrupted my pleasure at first. And I was delighted to find Croce sharing my practice: "A week after the premiere, I saw another performance. There was such euphoria onstage and in the pit that the final chaconne, loose ends and all, came together and held as if by miracle, and stars, demis, corps, orchestra, and audience were wafted together into Tiepolo skies." The invocation of Tiepolo gave me a happy twinge of rapport, for I too love the large, loose, breezy rococo of that Venetian.

I got into an argument with Nancy Goldner at either the rehearsal or the performance when I spoke of the Farrell-Martins variations as "competition variations." So it was gratifying to find myself almost directly addressed at the end of her fine column in the March issue of *Dance News:* "As in their first duet, the prevailing mode of white classicism switches to a lacier, more convoluted texture. The tone is more personal. Yet vestiges of impersonal nobility exist in the utterly noncompetitive nature of their solos." It was as necessary to her to call them noncompetitive as it was for me to call them competitive—we were each reading the ballet out of our own needs and natures. I enjoyed being involved in so detailed and lively a public conversation about art. Shortly after I met Goldner and began to read her writing, at Saratoga in 1974, I began to follow Arlene Croce's reviews in the *New Yorker*, and in 1978 I asked to review her first collection of critical reviews, *Afterimages*, for the *Hudson Review:* my review claimed that "a lot of us have thought for some time that Croce is about the best reviewer writing about any of the arts." This was a rejection of B. H. Haggin, of course, but it was not so much tacit as half-conscious: I am not sure I realized what I was saying about Haggin, although by that time I had ceased learning anything new from him and had come to feel that he himself had ceased responding freshly to art.

My conversations with ballet critics were matched by conversations on the State Theater promenade or at dinner or coffee before or after the ballet with other literary or artistic people or journalists who were not professionally involved with the ballet but whose lives were connected by admiration of the Balanchine Enterprise. These conversations, which have continued until the present and have been a major pleasure of my life, were how I personally experienced Balanchine's emergence into a role of prestige and authority in several realms of American culture. He ruled the ballet world, of course, since regardless of whether his critics approved, he had come to control ballet in America through the general acceptance of his preeminence and through his financial success. He also claimed a share of the world of general culture, since the subscription system at the New York City Ballet had done its job, however much we out-of-towners regretted having to buy our tickets in advance instead of paying $4.95 at the door for fine orchestra seats. But for me the most significant part of Balanchine's large audience was the highbrows, especially those in the vanguard of critical taste. Edwin Denby, who had written about ballet two or three times a year for the quarterly *Modern Music* in the 1930s and had reached a wider public only by substituting for Walter Terry at the *New York Herald-Tribune*, had become a major figure in the 1950s through his influence over Willem de Kooning, Frank O'Hara, and John Ashbery. What Denby and Haggin had preached to the few had become generally accepted, as the Balanchine Enterprise came to occupy a central position in American high culture from about 1950 until Balanchine's death in 1983.

In *Chaconne* we saw a new Farrell: after six years of exile, she had returned virtually transfigured. In everyday terms, she had finally lost her baby fat, but the change registered as a spiritualization of physique and a tranquility of spirit. She had become a woman, and she now controlled a powerful force not only of energy but also of sensibility. And now Balanchine made for and with her a succession of roles that became a repertory in itself, the harvest of what had blossomed years before; it was her own harvest, too.

*Chaconne* became the top New York dance ticket; for me, its spirit governed the entire atmosphere of the Balanchine Enterprise, and of New York as well, for the next several years. The spirit of the enterprise was like a river widening out into a lake: spacious, quiet, calm, out of time, not quite of this earth: the rest of this chapter is mostly a record of that extraordinary atmosphere. And the locus of this marvelous lake was New York City, my favorite place in those days, although I never lived there.

In the middle of this period and without contradicting its serenity, Balanchine composed two generous extravaganzas full of dancing and dancers and sets and costumes. *Union Jack* (1976) and *Vienna Waltzes* (1977) lie in the region of style Balanchine defined for the 1950s with the benign consumerization of classical ballet to be found in *Western Symphony* and *Stars and Stripes,* although the later ballets are grander and more richly rewarding of the attention they demand. Their creation seemed a gesture of the highest self-confidence and largesse on Balanchine's part—this is the respect in which they matched *Chaconne.* At first I thought that these two big shows might represent a flashback to the styles Balanchine had mastered early in his career, in the Charles B. Cochran Revues and the Ziegfeld Follies, but later it occurred to me that they are more closely connected with the less chic, more populist stage shows at Radio City Music Hall. It has been said that only as patriotic an immigrant as Balanchine—a big fan of Richard Nixon's—could have gotten away with celebrating America's Bicentennial with a tribute to England. And only as confident a choreographer and musician as the maker of *Concerto Barocco* could make two large late works in the genre and format of a Radio City Music Hall stage show.

The first section of *Union Jack* is a tour de force which uses a highly codified vocabulary of nondance movement to organize a ballet audience's attention. It consists of a military tattoo of seven Scottish and Canadian Guards Regiments marching to drumrolls and drumbeats. Seventy kilt-clad dancers file in slowly until the stage is full, then methodically shuffle in formation until your eyes almost blur trying to follow the complexity; they reassemble into their original order and exit in a condensed recap of the entrance; then they return, regiment by regiment, to dance to music that comprises English and Scottish folk tunes, Handel, and "Amazing Grace" and "A Hundred Pipers" thrown in for the group finale. The second act of the ballet pays tribute to the English music hall: it is a comedy skit with the Pearly King and Queen (Patricia McBride and Jean-Pierre Bonnefous as costermongers), joined at the end by a bottle of booze, their two children, and a donkey. The last section moves to London's West End of the twenties or thirties: there is a chorus-girl-and-boy number to hornpipes and "Rule Britannia" with Martins as a drunken randy sailor and Farrell as a Ginger Rogers-Betty Grable Wren.

The second and third sections are extended skits, and for some people they went on too long; the whole piece counted heavily on our devotion to the Balanchine Enterprise, but there was a lot of this devotion around. Balanchine was showing that he too enjoyed British marching regiments and British music halls, and he was reliving his experience in British musical revues. No very high level of connoisseurship here: the second and third sections were like big parties, and for me seeing Farrell as a Betty Grable-type Wren felt like being granted a wish. But the first section was something else: it generated great power and commanded an almost hypnotized attention and therefore achieved the serious impact of art, even if only as a kind of optical illusion.

*Vienna Waltzes* won an even greater and more complex loyalty—it was the biggest box-office hit the company ever had, and it gathered a large cult following of highbrow groupies as well. *Union Jack* was a huge joke that the audience was in on, and it gave a great deal of pleasure. But *Vienna Waltzes* sought to effect access to the general heart and mind of the whole audience. This ballet could have been based on any show with a Vienna waltz theme that was actually danced at the Radio City Music Hall any time between its opening in 1931 and its becoming just another auditorium in the 1960s.

Of the five sections, the first three are set to Strauss waltzes, absolutely basking in the obviousness of the choices: "Tales from the Vienna Woods" presents officers and their ladies at a ball in the Wienerwald, with soloists Karin von Aroldingen and Sean Lavery; "Voices of Spring" switches to classical dancing in the Wienerwald, with Patricia McBride and Helgi Tomasson as the woodsprites; "Explosion Polka" shows us a servants' ball in the Wienerwald, with Sara Leland and Bart Cook dressed to the eyeballs. Then the forest comes indoors in Rouben Ter-Arutunian's handsome set, and Franz Lehar's *Gold and Silver Waltz* becomes a *Merry Widow* sketch in an art-nouveau café at the Hotel Sacher, with Kay Mazzo as a lady in black and Peter Martins as a red-coated guardsman. Finally there is Suzanne Farrell, dancing her pre–World War I fantasies in a mirrored ballroom—not Nymphenburg but the nouveau-riche palace of some Hamburg shipping czar—to the Richard Strauss *Rosenkavalier* waltzes, with a thousand white winged ballgowns whirling under chandeliers.

What I admired in all this, and went to feed on again and again, was the spontaneity the seventy-two-year-old Balanchine brought to popular culture. I thought of him as being under the power of the same deep, alluring New York glamour that I had known in Allentown in the 1930s when I listened to a radio program called "Grand Central Station." The expert publicity for the ballet presented Balanchine as genius and impresario at once. He was said to have told his dancers that none of them knew how to waltz, so he had to show them, and I enjoyed being asked to believe, and believing, that nobody in the New York City Ballet knew how to waltz but that Balanchine did, that he could teach them and they could learn, and that in *Vienna Waltzes* I was, at last, seeing waltzing the way it ought to be done.

Farrell enlarged both *Union Jack* and *Vienna Waltzes* with her two-fold identity as the ideal Balanchine dancer. Her chorus girl in *Union Jack* summed up the popular part of his dream about American dancers; the wit and mischief of her impersonation passed beyond even her own apotheosis years before in *Slaughter on Tenth Avenue*—it was as final an achievement of style as Laurence Olivier's Archie Rice in *The Entertainer* in 1963. In *Vienna Waltzes* she brought such actuality to her rhapsody of longing and loss in the great empty ballroom that she transcended the mode and tone of popular art and reached the highest art—something *Union Jack* had neither achieved nor wished to achieve. Again it seemed that she herself composed what she danced, as if her own current of life had given her access to a central image of the romantic dream, just as it had seemed to be Greta Garbo's own current of life, her imagination and her own experience, that had made the world of Camille known to her. Because she is a dancer, Farrell could pass even beyond Garbo's range.

One detail of Farrell's performance stands out for me: when the dreaming girl finally dances with her imaginary lover, Farrell kept changing the hand with which she was holding her heavy French silk gown up behind her, and the effect gathered the elements of an entire civilization together: its animal power, its discretion, its fluency, its refinement, its competence, its breeding, its stresses. And my experience with art again came full circle. In the French film of *Gigi* back in the late forties I had been struck, perhaps more than I ought to have been, by the kind and degree of civilization implied when Gigi's grandmother instructs her in two competencies central to the education of a *grande cocotte:* how to choose jewels and how to eat Lobster à l'Amoricaine. Farrell's gesture reached sublimity through a union of stage business, choreography, and dancing that could have been achieved only in the intricate, intimate collaboration of Farrell and Balanchine. Farrell danced her section with an almost stern gravity, but after this ascent to the heights, the finale returned, in a coup de theatre, to the world of Ernst Lubitsch, of Fred Astaire and Ginger Rogers, an amalgam of *The Merry Widow* and "The Waltz in Swing Time,"

Suzanne Farrell and Jean-Pierre Bonnefous in *Vienna Waltzes,* 1977 (photo ©1994 Martha Swope; choreography by George Balanchine ©The George Balanchine Trust)

a huge, rich spectacle in which I enjoyed losing and finding Farrell among the other dancers.

At about this time, and almost overnight, *Who Cares?* revealed itself to me as a great work of art and became one of my favorite Balanchine ballets. It was one of my conversions. I was already familiar with the ballet and had an opinion about it: Gershwin the songwriter is a great composer for me, so I had a predisposition to like any ballet that used his songs, and I had always loved the pas de deux to "The Man I Love" and the "I Got Rhythm" finale—but the ballet as a whole stayed just outside the range of my interest. Not even Haggin's high admiration for it had won me over. One serious stumbling block to my appreciation of *Who Cares?* was the irritatingly distasteful men's group dance "Bidin' My Time," an eager-to-please, ballet-steps-to-show-tunes number with a series of jumping turns. I thought it corny, almost the only Balanchine dance of which I would say that. And this number infected my view of the rest of the ballet to the point that I nearly put it in the category of *Western Symphony* and *Stars and Stripes,* in which I had long since lost interest. I had liked those two ballets at first, and they had had great moments when they were new— Tanaquil Le Clercq's elegant rowdiness in the last movement of *Western Symphony,* Janet Reed's calendar-art Dulcinea coming on to Nicholas Magallanes's improbable cowboy in the second movement, Allegra Kent's witty cheerleader impersonation in the big pas de deux in *Stars and Stripes.* But these moments and the ballets as a whole could not survive the departure of their original dancers, and they had become the only Balanchine ballets to which I condescended. And that was where I was tempted to put *Who Cares?*

Then at some point in the late seventies I found myself interested in and liking a certain moment about a quarter of the way into the ballet, when things suddenly pick up—not the big shift when the principals arrive, but an earlier moment when the group dances are succeeded by pas de deux. It comes right after "Bidin' My Time," in fact; a couple move into a fast duet to "'S Wonderful" and initiate a surge of energy and invention, which they pass along to the other couples. It was when I noticed this development that I began to feel how the dance life in the piece really worked, and from then I made rapid progress in understanding the whole ballet and its value.

The first three easy and relaxed group dances have the job of establishing the popular genre—although I continue to think "Bidin' My Time" corny. These dances block out the stage space in simple, straightforward, square lines, making a kind of ground against which the figures drawn in the fast duets stand out with the complex irregularity of serious dance movement. The duets are set to four great songs, "'S Wonderful," "That Certain Feeling," "Do, Do, Do," and "Lady Be Good." ("That Certain Feeling" is danced by two couples in succession.) These dances have the appearance of ordinary show dancing, with jitterbugging steps, a little skit about a girl refusing a boy's invitation to dance, and a classic show-dancing climax in which the prettiest chorus girl is lifted the highest. But I had now caught on to the fact that the twists and turns of these couples have more than show-dancing inventiveness and create an energy which opens up the three-dimensionality of the stage and gathers to a climax in "Lady Be Good"—energy that offers the exhilaration of the great Balanchine. This energy and invention make *Who Cares?* a serious ballet and a great one.

The pas de deux bring the ballet up to serious power and invention, but the next dance, "The Man I Love," mounts to high eloquence, in an unusual tonality. The central body of *Who Cares?* consists of a suite of dances for the four principals, a man and three women: each woman dances a duet with the man and all four have solos, then they all perform a fast coda before the grand finale of "I've Got Rhythm." The suite begins with its grandest, gravest section, a pas de deux to "The Man I Love." It is longer and more spacious than the solos or duets that follow; it constantly circles back to its tune and its meaning in large clear

Patricia McBride and Jacques d'Amboise in *Who Cares?* 1970 (photo courtesy the Dance Collection, New York Public Library for the Performing Arts, Astor, Lenox, and Tilden Foundations; choreography by George Balanchine ©The George Balanchine Trust)

ballet figures that proceed with deliberation to occupy the whole stage and generate an emotion so far from show dancing that it does not even seem romantic. The piece has great freedom and openness—it is a "mood" number—but Balanchine's imagination and taste have cut away the self-pity and heavy breathing. It offered McBride what was perhaps her greatest role. Mysteriously normal, as always, she controlled the stage with a power that was quite different from charisma as ordinarily conceived; there was an edge to her yearning, a dry clarity to her expression of love. The extraordinary gesture of her right arm that begins the dance, which is like nothing else in Balanchine, is both a gesture of longing and a state-ment of intention, a sign of inner feeling but also a signal, even a command, to her lover. And the discretion of her rhetoric continued in the way she refused to woo or charm the audience in her solo "Fascinatin' Rhythm," a showstopper that doesn't try but never fails.

I had been admiring and studying McBride's performance since 1970 but it was not until my conversion to the whole ballet in the late seventies that I came to value the other performances. This happened in a complicated way. My conversion, which may have begun in 1976, had been furthered in 1978 by my acquiring a tape of the Canadian Broadcasting Company videocast of a performance of *Who Cares?* by the New York City Ballet that was shot in 1971, shortly after the ballet's premiere. Comparing this performance with those I was seeing at the New York State Theater gave me another of my upsetting experiences of the ephemerality of ballet. The original cast for *Who Cares?* had featured McBride, von Aroldingen, Marnee Morris, and Jacques d'Amboise, and at the point of my conversion they were all still dancing, and I remember thinking that they were all dancing well, except for von Aroldingen, whose work I had by then come to dislike almost automatically. I knew Croce's judgment that von Aroldingen had "trashed" her role in *Who Cares?* and while that seemed a strong way to put it, I assumed that Croce was talking about the smudginess of all of von Aroldingen's dancing at the time. But when I saw the videotape I saw exactly what Croce meant, which depressed but also excited and interested me in various ways, among them its demonstration of how inattentive I had been to *Who Cares?* from the start and how passively I had been watching it. The tape revealed von Aroldingen's role as astonishingly beautiful and original, individually detailed, characterized by inventively distinctive arm movements. On the tape von Aroldingen danced this marvelous role as if it had been made for her—as, of course, it had: the details of arm movement were Balanchine's special gifts to her, for they looked unlike anything she ordinarily did, unlike anything Balanchine had made before. I realized that I had for years been watching the ruin, or the trashing, of this original. Hers is a puzzling case, for von Aroldingen was in close contact with Balanchine during the seventies; she was taking care of him and organizing all his living arrangements, and he was creating important roles for her, both before and after Farrell's return. And he was known for attending all the performances of all his ballets. How could he have allowed this to happen? I haven't a clue.

I was also surprised by Morris's performance on this tape, although I must have seen her performance onstage at about the same time, since she did not leave the company until 1976. But I did not discover the song she dances, "My One and Only," until I got to know the tape, and that coincided with my new delight in the special quality of her dancing. There is a lovely, witty contradiction between the knowingness of the song and Morris's style—reserved, slightly prim, well behaved, pleased at being naughty. I didn't remember anything like those qualities when I saw her perform live in 1976.

What the videotape of *Who Cares?* did for me amounted to my first realization of the power of its medium in the experience of ballet, a fact and a consolation that has become important after Balanchine's death. Everyone agrees that videotapes make good reminders for people who have experienced the real thing in performance, but it is widely thought that the medium lacks the body and presence needed to carry a meaningful dance experience in itself. But when I taught Balanchine to undergraduates, many of whom had seen no ballet at all and no serious dancing in any form, the public broadcasting series of "Dance in America" tapes made a powerful impression on the students and I think a true one. In my classes we watched them many times, trying to describe what dance events look like and how they work; when we were finished, it was clear that a large majority of the class had felt the real power of the dance experience through this medium.

One section of *Who Cares?* was dropped a couple of years after the premiere: "Clap Yo' Hands," a fast coda for the four principals that was performed not to Hershey Kay's orchestration of a Gershwin song, but to a record of Gershwin's own performance on the piano. I remember liking the dance but not giving it special attention, for my attention was completely taken over by hearing the wonderful Gershwin performance coming over the sound system: an electrifying apparition of the spirit behind the whole ballet was intended and achieved. When I saw the piece again on the tape I concentrated on it for the first time and for the first time noticed that it uses the format of the final allegro in *Apollo:* a man and three women, Apollo and the three muses, now become one show dancer and his three partners. (*Serenade* belongs in this group too.) I now think that this grouping is little more than an oddity, a structure Balanchine liked, but I spent some time in the past trying to draw out more important implications.

By the time I saw the tape of *Who Cares?* Morris had been replaced by Merrill Ashley, with her powerful exactness, and the difference between the two dancers helped me to recognize the delightfully discreet refinement of Morris's dancing and personality. But Ashley had become a favorite. I had enjoyed her in small solos in the early seventies but my first serious look at her was in *Coppélia:* her "Dawn" variation in the third-act divertissement was unusually clear, but the mechanics of her articulation and pronunciation seemed too visible to be great dancing. Soon afterward, however, I was bowled over by the motor power and the juicy ping of her *Tchaikovsky Piano Concerto No. 2;* her elastic, exuberant power were part of the great refreshment in the revival of *The Four Temperaments;* and I followed her fondly from then on. So I was delighted when Balanchine, while basking in both his huge company as a whole and in the returned Farrell in particular, found time and energy to pay special attention to her. When he made *Ballo della Regina* for her in 1978 it was the coronation of a princess: the coda, in which her leg tells the time like an illuminated

Merrill Ashley in *Ballo della Regina*, 1978 (photo ©1994 Martha Swope; choreography by George Balanchine ©The George Balanchine Trust)

clock on a Times Square billboard, delighted the whole affectionate audience. In *Ballade* in 1980 she and Balanchine worked well to enrich and refine her lyrical dancing and they made a lovely piece, but in the end it failed to generate enough power in the theater—this time the choice of Fauré's music was not as successful as it had been in "Emeralds."

In 1978 Mikhail Baryshnikov joined the New York City Ballet in a thrilling development that I followed closely and with excitement, if in the end with great sadness. In 1982 I gave this account in a review of Gennady Smakov's biography of Baryshnikov for *Ballet Review:*

> At the first performance [of "Rubies"] at Saratoga in July 1978 (Smakov is wrong in saying it took place on November 14), Baryshnikov was quite remarkably bad, thoroughly out of style and even self-defeating in technique, since the boldness of his dancing made his bad Balanchine accent almost shocking in its impact. But by the next January, and in the TV version from the White House, he had achieved beautifully natural continuity and grace in *Rubies:* the accent was still a bit foreign, but the progress had been so great and so fast that there didn't seem any reason why he should not become the fully worthy successor to Villella in this role in which we had so long and so sorely missed Villella's rare combination of force, speed, wit and charm. But by June 1979, Baryshnikov's performances in exactly this role were some of the signs that his experiment with the company style had, in fact, been discontinued. The performance was still secure and correct technically, but the style was going wrong in a central way: Baryshnikov was beginning again to separate the episodes of the piece into little "numbers," thereby isolating himself from the other dancers and breaking that ideal continuity basic to Balanchine classicism. But he didn't look at all like someone who was miscast [this is what Smakov claimed]; he looked like someone who had given up on a project that he had been well on the way to mastering.

And I explained what had happened:

> During Baryshnikov's stay at the City Ballet, Balanchine's health was in such a condition as to limit his physical activity to a considerable extent for much of the period. Baryshnikov must have expected that in joining the City Ballet he would get some roles made for him by the greatest choreographer in the history of ballet, and one wonders how his willingness, or even his ability, to work fruitfully and comfortably with the company was affected by his becoming aware that Balanchine's health

made it unlikely that there would be new roles for many months at least. Many of Baryshnikov's decisions have been motivated, he has himself told us, by his intense awareness of the passage of time, unusually intense even for a dancer. In this instance that awareness may have amounted to real pain.

Balanchine worked on *The Prodigal Son* with him and they achieved a superb alternative to the dazzling Villella performances that remained fresh in my memory. It was Baryshnikov's performance of *The Steadfast Tin Soldier* that was chosen to be preserved on video, a marvel of delicacy, power, and wit, completely realizing what must have been Balanchine's intentions. His *Prodigal Son* is also on videotape, as is his *Tchaikovsky Pas de Deux:* in this respect the Baryshnikov-Balanchine story ended more happily than the Balanchine-Villella story, since Villella's dancing is available now only in the clumsy cinematography and faded colors of the videotape of the film of *A Midsummer Night's Dream.*

*Walpurgisnacht Ballet,* a setting of the ballet music from Gounod's *Faust,* is a part of the Farrell story, a part of the repertory story, and a part of the late Balanchine story; and for me it offered the most convincing evidence of Balanchine's inclination toward near-parody in repertory building. I ended a *Salmagundi* symposium talk with this account:

> It offers many new delights, including a sumptuous new role for Farrell, which she dances with smiling, glowing pleasure. But what makes everybody smile about the experience afterwards, I think, is the pleasure of recognition, though "recognition" in this respect is a virtual sleight of hand on Balanchine's part. Even if one can't or doesn't want to name the stylistic elements involved—the soigné bland charm of the music, the establishment decorum of the orgiastic abandon, the numberless infinities of gradations in the hierarchy of dancers on stage, from étoile to apprentice coryphée—one recognizes with a virtual sense of accomplishment that a certain exact thing is being done. And it's being done with a wittily sharp inflection that poises itself captivatingly on the brink of parody. With *Walpurgisnacht Ballet,* then, as with other middle ground ballets in the Balanchine repertory, one feels that a certain "place" in the repertory of possible ballets has been at one and the same time defined and most satisfyingly filled.

When Farrell returned, Balanchine dropped *Liebeslieder Walzer* from the repertory, and I was sure he did so because he could not bear to take the role away from von Aroldingen yet did not want to see it danced by anyone but Farrell. I believed this even before Balanchine gave me evidence of it by composing another German romantic ballet, *Robert*

*Schumann's "Davidsbündlertänze"* (1980), which moved me because in the deepest way it was a ballet about and for both von Aroldingen and Farrell. *Liebeslieder Walzer* and *Robert Schumann's "Davidsbündlertänze"* share something of the same apparatus: the piano on-stage, the ballroom atmosphere and its ambiguity, the familiar connection between Schumann's music and Brahms's. Both ballets are about two kinds of dance illusion and two kinds of dancer. But *Liebeslieder Walzer* is a Mozartian marriage of spontaneity and intricate workmanship, while *Robert Schumann's "Davidsbündlertänze,"* despite magnificent sections, is not finely and fully worked. There is, however, a connection between this ballet's sketchiness and its autobiographical implications, whereas the Brahms ballet, while unparalleled in emotional power, reaches objectivity.

The doubleness of both ballets consists of different ways of representing women in ballet and of having them partnered. Balanchine's axiom "Ballet is woman" has always implied the near-invisibility of the woman's partner, who is often only a means of extending the dimension and range of her imagery. Yet the near-invisibility of the partners in *Liebeslieder Walzer* is, so to speak, invisible, and it is true that women are more prominent than men in almost all romantic pas de deux, except for those danced by Fred Astaire—an immense exception, to be sure. The relationship between Farrell and d'Amboise in the Schumann ballet is an extreme example of Balanchine's practice with male dancers, while the relationship between von Aroldingen and Adam Lüders, who represent Clara and Robert Schumann, is an explicit exception that proves the rule of the partner's invisibility, even as it illuminates its meaning and motive, its fruitfulness and also its psychological and emotional cost. In this ballet Balanchine cherishes women's loving concern, but he also wants them to be absolutely free, and so *Robert Schumann's "Davidsbündlertänze"* has two literal, physical centers: one is Farrell's bravura solo of self-delight, the other Clara's worried, lonely search for Schumann, which is followed by Schumann's self-enclosed agony and delusion. Farrell is self-sufficient and happy when alone, Lüders's aloneness is the illness of alienation, but von Aroldingen is never alone, she is entirely given over to concern for her partner.

Farrell and von Aroldingen, both forceful, both beautiful, inhabit the same ballet but they are neither aware of nor in touch with one another. Farrell takes part in the celebratory dance for three of the couples (the Schumanns do not—it is Balanchine's eerily beautiful and painful invention to have the Band of David meet without its founder), but she is generally by herself with her invisible partner, not in a social realm at all. When Lüders and von Aroldingen move out of the social world, it is because their private suffering will not allow them to stay: no shift in mode of illusion takes place. Farrell's dancing is fantastically bold and adventurous, and very moving, but it is not exactly dramatic; von Aroldingen's dancing is refined and pure (it was almost shamingly moving to see Balanchine call forth her beauty, which we had so often and so justifiably doubted, in tribute to this most faithful dancer and friend), but it is also always dramatic—tender, worried, solicitous, lonely—it is never dancing in and for itself, never abstract or plotless, always in the service of character, relationship, emotion, motive. *"Davidsbündlertänze"* shows Balanchine again, as in *Liebeslieder Walzer,* attempting to juxtapose these two ways of dancing in the same ballet.

But the attempt is more riskily overt in the later ballet and in comparison with *Liebeslieder Walzer, "Davidsbündlertänze"* has the sketchiness of a first draft—hardly ever before encountered in Balanchine's work. In *Liebeslieder Walzer* the complex symmetry of the pairings and groupings had seemed to arise without plan directly from the music; one feels in touch with all four couples all the time, as for instance, in McBride's two brief appearances before her final pas de deux in the second part. In *Robert Schumann's "Davidsbündlertänze"* the narrative about Clara and Robert Schumann and the relation between that narrative and the Farrell role is fully realized, but the same cannot be said about the roles or relation to the whole of the two other couples, Heather Watts and Peter Martins, Kay Mazzo and Ib Andersen, who are not placed exactly, whose identity is not securely established. The entire ballet refuses to come into focus; but the magnetism between the double centerpieces is strong enough to hold the work together.

I cannot guess what proportion of the audience for *Robert Schumann's "Davidsbündlertänze"* caught its autobiographical implications. The drama of survival is here oddly upside down: if this ballet survives, later audiences may see its autobiographical elements more clearly than current audiences because the relevant facts may then be more firmly in the public domain. Yet Balanchine's personal and professional infatuation with Farrell throughout the 1960s and his enthronement of her as his final conception of classical dancing was widely known when the ballet was made in 1980, as was the fact that his ballets had been dramatizing his relationship with her from the beginning of her career. His deep dependency on the affection and concern of von Aroldingen after Farrell left the company in 1969 was also widely known. The break with Farrell and his turn to von Aroldingen for solace were perhaps new experiences in his relationships with women: the first time he had completely lost control and self-control in relation to a woman he loved (although he actually serenaded Vera Zorina at her window once, in the 1930s) and the first time a woman had taken care of him since he was a child. Balanchine's age seems adequate explanation for the new openness of autobiography in *Robert Schumann's "Davidsbündlertänze."* But now I catch another autobiographical implication more painful to contemplate,

Karin von Aroldingen in *Robert Schumann's "Davidsbündlertänze,"* 1980 (photo ©1994 Martha Swope; choreography by George Balanchine ©The George Balanchine Trust)

particularly if Balanchine was himself aware of it (my guess is that he wasn't, that it is available only to us through what we know now about his final illness). I have in mind the possibility that his experience of his mysteriously failing powers in those last years influenced his representation of Schumann's growing insanity and may in fact have been the (perhaps unconscious—let's hope) reason for his having chosen both the music and the narrative subject.

These meanings form a major part of the identity of *Robert Schumann's "Davidsbündler-tänze,"* and although they may not have been visible to the general audience, many undeniable meanings in works of art have been visible only to part of the public. And I am not only certain these meanings will be visible as strengths or weaknesses if the ballet survives—I even believe that these meanings will ensure the ballet's survival in an effective form. Such facts create the legends that keep a work of art popular. We shall not even need Antony Tudoresque names for the two women ("She who worries" and "She who is alone") to help audiences recognize them, and although Farrell and von Aroldingen might seem as hard to replace as Violette Verdy in her roles, I think that the relation between the two kinds of dancing in *Robert Schumann's "Davidsbündlertänze"* will be easily visible however the roles are danced.

For the Tchaikovsky festival of 1981 Balanchine made a ballet that almost explicitly identifies itself as a "late work," even a last work: *Mozartiana*, to the Suite No. 4 for orchestra. It is full of reminiscence and tribute. The music is an orchestration of Mozart pieces, which Tchaikovsky chose with thrilling intuition and taste: the motet "Ave Verum Corpus" (K. 518) and a handful of piano pieces, including a conventionally Mozartian set of variations on a melody from a comic opera by Gluck (K. 455); a decidedly nonrepresentative minuet (K. 355) that is filled with exciting harmonic clashes; and a miraculous late polyphonic gigue (K. 574), which Mozart inscribed in the Leipzig court organist's album, while remarking to a friend with whom he had been examining Bach manuscripts at the same time, "One can still learn something from this composer," and perhaps writing the gigue on the spot as a tribute.

As this music enabled Balanchine to look back through Tchaikovsky to Tchaikovsky's favorite composer, Mozart, so his own choreography enabled him to look back through his own work. It was his third setting of a score he had first mounted on the Les Ballets 1933 company in Paris. There is a powerful photograph of Tamara Toumanova in this ballet, in which she looks immensely strong and handsome and full of presence. When Balanchine revived and slightly reworked the piece in 1944 for the Monte Carlo company, the ballerina was Alexandra Danilova—radiant, charming, spontaneous, grand. Now, at the end of his career, he not only cast Farrell but dressed her in an ambiguously somber white tulle ballet skirt with a black overskirt. The ballet opens—in one of Balanchine's rare disregards for the composer's intentions—with a prayer set to the "Ave Verum Corpus" and composed of some unnervingly representational gestures of prayer—hands clasped, then raised to heaven. I was bothered by these immediately, anxious about them and about myself ("Am I going to like this?"), while Nancy Goldner was delighted by the large, full richness of the imagery in front of her, which reminded her of a Bellini madonna. The whole ballet is suffused by the elusive tone of the costume and the prayer, even the quick gigue that comes next, and even (and this is especially peculiar) the rococo ornamentation of the full-scale theme and variations that end the suite. I remembered the earlier *Mozartiana* as sweet, sunny, and social, but the new ballet, while it forms an extraordinarily unified tiny society with its eleven dancers, who include four little girls, does not feel quite sociable. It is a celebration of Farrell's and Balanchine's own style and technique without being a love poem or an elegy, although it has some implications of both. And it carries the mode of *Chaconne* to its ideal destination.

The competition variations in *Chaconne* had been rococo in ornament but heroic in scale and phrasing—a couple of them are set across the strophes and even across bar lines in a continuous outpouring of energy. The variations in *Mozartiana*, while they add up to a grand summation, are individually on a small scale, even dangerously so—Farrell now calls to mind not a goddess but the Dresden shepherdess of cliché rococo. Never before Farrell could Balanchine have achieved so full-bodied a presentation of charm and delicacy of ornament. And *Mozartiana* seemed to show me how much Balanchine had wanted to enter this mode, yet how afraid he had been that the result might look merely charming and trivial. Farrell's quick leaps to the downward curling cascades in the second, "B," phrase in the minor variation actually mimic the ornaments of the music. I had earlier thought of Balanchine as expressly avoiding such imitation in setting highly ornamented music, and I had certainly thought of his musicality as being quite different from this kind of partnership with the music. The dances set to the richly decorated melodic line of the slow movements of *Stravinsky Violin Concerto*, for instance, do not imitate the twists and turns of Stravinsky's ornamented melisma but instead set up in counterpoint a large arc of movement that has no ornamentation. And the same is true of the figurations, musical and choreographic, in the slow movement of *Concerto Barocco*. But in *Mozartiana* Balanchine's note-for-note mirroring, with the help of Farrell, escapes the trivial and mechanical as mysteriously as Mozart can.

The somber cast of *Mozartiana* was probably a sign of the preoccupation with death that Balanchine's work began to show in the last years of his life. I was slow to catch this meaning and probably unwilling to face it. The life of the Balanchine Enterprise meant so much to me that I refused to accept that it had to come to an end. I had scolded other writers for failing to take into account Balanchine's illness when Baryshnikov was with the company, but I myself had paid little attention to it, much less worried about it. I studied the way *Robert Schumann's "Davidsbündlertänze"* reflected Balanchine's relations with von Aroldingen and Farrell, but I did not see that the choreographer might be contemplating his own death. I was surprised by the representationalism of his handling of Schumann's suffering, but it could not jolt me into seeing that he might be identifying with that suffering. (A more poignant possibility, which I was not alone in missing, is that Balanchine may have been identifying also with Schumann's madness, since he may have thought that he himself was going mad in 1980; the medical opinion now is that as early as that year he may have begun to experience the delusions that are part of the Creutzfeldt-Jacob syndrome that killed him.) The fact that *Robert Schumann's "Davidsbündlertänze"* is not as fully worked as Balanchine's other big ballets did not strike me as a sign of failing powers. And I failed, in almost deliberate blindness, to connect the white tulle overlaid with black in *Mozartiana* with the possibility that Balanchine was thinking about death; in my displeasure over his leaving the sunny early *Mozartiana* behind, it did not occur to me there might be a personal reason for making the change.

But not even I could remain unaware of the personal implications of his setting of the Adagio Lamentoso from the *Pathétique* Symphony at the Tchaikovsky festival in 1981. I was moved at his candor in choreographing for music that was widely held in disrespect for its lack of reticence in despair. And there was nothing reticent in Balanchine's frank setting. He composed a pageant, not a ballet, a rite of mourning, of celebration and sanctification of his own death: it was oddly old-fashioned and even inept, yet I was moved to tears as its awkward sincerity reminded me of pageants in my church fifty years ago—an amazing quality to find in the work of this sophisticated theatrical artist. The piece was performed only twice, a dramatic procedure that recalled the *Requiem Canticles* Balanchine had set to Stravinsky's tribute to Martin Luther King, Jr., in 1968, and which is described accurately in *Choreography by George Balanchine:* "Choreographed as a religious ceremony and performed once. The corps de ballet, in long white robes and bearing three-branched candelabra, moved on the darkened stage; a lone woman seemed in search among them, and at the end a figure in purple representing Martin Luther King, Jr. was raised aloft." And here is that same author's description of the "Adagio Lamentoso" in 1981: "Women mourners dance in grief; angels with tall white wings and hooded figures in purple are followed by a procession of monks who prostrate themselves to form a living cross; a child enters carrying a candle. To the final chords, the child extinguishes the candle."

Everyone knew that the child was Balanchine.

# POSTSCRIPT

Although I did not know Balanchine personally, my attachment to the Balanchine Enterprise was so close and strong that I took his death very personally indeed. It took some time for its impact to reach me. I did not attend the funeral service in the Cathedral of Our Lady of the Sign because I have never formed the habit of going to funerals, and I therefore did not allow myself to experience the realization of death that the funeral might have given me. So my relation to the Balanchine Enterprise remained for some time what it had been before Balanchine's death: I went to the New York City Ballet just as often, and I enjoyed it and thought about it just as much. Suzanne Farrell, Patricia McBride, and Merrill Ashley were dancing marvelously, and the work of Darci Kistler and Kyra Nichols, the two most prominent younger ballerinas, was a new chance for those comparisons I loved to make between dancers. Much was recognizably Balanchinian and often excitingly so. If the fact of Balanchine's death did cross my mind when I was watching these performances, it was because I sensed that the dancers were performing with special intensity in his memory. And I think that this was, in fact, the case.

This sense was reinforced by a revival of *Liebeslieder Walzer* in the spring of 1984, ten years after it had last been shown. It was mounted by Karin von Aroldingen, to whom Balanchine had left the rights and who had already mounted it in Vienna. The ballerinas were Farrell, McBride, Stephanie Saland, and Nichols; the first two were entirely familiar with the work, although Farrell had not danced it since she left the company in 1969; Nichols and Saland had never danced the ballet before, but they were both Balanchine trained, even if neither had undergone the focused initiation into the Balanchine style that comes with having a role made especially for her. Farrell's consummate performance enchanted me with the subtle points of dramatic emphasis she had learned to make. McBride's loving warmth made her appear to be relishing this return to early lyricism after the idiomatic "McBride" dancing she had been doing for many years in "Rubies" and *Who Cares?* The revival seemed to prove that Balanchine's dancers could perform in his style and spirit without his immediate presence and even after a considerable lapse of time—and I think that others shared my perception.

*Liebeslieder Walzer,* which I had thought so much about in the early 1960s, had been brought back to my mind by *Robert Schumann's "Davidsbündlertänze,"* and the revival allowed me to check conclusions I had come to about the relation between them. I confirmed my sense that the earlier work was far more fully achieved than *Robert Schumann's "Davidsbündlertänze,"* and my admiration of *Liebeslieder Walzer* consequently increased even beyond my earlier enthusiasm, but I was relieved to discover that the comparison did not lessen my pleasure in the Schumann, as such comparisons sometimes had done in the past. And another comparison I could not help making, between Kyra Nichols and Violette Verdy, whose role Nichols was taking, was not invidious either, even though Nichols's lack of Verdy's dramatic power did give me a problem when I wrote about the revival: "The beautifully realized double center and double mode of *Liebeslieder Walzer,* to which Verdy was the guide, has in fact all but disappeared in the revival, in which Verdy's role has been taken by Kyra Nichols, a first-rate dancer who doesn't make Verdy's sort of dramatic points. . . . One is no longer following a character and her story."

In my optimistic mood, I took the loss philosophically and, indeed, felt a positive pleasure in comparing Verdy's remembered performance with Nichols's lesser one.

Yet what remains is beautiful and moving, for Nichols after all is a generous and deep dancer, marvelously trained, who gives the steps rich, full intonation. She has a distinctive accent too, an accent rather of physique than of style or dramatic intention. She lacks a striking stage mask and has had trouble managing her smile, but the way she carries herself and the configurations her body makes have great distinction. Her mere presence creates a meaning—the poise of her head over the held-back wide curve of her shoulders suggests to me the breeding of a princess of the blood. The dramatic imagery of this role in the new *Liebeslieder Walzer,* though rather blandly inflected, gets some resonance from Nichols's eloquent physique. And she dances the formal second section supremely well.

Nichols has continued to be a beautifully finished dancer, but only occasionally an exciting one for me. She and Kistler are far and away the major dancers at the New York City Ballet today.

But there was a complication to my happy reaction to the *Liebeslieder Walzer* revival, in Peter Martins's decision to stage the ballet with a second cast, consisting of Maria Calegari, Valentina Koslova, Judith Fugate, and Heather Watts. Their bland, colorless run-through made no impression at all. Nor could it have: of the four, only Calegari was a major dancer, and no one was on hand to teach them the details of attack, coordination, phrasing, and nuance out of which a real performance of this most richly molded work might grow. I wondered why there need be two casts, anyway, and what purpose double casting was supposed to serve. If the inadequate and unprepared dancers in the second cast had demanded to dance in this ballet, it was the job of the director of the company to refuse. For the New York City Ballet was reviving one of Balanchine's greatest ballets, and it was mere common sense to make sure that a great performance would result, that *Liebeslieder Walzer* would actually be danced, instead of merely scheduled. I wondered how the ballet struck people who had never seen it and who watched the second cast instead of the first. Perhaps they noticed that something was wrong but told themselves the dancers were having an off night. Perhaps they thought that *Liebeslieder Walzer* was a lot harder to understand than they had expected, since they weren't getting much out of it. Or—worst of all—perhaps they talked themselves into believing that they were having a great experience of a great work.

I tried to phrase my concern about this second cast diplomatically when I wrote about the revival for *Raritan* in 1985:

> There remains a sour note to strike, though nothing clear-cut can be learned from it. *Liebeslieder Walzer* is actually alive only in the performance of the dancers I have just been speaking of; for reasons perhaps understandable from the point of view of company morale but not from the point of view of theatrical reality, the NYCB administration decided to assign this uniquely difficult ballet to an entirely different cast, which has so far proved inadequate. What that decision and that failure means about survival and revival isn't easy to work out.

By the end of the decade I had figured out what it meant.

By 1985 it had become impossible not to be concerned about the diminishment of Farrell's dancing, which, as may be imagined, I kept track of with intense personal involvement. One of her hips had been seriously injured, and she had been performing in pain throughout the early eighties, although her suffering was not apparent to the audience. Then came signs of serious trouble: in the middle of confident, steady performances, there would be sudden terrible lapses. There is a passage in *Monumentum,* for instance, where she must plunge into a deep unsupported arabesque and balance herself in it for a moment, then do it all over again a moment later: it became impossible to predict, by us and certainly by her, whether she could hold those balances. Yet it was thrilling to see her throw herself into the first arabesque without holding back, and then, even if the first had not worked, to throw herself just as fully into the second—this was Farrell's courage raised to heroism. But the next stage was harder to watch, because I had to question whether it was wise or even right for her to keep on dancing *Mozartiana.* By 1986 her performance of this key role was only a sketch of what it had been, a lovely stage picture without dance force; I no longer felt the phenomenal power that used to infuse and intensify the exquisite detail. And *Mozartiana* itself ceased being really there for me, as well, since it works only when the ornamentation is projected with full body power—otherwise it falls back into mere eighteenth-century prettiness and charm. It was precisely the dimension of Farrell's dancing that Balanchine had used to embody his large conception of rococo art, and it was desolating to see Farrell's injury weaken it. But she continued to dance other roles wonderfully until she took sick leave late in 1986. After her hip replacement in 1987, she appeared onstage a few times in the avatar of a glamorous actress, though not a dancer as she herself had taught me to define dancing.

I think it was while I watched Farrell's power diminishing that I began at last to feel the full impact of Balanchine's death and the dissolution of the Balanchine Enterprise. The depression that took me over then, at the end of the eighties, was entirely predictable but, as is often the case, it baffled me anyway: I had a vague awareness of what was happening to me but couldn't bring it into focus. It should have been obvious that I was grieving for the loss of one of my sources of life, but I couldn't grasp that, nor was it clear to me that it was this grief that was spreading through every part of my life and work. Going to New York became almost intolerable. I was prepared not to take pleasure in the New York City Ballet, but I wasn't prepared when that central disappointment infected everything else, leaving me incapable of excitement about or even interest in the city I loved. When grief subsided and depression lifted, it was again to Balanchine that I turned as I began to examine more closely exactly what was taking place on the stage of the New York City Ballet. And I found that my depressed view had not been so far off the mark, after all.

The first thing to say about the present condition of the New York City Ballet is that nothing and nobody could have kept it from dissolution. A friend of mine thinks that

Balanchine realized this, since he had to know the dimension of his genius and what it had cost to achieve his results. Balanchine was not simply the choreographer of the New York City Ballet—he ran every part of it. He would not or could not delegate authority, and his genius and energy were such that he did not have to. There was a repetiteur on hand to see that the dancers remembered their steps, but for the rest he had and wanted only himself; he was teacher and coach to the entire company, as well as the balletmaster who kept the repertory in shape. In this capacity he followed his own taste and interest; some ballets were allowed to be less well presented than others, and some he allowed to go dead for awhile, as he did with *The Four Temperaments* during the late fifties and sixties, although I did not realize that until Balanchine himself brought it back to life in 1974. Perhaps he let it die because he knew he could revive it.

In any event, he was the only one who could bring *The Four Temperaments* back to life and the only one who could keep his ballets really alive in repertory: a different administrative setup, with assistants and coaches teaching the ballets to the dancers, was never tried and would not have worked. Every element in the life of the Balanchine Enterprise came from the daily, detailed attention of the genius who had created it, and that's the way it had to be. This source of life and maker of life was not simply a difficult act to follow: Balanchine was a once-in-a-millennium phenomenon, and what he uniquely created was bound to dissolve soon after his death.

He himself chose Peter Martins as his successor, whose unenviable job it was to try to keep the inevitable from happening for as long as possible. In the beginning he was not unsuccessful, for the Balanchine spirit in many performances in 1983 to 1985 was living art, not careful memory or curatorship. This may have been due to a wise passivity on Martins's part, which had the effect of deliberate noninterference with ballets that were surviving well on memories of the past. Would that he had kept to so intelligent a policy. But already in 1984 he began making changes—that second cast for *Liebeslieder Walzer*, for instance. That disappointment offered a preview of the colorlessness of the Balanchine performances now. Martins went on to change Balanchine's entire way of ranking and casting in accordance with the same principle: just as he had thrown four inexperienced dancers into that most difficult ballet, so now he promoted to the rank of principal, secondary dancers whom Balanchine had not promoted and then threw them into leading roles in the Balanchine repertory. The new principals could not handle leading roles with any more power or color than the second cast had handled *Liebeslieder Walzer*. They could get through the steps, as Calegari, Koslova, Fugate, and Watts had gotten through the steps, but getting through the steps is not what a principal does in a company that bears Balanchine's stamp.

In a Balanchine ballet the leading role is not just the name at the top of the program, it is the organizing center. *Concerto Barocco* and *Raymonda Variations* and all the rest take their identity, their very being, from what the ballerina dances: from her we learn what the ballet means and is. Focusing a whole ballet takes genius, which has nothing to do with having been around for a certain number of years. Throughout his career Balanchine promoted young dancers to the rank of principal because it did not matter how old they were if they could do the principal's job of showing what a ballet was about, what it was. And he kept the same dancers in leading roles for long periods of time for the same reason: because there were no other principals available who could carry them. Other dancers may have longed to dance these roles, and an evenhanded justice might have given them their turn, but for Balanchine, his ballets came first and they had to be served properly. If a ballet could only be carried by Farrell, then Farrell it had to be.

Many fine dancers who had served the company long and faithfully, sometimes with distinction, nevertheless lacked the genius necessary to carry a whole ballet, and Balanchine in consequence neither promoted them nor assigned them leading roles: he would never have given *Concerto Barocco* to someone who could not carry it. Some of his decisions were hurtful, and a couple of them may have been unfair and mistaken; Balanchine was not infallible. But his way of casting made sense and deserved Martins's attention.

Perhaps Martins disregarded it because he thought he could not get away with it, as conductors today cannot hire, promote, or fire musicians the way their predecessor did fifty years ago. Or he may have thought Balanchine's methods unjust—during his years as a dancer he may have heard, and himself have spoken, too many complaints about Balanchine's tyranny. And he almost certainly lacked the personal authority to carry off Balanchine's system. But Martins's whole performance as director, not least his choreography (in ballets that feature two leading couples instead of one), shows that the distinction I'm making between principals and soloists may simply not have mattered to him, if, in fact, he even saw it.

The new dancers he has brought forward confirm this. Damian Woetzel is the best of them, with winning energy and a big technique that make his every entrance on stage an event; but he is the only new dancer of whom this can be said, and he remains seriously unformed. Someone should be teaching him how to carry more weight in the company than he does, how to dance with grander authority. Wendy Whelan deploys formidable strength excitingly and exactly, but she badly needs a teacher to diversify her stiff and monochromatic style. Martins seems unable to help these gifted young people. The other new dancers are far less gifted, almost interchangeable in their anonymity—it is hard to figure out how some of them were chosen. Balanchine is said to have disliked stars, and conceivably Martins is being loyal to this principle. In an interview given while she was mounting *Mozartiana* on the Boston Ballet in 1994, Farrell talked to Christine Temin of the *Boston Globe* about the present condition of the New York City Ballet: "What I miss onstage is the *personages*. We have good dancers, but not necessarily more interesting ones. There used to be a poise, elegance and flamboyance that's gone now." She, at least, never misunderstood what Balanchine meant about stars. His choreography was the biggest star, of course, but his absolute power over the stage did not keep him from wanting it filled with vivid and beautiful people. How could he show his ballets properly without such dancers to project them? And when he picked dancers he looked for some special distinction rather than for the famous Balanchine look, as one can tell by looking at the dancers he actually chose.

I miss the personages, but I also miss the company's dancing style as a whole, especially the fast dancing: brilliant, full, life-sized, sincere, generous, humane. Throughout the fifties and sixties I could tell that the dancing at the New York City Ballet was getting better because I was getting happier as I watched it. And I knew that Balanchine wanted this. Even his applause machines were works of high art. There was a period when the finale of *Coppélia* was my favorite thing in ballet. And at the end of a particularly great performance of *Symphony in C,* when fifty dancers filled the stage with disciplined, free vitality, I felt an exhilarated happiness. My friends felt it too, we defined it in the same way, and we agreed about its value. When that exhilaration failed to come—for it did not come at every performance—we agreed about that too, for this happiness was too important to fake. It was one of the great things in our lives, and one of the great things in the century.

George Balanchine (photo by Tanaquil Le Clercq)

# WORKS CITED

Barnes, Clive. Ballet reviews in the *New York Times*. Cited in Reynolds, below.

*Choreography by George Balanchine*. New York, 1983.

Clifford, John. Interview in *I Remember Balanchine,* edited by Francis Mason. New York, 1991.

Croce, Arlene. *Afterimages*. New York, 1977.

———. *Going to the Dance*. New York, 1982.

———. *Sight Lines*. New York, 1987.

Danilova, Alexandra. *Choura*. New York, 1986.

Denby, Edwin. *Dance Writings*. New York, 1986.

Farrell, Suzanne. *Holding on to the Air*. New York, 1990.

Garis, Robert. "Balanchine: change, revival, survival," *Raritan* 5:2 (Fall 1985): 1–34.

———. "Balanchine-Stravinsky: Facts and Problems," *Ballet Review* 10:3 (Fall 1982): 9–23.

———. "Ballet and Balanchine," *Partisan Review* 32:4 (Fall 1965): 581–88.

———. "Ballet 66," *Partisan Review* 33:4 (Fall 1966): 596–606.

———. "Beginnings, Balanchine," *Raritan* 2:4 (Spring 1983): 47–69.

———. "The Balanchine Enterprise," *Ballet Review* 21:1 (Spring 1993): 24–44.

———. "The New York City Ballet," *Partisan Review* 35:4 (Fall 1968): 573–83.

Haggin, B. H. *Ballet Chronicle*. New York, 1970.

———. *Discovering Balanchine*. New York, 1981.

———. *Music in the Nation*. New York, 1949.

———. *Music Observed*. New York, 1964.

———. *Music on Records*. New York, 1943.

Harris, Dale. "Balanchine: Working with Stravinsky," *Ballet Review* 10:2 (Summer 1982): 19–24.

Harvey, James. *Romantic Comedy in Hollywood from Lubitsch to Sturges*. New York, 1987.

Kirstein, Lincoln. "Working with Stravinsky," *Modern Music* 14:3 (March 1937): 143–46.

Martin, John. Ballet reviews in the *New York Times*. Cited in Reynolds, below.

Martins, Peter. *Far from Denmark*. New York, 1982.

Newman, Arnold, Robert Craft, and Francis Steegmuller. *Bravo Stravinsky*. Cleveland, 1967.

Reynolds, Nancy. *Repertory in Review: 40 Years of the New York City Ballet*. New York, 1977.

Shaw, George Bernard. *Music in London*. London, 1932.

Stravinsky, Igor. *An Autobiography*. New York, 1962.

———. *Selected Correspondence*, Volume 1, edited by Robert Craft. New York, 1981.

Stravinsky, Igor, and Robert Craft. *Dialogues and a Diary*. New York, 1963.

———. *Themes and Episodes*. New York, 1966.

Stravinsky, Vera, and Robert Craft. *Stravinsky in Pictures and Documents*. New York, 1978.

Taper, Bernard. *Balanchine*. New York, 1984.

White, Eric Walter. *Stravinsky*. Berkeley and Los Angeles, 1979.

# INDEX

New York City Ballet has been abbreviated NYCB